Environment and Sustainable Development

About the Editors

Ms. Seema Sahdev is serving as an Associate Professor in Department of Geography at Kalindi College, University of Delhi. Ms. Sahdev did her M.Phil. degree from Delhi University and pursuing her Ph.D. from Jamia Millia Islamia. Ms. Sahdev had worked on the various Administrative Post of the College and organized various awareness programmes related to disaster management for students as well as faculty members. Ms. Sahdev published her research paper in National Geographical Journal of India and Goa Geographers. She has convened one International Conference and one National Seminar related to environment, resource management and sustainable development. Her specialization is in Electoral Geography, Environmental Geography and Geographical Information System (GIS).

Dr. Manish Kumar is serving as an Assistant Professor in Department of Geography at Kalindi College, University of Delhi, is professionally a Geographer. From January 2009 to December 2014, Dr. Kumar served as Programme In-Charge of M.Sc. Remote Sensing and GIS Course of Kumaun University, Uttarakhand. Dr. Kumar has worked as Research Associate on UNDP Project on "'Rurbanization': Making Small Towns Hubs of Rural Productivity at Delhi Policy Group." Dr. Kumar has also served as Visiting Faculty at School of Planning and Architecture, New Delhi. Dr. Kumar holds a Ph.D. from Kumaun University, Nainital, Uttarakhand. He also holds a Post-Graduate Diploma in Remote Sensing and GIS from Indian Institute of Remote Sensing, ISRO, Dehradun, Uttarakhand. His area of research domain includes application of remote sensing and GIS in urban and regional planning, urban heat island, land-use and land cover dynamics, climate change, snow cover dynamics etc.

Environment and Sustainable Development

A Geographical Appraisal

Edited by
Seema Sahdev
Manish Kumar

CONCEPT PUBLISHING COMPANY PVT. LTD.
NEW DELHI-110059

ISBN-13: 978-93-5125-189-7

First Published 2018

Published and Printed by:

Concept Since 1974

Concept Publishing Company Pvt. Ltd.
A/15-16, Commercial Block, Mohan Garden,
New Delhi-110059 (INDIA)
Phones : 25351460, 25351794, *Fax* : 091-11-25357109
E-mail : publishing@conceptpub.com
Website: www.conceptpub.com

Cataloging in Publication Data--Courtesy: D.K. Agencies (P) Ltd. <docinfo@dkagencies.com>

Environment and sustainable development : a geographical appraisal / edited by Seema Sahdev, Manish Kumar.
pages cm
Contributed articles.
Includes bibliographical references and index.
ISBN 9789351251897

1. Environmental management—India. 2. Sustainable development—India. 3. Environmental geography—India. I. Sahdev, Seema, editor. II. Kumar, Manish (Assistant professor of geography), editor.

LCC GE320.I4E58 2017 DDC 333.720954 23

Preface and Acknowledgements

Every ecosystem has a limited capacity to produce and assimilate when these limits are exceeded, the ecosystem degrades and becomes dysfunctional. A dysfunctional ecosystem cannot sustain its contribution and slowly dies. So, there is need to discuss how the carrying capacity of an ecosystem defines the limits within which the development process can be sustained. We need to discuss that how various sector of economy can be made more supportive of sustainable development. The inclusion of resource depletion and its appraisal as part of this book examine the political and economic processes. These processes imply that natural resources are optimally allocated and sustainably used only when the exploitation of resources are made consistent with future as well as present needs.

Policies of ecological capabilities are based on information technologies for preparing, planning and successful implementation of the environmental management initiatives. Through better management and technology, the carrying capacities of various ecosystem can be enhanced. Keeping these facts in mind the comprehensive account of environment with sustainable viewpoints are presented in this book.

In this regard, we thank all the contributors in producing this edited book through their research papers in a more realistic manner. We are highly thankful to our Principal Dr. Anula Maurya for her encouragement and support. Sincere thanks to Prof. R.B. Singh from Department of Geography, Delhi University for his valuable cooperation in the preparation of this book. In the last we thank the publisher Mr. Ashok Kumar Mittal, Concept Publishing Company Pvt. Ltd., New Delhi for their help at various stages of preparation of this book.

New Delhi

Seema Sahdev
Manish Kumar

Contents

PART II
ENVIRONMENTAL ETHICS AND SUSTAINABILITY

PART III
SPATIAL INFORMATION TECHNOLOGIES IN ENVIRONMENTAL MANAGEMENT

List of Contributors

Dr. Amit Kumar Ray, Centre of Excellence for Natural Resource Data Management System, Department of Geography, Kumaun University, SSJ Campus, Almora, Uttarakhand, Pin-263601. Email ID: rayamitkumar77@gmail.com

Dr. Anjan Sen, Assistant Professor, Department of Geography, University of Delhi, Delhi-110007, Email ID: dr.anjansen@gmail.com

Ankur Srivastava, Research Scholar, Department of Geography, Delhi School of Economics, University of Delhi, Email ID: anku.pre@gmail.com

Dr. Anula Maurya, Principal, Kalindi College, University of Delhi, East Patel Nagar, Delhi-110008, Email ID: anulamaurya@yahoo.co.in

Ashok Kumar, Research Scholar, Department of Geography, Jamia Millia Islamia, New Delhi-110025, India.

Awadh Narayan Choubey, Research Scholar, Department of Geography, Jamia Millia Islamia (A Central University), New Delhi-10025. Email ID: awadhonline@gmail.com

Dr. B.W. Pandey, Associate Professor, Department of Geography, Delhi School of Economics, University of Delhi, Delhi, Email ID: bwpdsegeo@gmail.com

Dr. Daljit Singh Chhiller, Associate Professor, Swami Shraddhanand College, University of Delhi, Alipur, Delhi-110036, Email ID: daljitchhiller@yahoo.com

Dr. Ganita Bhupal, Assistant Professor, Department of Economics, Rajdhani College, University of Delhi, Email ID: ganita.bhupal@rajdhani.du.ac.in

Harish Kumar, Research Scholar, Department of Geography, Delhi School of Economics, University of Delhi, Delhi, Email ID: hkharishkumar.162@gmail.com

Prof. Haseena Hashia, Professor, Department of Geography, Jamia Millia Islamia, New Delhi-110025, India, Email ID: hhashia@jmi.ac.in

Dr. Indu Chaudhary, Assistant Professor, Department of Economics, Kalindi College, University of Delhi, Delhi-110008, Email ID: induchy@rediffmail.com

Dr. Manish Kumar, Assistant Professor, Department of Geography, Kalindi College, University of Delhi, East Patel Nagar, Delhi-110008, Email ID: manish.ks1@gmail.com

Dr. Mansi Sachdeva, Assistant Professor, Department of Economics, Kalindi College, University of Delhi, Delhi-110008, Email ID: mansisachdeva004@gmail.com

Dr. Monica Ahlawat, Assistant Professor, Department of Geography, B. R. Ambedkar College, University of Delhi, Email ID: monica_ahlawat@yahoo.co.in

Dr. Neeti Yadav, Assiatant Professor, Department of Botany, Daulat Ram College, University of Delhi, Delhi-110007, Email ID: neetiyadav2008@gmail.com

Dr. Neha Arora, Assistant Professor, Department of Geography, Shaheed Bhagat Singh College, University of Delhi, Delhi, Email ID: nehaarora.geo@gmail.com

Dr. Netrananda Sahu, Assistant Professor, Department of Geography, Delhi School of Economics, University of Delhi, Delhi-110007, India, Email ID: babunsahu@gmail.com

Om Jee Ranjan, Research Scholar, Department of Geography, Delhi School of Economics, University of Delhi, Delhi, Email ID: omjeeranjan@gmail.com

Dr. Pankaj Kumar, Assistant Professor, Department of Geography, Delhi School of Economics, University of Delhi, Delhi-110007, Email ID: pankajdsedu@gmail.com

Dr. Poonam Sharma, Associate Professor, Department of Geography, Shaheed Bhagat Singh College, University of Delhi, New Delhi, Email ID: poonamsharma299@gmail.com

Dr. Prabuddh Kr. Mishra, Department of Geography, Shivaji College, University of Delhi, New Delhi, Email ID: prabuddh@shivaji.du.ac.in

Pravendra Singh Birla, Research Scholar, Faculty of Education, Dayalbagh Educational Institute (Deemed University), Dayalbagh, Agra-282005 (U.P.), Email ID: pravendra.20@gmail.com

Dr. Preeti Tewari, Associate Professor, Department of Geography, Shivaji College, University of Delhi, New Delhi, Email ID: pretewari@yahoo.co.in

Priyanka Mittal, Research Scholar, Faculty of Education, Dayalbagh

Educational Institute (Deemed University), Dayalbagh, Agra-282005 (U.P.), Email ID: priyanshimittal1984@gmail.com

Prof. Rana P.B. Singh, Professor & Vice-President ACLA, Asian Cultural Landscape Association (SNU Seoul, Korea), Dept. of Geography, Banaras Hindu University, Varanasi, India, Email ID: ranapbs@gmail.com

Dr. Ranjana Roy Mishra, Assistant Professor, Department of Botany, Kalindi College, University of Delhi, East Patel Nagar, New Delhi-110008, Email ID: royranjana_123@rediffmail.com

Rashmi, Research Scholar, Department of Geography, Delhi School of Economics, University of Delhi, Delhi-110007, Email ID: rashmithakur1990@gmail.com

Rini Mazumdar, Research Scholar, Department of Geography, Delhi School of Economics, University of Delhi, Delhi, Email ID: mazumdar1989@gmail.com

Saidur Rahaman, Research Scholar, Department of Geography, Delhi School of Economics, University of Delhi, Delhi-110007, Email ID: saidur.rahaman09@gmail.com

Dr. Saloni Bahri, Assistant Professor, Department of Botany, Miranda House, University of Delhi, Delhi-110007, Email ID: saloni3bahri@gmail.com

Sandesh Yadav, Research Scholar, Department of Geography, Jamia Millia Islamia, New Delhi-110025, India, Email ID: sandesh_official@yahoo.in

Ms. Seema Sahdev, Associate Professor, Department of Geography, Kalindi College, University of Delhi, East Patel Nagar, New Delhi-110008, Email ID: seemasahdev@yahoo.com

Shahid Jamal, Research Scholar, Department of Geography, University of Delhi, Delhi-110007, Email ID: shahidjamalkmc@gmail.com

Dr. Somdutta Sinha Roy, Assistant Professor, Department of Botany, Miranda House, University of Delhi, Delhi-110007, Email ID: somduttas@gmail.com

Dr. Sushma Moitra, Assistant Professor, Department of Botany, Miranda House, University of Delhi, Delhi-110007, Email ID: sushmamoitra@gmail.com

Tariq Ahmad Ganaie, Research Scholar, Department of Geography, Jamia Millia Islamia, New Delhi-110025, India, Email ID: tariqahmadg7@gmail.com

Dr. Taruna Bansal, Assistant Professor, Department of Geography, Jamia Millaia Islamia (A Central Univesity), New Delhi-110025. Email ID: tbansal@jmi.ac.in

Prof. V. Madha Suresh, Professor, Department of Geography, University of Madras, Chennai. Email ID: suresh geography@ gmail.com

political, economic or social, to get a balance view of achieving a more sustainable way to manage resources. The knowledge acquired through case studies will be helpful in developing the model of sustainable resource use.

The twenty four chapters included in this book are contributed by academicians, scientists and researchers at different stages of their working career. The chapters in book is divided into there parts—Resource Depletion and its Appraisal, Environmental Ethics and Sustainability, and Spatial Information Technologies in Environmental Management.

PART I
RESOURCE DEPLETION AND ITS APPRAISAL

We are aware of the fact that the sustenance and welfare of human being depend upon the exploitation of different kind of natural resources. The advancement of social and cultural revolution has started the conflict between man and nature. In many countries due to tremendous increase of population, most of the natural resources are being rapidly consumed. At present rate of consumption, the fossil fuels may be drastically depleted leading not only severe energy crisis, but their rapid consumption has affected adversely the quality of our environment. In nature, use of renewable or non-renewable resources beyond their rate of replacement is considered to be resource depletion. However, Ministry of Environment and Forests, Government of India and Department of Environment and Forests of each State Government have been deeply engaged in the protection, preservation and conservation of resources. Several possible policies, programmes and implementation strategies have been evolved from time-to-time by these Governmental Organizations towards their effort for better resource management. In spite of all these actions, resource depletion is increasing day-by-day because developmental activities are promoted without consideration of accountability of natural resources and required environmental carrying capacity. There is need of hour to dominate and manage natural resources for our use. We should invigorate Earth-sustaining forms of economic development and to dissuade Earth-degrading form of economic growth. The developing of natural resource accounts and budget is one of the strategy which allow us to make sure that natural resources are optimally allocated and sustainably used. A carrying capacity based planning process and innovative technologies for resource use is highly essential for achieving sustainable development. **Pandey** *et al.* have elaborated the importance of fresh water and focused on their character as a limited renewable natural resource and its availability and suitability is vital for entire living things. *Fresh water resources are allocated irregularly in space and time perspective and due to major population demand is in critical situation.* Water pollution and water diversions intimidate to interrupt social and economic development in many areas as well as the health of environment. Authors have also discussed the availability and the importance of groundwater resources. **Sushma Moitra** *et al.* has elaborated that every growing city would put pressure on existing environmental resources. This chapter deals with issues of biomedical waste especially with reference to Delhi. Biomedical waste is generated from healthcare establishments like clinics and hospitals as well as research institutions that handle humans or animals. Different categories of biomedical waste range from human tissues and organs, waste sharps such as needles, syringes, glass etc. to cotton and plaster contaminated with blood and body fluids. The rules governing biomedical waste disposal are meant to ensure that toxic and hazardous waste remains segregated and are disposed off in a manner such that the community is not at risk. There are special agencies that handle biomedical waste. Handling of such waste requires periodic monitoring. The biomedical waste management cell has been created in Delhi Pollution Control Committee. There are three common biomedical waste facilities in Delhi that have facilities of autoclaving, shredding and effluent treatment. **Ranjana Roy Mishra** discussed how religion helps in biodiversity conservation in India with special reference to sacred plants. Dr. Mishra described how diversity of culture and beliefs in our country help in the conservation of many plants. India has a diverse culture and Indians are very religious. Respect for nature and environment is common to all religious faiths. Large numbers of God and Goddesses are worshipped in India. Each one of them is associated with at least one plant like Goddess Lakshmiji is associated with Kamaland Lord Krishna is associated with Kadamba. Devotees offer prayers to them with these plants or their parts. There are also a lot of festivals and ceremonies celebrated throughout the year in different states in different manners. During these festivals and ceremonies different types of plants and their parts are required which helps in conserving many plant species. **Shahid Jamal** and **Anjan Sen** have focused the technical intelligence of Craftsmanship. The authors have given the example of craftsmanship who is mainly involved in Saree weaving in India. The iconic sites under UNESCO are from five Indian states: Madhya Pradesh, Uttar Pradesh, Maharashtra, Andhra Pradesh and Assam. Craftsmanship is not only a profound understanding of materials, and of the tools with which materials are fashioned, but most importantly it involves a genuine pride which drives an individual to craft and weave as well as can be done, beyond what is required, beyond economic considerations of reward. **Neeti Yadav** highlighted the importance of India's wealth of medicinal plant biodiversity which is used by various tribal's and local people to cure different ailments ranging from simple fever, diarrhoea, ulcers, swelling, bone fractures, skin care, night blindness, toothache, asthma etc. Dr. Yadav examined how unchecked commercialization, habitat loss and habitat degradation have placed many medicinal plant species at a risk of extinction. Therefore, she pointed out an urgent need for their conservation. The present chapter discusses the various *in vitro* protocols developed for some of the selected endangered and economically important medicinal plants of India such as *Tinospora cordifolia, Pterocarpus santalinus, Stevia rebaudiana* and *Tylophora indica*. **Ganita Bhupal** tried to analyze the role of household behaviour in terms of firewood consumption as a response to the economic development in various districts of Bihar. She took the data of households of urban and rural areas of Bihar using firewood as a fuel in 2005-06 and 2011-12. Bhupal found that in majority of rural and urban areas, the per cent of households using firewood has increased by a large amount. **Pankaj Kumar**, **Saidur Rahman** and **V. Madha Suresh** in his chapter did SWOT analysis for agriculture and allied sectors of Malda district in West Bengal and identified positive and negative impacts due to agricultural land use change. **Ashok Kumar** *et al.* highlighted the impact of quarrying on various elements of environment such as quality of air, noise pollution, large scale deforestations, habitat fragmentation, loss of biodiversity, landscape degradation and many more. Their study aims to realize the necessity for assessment of quarrying on environmental conditions and the human beings living in the neighbouring region. The study begins with the discussion on changes in Land Use and Land Cover (LULC) during the period 2005-2012 in the study area. Further, the study moves ahead with identification of major quarrying sites and coverage of their details (Geology, Lithology, stone reserves etc.). In its main course, the study narrows down on "How quarrying degrading the environmental conditions of quarrying sites and their neighbouring regions?" and further, answers the question that "what is the nature of impact of quarrying on environmental conditions and the public health of the neighbouring regions?" In this study, the environmental conditions are being assessed in terms of air quality and the noise levels and the public health in terms of respiratory diseases due to degraded air quality and the behavioural and psychological impacts due to increased noise levels in the study area.

PART II
ENVIRONMENTAL ETHICS AND SUSTAINABILITY

Environmental ethics is a discipline that concerns itself with the moral relationship of human beings to the environment and is also concerned with determining the value and moral status of the environment. Ethics is an action concept which requires courage and character to meet the challenge when rapid rates of environmental change leave little time for people living within ecosystem to adapt, when the pace of gradual change is accelerated to the point where change destroys ecosystem and human livelihood system. Out of such realisation has grown the nation of sustainable development Development therefore was redefined to mean only that economic and social growth that was equitable and that could be sustained over time. The concept of sustainable development is closely linked to the carrying capacity of ecosystems. The concept of carrying capacity implies that improvement in the quality of life is possible only when the patterns and levels of production, consumption activities are compatible with the capacities of the natural environment as well as social preferences. The carrying capacity of an organism or a system is its ability to meet demands and withstand pressure without doing permanent change to itself or compromising its ability to meet future demands and withstand future pressure. For an ecosystem, this could mean its ability to tolerate extraction (its productive capacity) and withstand pollution (its assimilative capacity without getting degraded. Therefore, one way of ensuring sustainable development is to ensure that the process of economic growth does not take from nature more than its is able to regenerate and does not pollute the nature beyond its ability to assimilate.

Sustainability is an ultimate goal for both preserving nature and improving the lives of people everywhere. Sustainability implies that human well-being and environment health need to be complementary, not contradictory aims. Environmental problems and their solution occur at the intersection of natural systems and the human systems that manipulate the natural world. The integrated approach is essential to work toward sustainable solution in our environment.

Environmental protection, as a component of a sustainable development consistent with poverty eradication, is imperative in resource management. So, the human dimension has to be incorporated into planning with an emphasis on sustainable development. Voluntary agencies and environmental group be encouraged to expend their activities, so that, sustainable development is possible. The emergence of the concept of sustainable development in recent years has brought in the general realization that societal perception must shift towards ecological determination so as to achieve qualitative growth within the limits of the ecosystem's carrying capacity. A carrying capacity based planning process, innovative technologies for enhanced material and energy, affectively of production and consumption, structural economic change towards less resource-intensive sectors and preventive environmental management through increasingly. Interventionist policies of ecological capabilities, is highly essential for achieving sustainable development.

Sustainable development is a process in which the exploration of resources, the direction of investments in orientation of technological development and institutional change are all made consistent with future as well as present needs. Ethical Guidelines for sustainable living involves a respect for all life and for the process that sustain it. We should try to understand and cooperate with the rest of nature. We should work with the rest of nature to sustain the ecological integrity, biodiversity and adaptability to earth's life support system for us and other species. **Rana P.B. Singh** in his chapter discussed that the ethical values and sustainability is geographer's art as Geography is defined as the study of the Earth as home of humanity. This helps in understanding and interpreting the scared power inherent within a landscape. An awakened walk on the path of divine Nature a major concern of the new age movement may lead to the deeper and sensible quest. **Haseena Hashia** in her chapter discussed about Anthropocentrism, Biocentrism and Ecocentrism as major ethical perspective and explained that the concept of sustainable development is based on the idea of the essential needs of the world's poor, to which overriding priority should be given. It is also based on the idea of limitations imposed by the state of technology and social organization on the environment's liability to meet the present and future needs. **Anula Maurya** suggested that the implementation of environmental laws and policies will be effective only with public support and participation which require an awareness and clear understanding of key environmental problems. **Pankaj Kumar** and **Rashmi** elaborated that environment is a complex of many variables which surrounds man as well as all living organisms. Further, authors explained that an environmental issues arises when quality or quantity of any environmental factor which directly or indirectly affects the health and well-being of man in an adverse manner along with this these landscapes is heavily changed by human beings. They also argued that anthropogenic impact on natural environment is one of the most burning issues of the present times and a subject of discussion in geographical literature. The problems like—acid rain, ozone depletion, global warming, water pollution etc. are the important issues of today's concern. To solve these problems the local native community people would come up and take the initiative to conserve environment in a small step which will become a major weapon in future in conserving environment. **Indu Chaudhary** and **Mansi Sachdeva** have discussed that climate change has been a topic of discussion not just among the veterans, but also among the populace in general. This is not surprising because changes in the climate have lately become more visible and real with some of them being irreversible. The more disturbing fact is that not only the present generation is impacted, the future generations is equally at peril. Consequently, the issue of climate change has forced the think tanks of various nations to come together on several occasions and take concrete steps as demonstrated by the Kyoto Protocol in 1997 and the more recent climate convention in Paris in December 2015. It is in this context, the study analyzes the impact of environmental regulation on climate change using a regression analysis of the Annex-A and Annex-B countries of the Kyoto Protocol. In doing so, authors press upon the need for environmental regulation and discuss the different forms of environmental regulation with special focus on economic incentives. **Preeti Tewari** suggested that the economic, social and political dimensions are intricately interlinked and development cannot be truly sustainable if any one aspect is overlooked. She highlighted a sustainable economic system should be geared towards the reduction and elimination of poverty. Special attention should be paid to the working poor to help them increase their incomes to a level that enables them not just to remain alive, but also to rise out of absolute poverty. **Pravendra Singh Birla** and **Priyanka Mittal** in his chapter highlighted about the objectives and areas of environmental education and also identified role of environmental education in Indian context and highlighted problems that India face regarding environmental education and suggested that the success of the effective government strategy to promote environmental education in India will depend upon the close synergy and partnership between the MHRD and the MOEF, their key institutions, State Governments, NGOs as well as educational institutions throughout the country and has suggested four areas of environmental decision-making i.e., the types of environmental issues on which decisions might be made, the physical setting of the prospective environmental decision, including its spatial scale, the type of social groups and individuals who might interact in a process leading-up to an environmental decision and the time frame within which the decision must be made. **Ankur Srivastava** and **Poonam Sharma** conducted cases studies from Himachal Himalayas to identify environmental issues in development and pointed out that the impact of environmental issues immerging from developmental process is clearly visible on a large scale. The ongoing concrete development in the region mainly include road network expansion along river side, hydro power development, tunnel construction, tourist bases, ski villages etc. Its impact can be traced out in form of stress on ecosystem services affecting land, water, air along with its related attributes. Frequent landslides, dying natural water sources, degrading local ecology, disappearing flora and fauna are few to count evidences from the concerning area. **Monica Ahlawat** studied the actual condition of women in nature and focus on the systematic pattern of discrimination against women at every level and emphasizes the decisive role played by traditional cultural norms in determining the position of women in agrarian society. She also suggested that to achieve substantial growth in production depends partly on women and progress towards greater quality of for women. **Prabuddh Kr. Mishra** in his paper stated that Environmental education provides students with the knowledge, skill and experience, essential to become successful community leaders as well as making intelligent decisions pertaining to the management of their natural resources.

PART III
SPATIAL INFORMATION TECHNOLOGIES IN ENVIRONMENTAL MANAGEMENT

Policies for sustainable development are based on an assessment of the information available about the environmental issue. Sharing data and information is must for rapid response. We all need the analytical tools to get the validity of this information. Without this, environmental policy may be misguided, resulting inseparable damage to our environment. In this regard most imperative is generating awareness among all section of society regarding human advancement and developing human resource to meet the challenge of implementing spatial information technologies. Information technologies are indispensable for the preparing, planning and successful implementation of the environmental management initiatives. Spatial information technologies include geographic information system (GIS), global positioning system (GPS), remote sensing and spatial data management. The implementation of spatial information technology depends on the development of appropriate spatial data infrastructure which include technologies, policies and people to provide, accurate sustainable development throughout all levels of government and the academic community to contribute to economic growth, environmental quality, disaster management, urban planning, agricultural planning and land management etc.

Some of the chapters in this book discussed about the spatial information technologies which encompass a crucial role in environmental management provides it is integrated suitably in the decision-making process. **Seema Sahdev** and **Manish Kumar** have focused on changing green space over National Capital Territory of Delhi. Two multi-temporal satellite images of Landsat 7 and 8 have been used over a period of nearly one decades (i.e., 2003 to 2016). The authors however, significantly highlighted the destruction and degradation of vegetative area around National Capital territory of Delhi in the modern times due to rapid and haphazard urbanization, making urban settlements major source of GHG emissions and at the same time making them more vulnerable to global environmental change impacts like global warming and climate change. Hence, green cover changes monitoring become very crucial in decision-making and conserving green space in cities and at this stage significant contributions can be provided by remote sensing technologies. **Amit Kumar Ray** has conducted study on Landslide hazard Zonation Landslides along the Yamuna and Bhagirathi (Ganges) River valley in Uttarkashi district. This area is experiencing frequent landslides during the last two decades in Uttarakhand. These landslides adversely affect both human and animal lives, cause enormous damage to properties, and blocks communication within and with other parts of nation and lead to additional financial burden on the state and national economy. Dr. Kumar has acquired and used various data from different sources such as land use land cover, road proximity, drainage, geology, slope and landslide locations. Multi-Criteria Evaluation (MCE) techniques have been used to evaluate the stability of landslide disaster to produce landslide hazard zonation map. Dr. Kumar has classified study region into five classes i.e., "very low hazard", "low hazard", "moderate hazard", "high hazard" and "very high hazard". The results reveals that large part 26.33% area of these tehsil falls under very high to high hazard zone, 16.93% in moderate hazard zone, 8.58% in low hazard zone and 48.16% under very low hazard zones. **Daljit Singh Chhiller** has observed that Remote Sensing and GIS are the two Geo-Spatial Technologies increasingly used in Geographic Research. The high cost of the software's used to apply these technologies to geographical data did not allow expansion of its use in India except in the projects which are financed by some funding agencies. Moreover, its use for individual research by teachers and students in absence of license access to these technologies was highly restricted. Even if a license is purchased by the educational institution, its maintenance cost further inhibits is use. In this chapter Chhiller mainly highlighted how QGIS, open source GIS software helps in overcoming these problems. By adopting UBUNTU, an open source operating system and QGIS, an open source GIS software any department of Geography can establish a GIS laboratory where not only teachers, but students may learn its applications and start using it in a big way. **Netrananda Sahu** in his chapter stated that understanding of climate variation due to natural and a human induced cause is a challenging research and societal issues. And told about linkages between Global Environmental Change and Indian Ocean Dipole. A cooler than normal water in the tropical eastern Indian Ocean mode plays an important role as a modulator of the Indian Monsoon rainfall and influences the Indian summer monsoon—ENSO relationship is due to positive IOD which is identified. Although Indian Ocean Dipole Mode Index is defined as the difference in SST anomaly between the tropical western Indian Ocean and the tropical south-eastern Indian Ocean. **Neha Arora** formulated a model of sustainable agriculture and environmental protection for the future agricultural development of the state with the help of flow chart and to analyse different components of sustainable agriculture that will ensure resource conservation i.e., land, water and air for protecting land, integrated crop management, integrated nutrient management and integrated pest management holds importance. For protecting water resources measures like canal water management, micro-irrigation technique rain water harvesting is useful. **Awadh Narayan Choubey** and **Taruna Bansal** have tried to analyze the demographic, social and economic changes witnessed along the Delhi-Agra Corridor from 1991 to 2011. They have examined the land use/land cover changes witnessed by the corridor.

Part I
Resource Depletion and Its Appraisal

1

Water Resource Potentiality, Problems and Its Management

B.W. Pandey, Om Jee Ranjan, Rini Mazumdar and *Harish Kumar*

Introduction

Water is the most important natural resources for all life on Earth surface (Singh and Pandey, 1996). The water availability and its quality have played a very important role in pláces where people can live, and also their quality of life. About 97 per cent of total water is in the oceans in form of salt water and remaining three per cent is fresh water. The majority of fresh water that is about 69 per cent is locked-up in glaciers and icecaps and remaining fresh water is in the form of ground water (Singh and Pandey, 1993). The fresh water, human is most familiar with, as a rivers, lake and waterfall is only about 0.3 per cent of total (Fig. 1.1).

Awareness of its limited availability in surface and time has necessitated the designing of new globally feasible management of water arrangement aiming at striking a balance between the use of water as a basis for livelihood and its protection to help make sure its sustainability through present to future generations (Agarwal *et al.*, 2000).

Our Global Water Resource

Matter of fact is that authentic assessment of stored water as a resource in various and different physical states are difficult to actual estimation, but our scientist and geographers are trying to present an approximated data to understand the actual values of

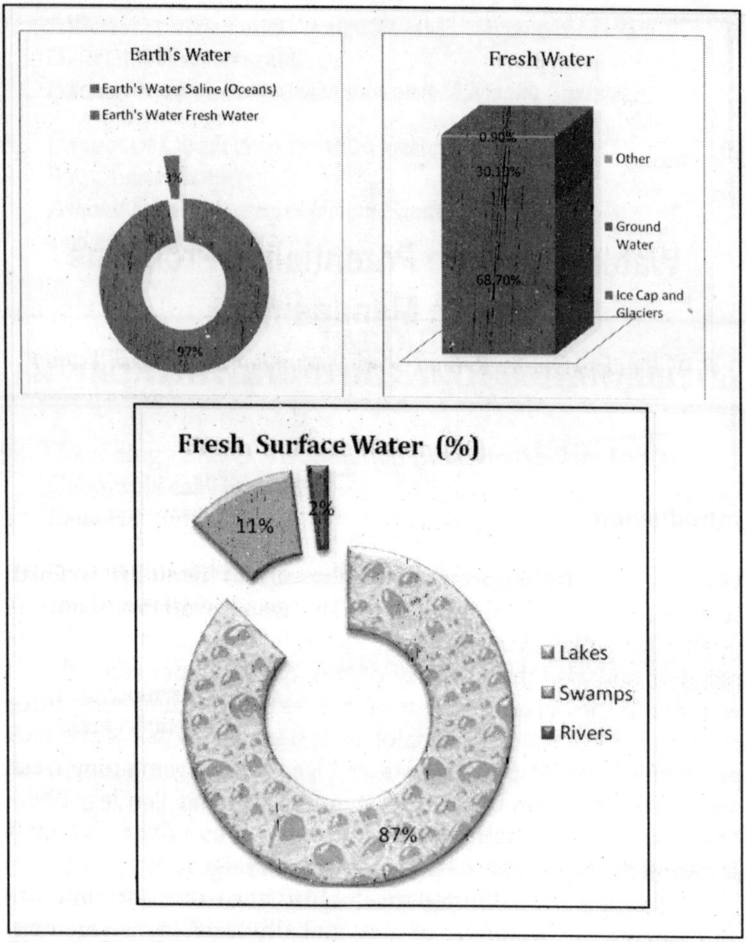

Fig. 1.1: Distribution of Earth Water
Source: Igor Shiklomanov's Chapter "Water Fresh Water Resources" in Peter H. Gleick (ed.), 1993.

water bodies and its forms. According to Shiklomanov (1993), the quantity estimation of water stored in underground ice in permafrost region, bogs and marshes, on amount of soil moisture can only be gauged by scientists but at other hand, much more reliable estimates are available in these days of water stored in the oceans, in lakes, in polar and in glaciers and in ground water. Approximately 35 million km^3 (about 2.5%) of the total stock water is available in the hydrosphere (Fig. 1.2).

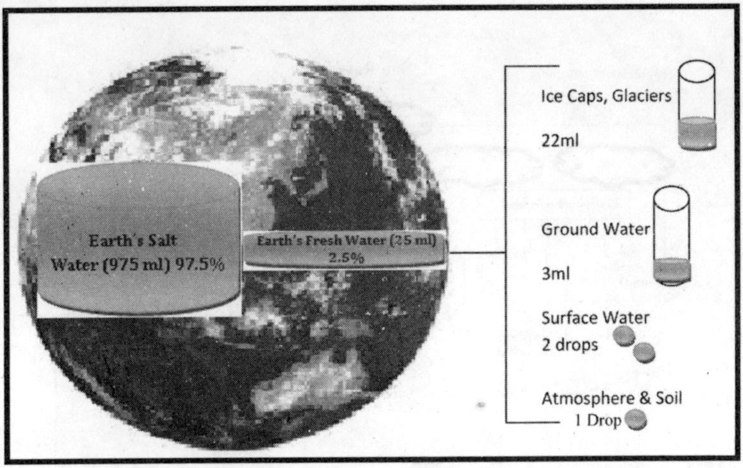

Fig. 1.2: Distribution of Fresh Water in the World

Source: Sketch by O.J. Ranjan and data adopted by Igor Shiklomanov's.

The Global Water Cycle

Water resource is renewable because it has the continuous movement from ocean to air and land then back to the ocean. This hydrological cycle is a prime phenomenon in meteorology. The sun ray's fall on the surface water thereby surface water get heat and convert into evaporate (gas). This water vapour rises and goes to the earth's atmosphere where it release heat and condenses into liquid droplets. Condensed droplets started to combine and grow until they fall to the earth as a precipitation in liquid or solid (snow) form and it is temporarily stored in lakes, ponds, underground, and glaciers, but every stored water bodies finally returns to the oceans except those water which is used by living organisms because they evaporated directly into the atmosphere.

The evaporation phase of the cycle is responsible to purify water which is available as fresh water on the earth surface and it streams transports minerals across the world; maintenance the most of life and ecosystems on the earth planet and responsible for reshaping the geological features of the Earth surface, through processes including sedimentation and erosion.

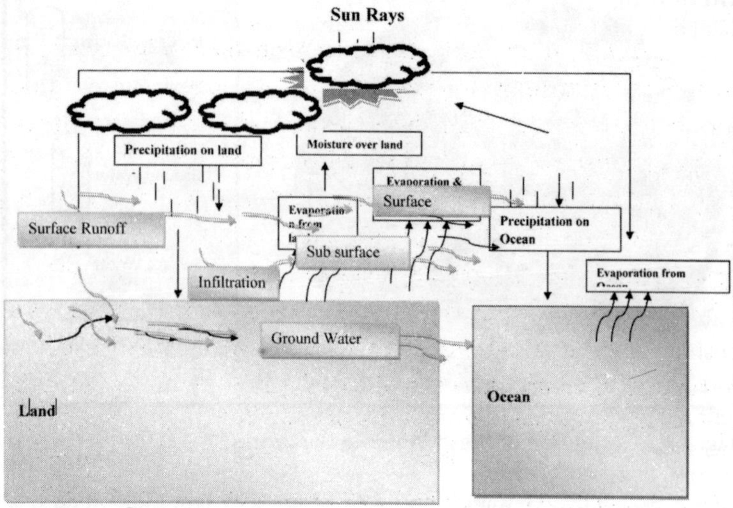

Fig. 1.3: Global Water Cycle
Source: Sketch by O.J. Ranjan and Idea adopted by NOAA National Weather Service, 2015.

Utilization of Water Resources

Natural fresh water resources (lakes, rivers, streams, ice pack, groundwater and precipitation) are essential element for Agricultural, Industrial, Household, Recreational activities and activities of ecosystem. It is the renewable resource, but it is gradually decreasing and demand of water is rapidly increasing in many part of world where population is recklessly increasing.

Uses of Fresh Water in Agricultural Sector

Floras require water for growth, reproduction and photosynthesis. This uses of water is not recoverable completely because some amount of water get spend on the chemical make-up of the plant. Agricultural sector is a biggest user of fresh water and it is estimated on global scale that the 67 per cent of water are used for irrigation purpose per year (UNESCO, 1999) and approximately 17 per cent of total agricultural land is irrigated, but its produces about 40 per cent of the world's tood (FAO, 2002) (Fig. 1.4). The irrigated cropland is gradually expanding while water logging and siltation like situations continue to decrease its productivity (Glecik, 2002). In-spite of this it is the contemporary inevitability to increase the irrigated cropland but irrigation per capita has been decline about 10 per cent the past decade because of rapid population growth (Postel, 1999; Gleick, 2002).

Industrial Uses of Fresh Water

Usages of water for Industrial purpose are lower than agricultural usages and it is estimated that around 20 per cent of total fresh water resources are used. Among these 57 to 69 per cent of total fresh water is used for hydropower and nuclear power production and 30 to 40 per cent for industrial processes, and only 0.5 to 3 per cent for thermal power generation (Shiklomanov, 1993). Most of the major industries use water for power generation and as a cooling system, in chemical processes, in manufacturing plants and as a solvent.

Most of industries need lot of water for processing the related machines, such as a steam turbine, as a chemical solvent etc. After Industrial used untreated water became a serious threat now-a-days. It create many types of pollution such as chemical pollution, thermal pollution, water pollution etc. so, it is necessarily requires purification techniques both in water supply and discharge.

Uses of Fresh Water for Household

Worldwide Fresh water consumption for household purpose is about 15 per cent in the form of drinking, cooking, sanitation and bathing and other basic requirement and household-wise consumption rate is around 50 litres per household in a day, excluding water for gardens (Peter Gleick, 2002) (Fig. 1.4).

Average consumption of fresh water in developed countries is about 10 times more water daily per person than the person of developing countries. The person of developed countries uses 500-800 litres per day whiles 60-150 litres per day per person is consuming rate in developing countries. Herein in third world, withdrawal rate of water represents only 50 to 100 litres per person in a day (UNESCO, 2001).

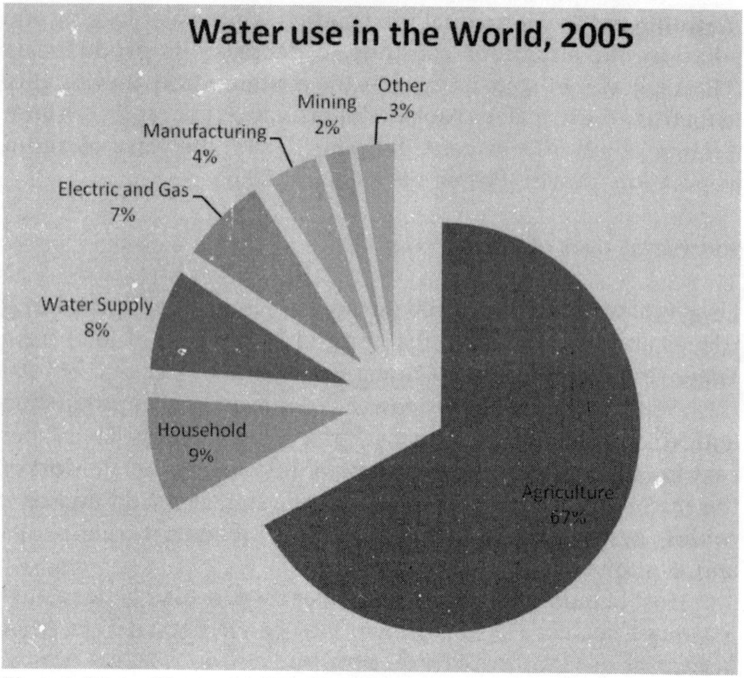

Fig 1.4: Water Use in the World, 2005
Source: United nation water cooperation-2013 facts and figures, 2016.

Recreation and Water Consumption

Recreation is a constitutive and crescent activity. It is an activity in which people refresh the body and mind. Recreation always involves some degree of exercise as well as visiting areas that contain bodies of water such as parks, wildlife refuge, wilderness areas, public fishing areas, and water parks.

Recreation is generally non-consumptive usage of water. Recreational usage of water may be reducing the availability of water for other users at specific times and places. As an example water retained in a reservoir to allow boating in the late summer is not accessible to farmers during the spring planting season and water released for whitewater rafting may not be accessible for hydroelectric generation during the time of peak electrical demands.

Activities of Ecosystem

There are many negative effects of human activities on ecosystem which includes land reclamation, urbanization, industrialization, grazing, hunting, agriculture etc. Humans have been weakening ecosystem services through changing habitat and changing ecosystem structure over the ages. Building of dams on river leads to change in the topography and subsequent change in the surrounding habitat. Humans are destroying forests for fuel-wood and arable land for agriculture. The above mentioned activities are leading to drop in the water table throughout the planet.

Global Water Problems

Water is important for the progress of human beings and sustainability of our habitat, but it is a resource which has its vulnerabilities quantitatively and qualitatively. As People Action International (PAI, 1997) states, "water is the basis of existence of life on this planet. Our lives are integrated with water in multiple ways".

Shortage of water is becoming a burning issue in the world in this time. Today about 14 billion cubic metres fresh water are available for human use and by 2025 water affordability is expected to decrease to around 5100 cubic meter per person (World Bank, 2009). According to PAI (1999) estimation, there were 31 countries with a total population of 458 million which faced water pressure in 1995. Twenty per cent of the world's population which is approximately a billion people requires access to safe drinking water (Simonovic, 2000). Likewise almost 50 per cent of the world's population or more than 3 billion people require access to sanitation (Cosgrove, 2000) and almost 80 per cent of all illnesses and about one third of all deaths (about 7 million die in every year) in countries of third world are related to water. Every eight second a child dies from a water-related illness, which is about 4 million a year. About 50 per cent of the. total rivers and lakes on this earth are extremely polluted. Pollution has created millions of environmental refugees (Serageldin, 1999).

Many biggest cities, such as Beijing, Buenos Aires, Dhaka,

Lima and Mexico City, depend heavily on groundwater for their water supply, but this type of overuse is not sustainable, because it takes many years to fill aquifers. Most of the world's megacities are located on coast lines, where aquifer depletion leads to saltwater intrusion and the pollution of freshwater (UNEP, 2000 and Cosgrove, 2000). Countries like Bangladesh, the Philippines and Thailand face water losses of 50 per cent. In Middle East countries like Jordan, Yemen and others with rising water shortage, more than 40 per cent of the accessible water cannot be traced. Rapid population growth and increasing water consumption for agriculture, industry and municipalities have too heavily stressed the world's freshwater resources. It is not surprising that, in some areas the demand for water already exceed nature's supply with a growing number of countries expecting to face water shortage in the near future. Water scarcity is becoming the greatest threat to food security, human health and natural ecosystems.

Water Pollution

Water pollution occurs when lethal substances enter water bodies such as lakes, rivers and oceans and gets dissolved in them or keep floating in the water. This degrades the quality of water. Not only does this spell disaster for aquatic ecosystems, the pollutant also seep through and reach the groundwater, which might end up in our households as impure water we use in our everyday activities which includes drinking. It means anything that is added to the water, above and beyond its ability to break it down, is pollution.

Water pollution has two major sources which is point and non-point sources. Point sources are the one who's discharging the pollutants directly into water and non-point sources are unable to trace because they do not have one single source of pollutants.

Every day, about two million tons of dirt, industrialized and agricultural waste is discharged into the world's water, which is equivalent to the mass of the entire human population of 6.8 billion people. The UN estimates that the amount of wastewater produced annually is about 1,500 km^3, six times more water than exist in all the rivers of the world (Ward, 1996 and Weyer *et al.*, 2001).

Water Resource Management

Water resource management is the organization of water resources under set policies and regulations. It is the activity of better management for planed allocation with optimum usage of Water resource. An abundant natural resource in past time is becoming a precious commodity due to droughts, misuse and exploitation by human being (Fry, 2008).

Scope of Water Resource Management

Water resource management in any country becomes a burning issue without better management of water recourses and due to these sustainable environment cannot be achieved (SIWI, 2005). In some places water is abundant, but getting it to people is difficult because of lack of infrastructure and because of restricted access and as a result of political and socio-cultural issues. In other places, people's demands go beyond what the natural resource base can handle, and not everyone is assured access to water. In every part of the world, water users tend to focus first on meeting their instant needs. Across southern Africa, foresters have established plantations across wide swaths of highlands. But the water cycle is interrelated and knows no national boundaries. Water evaporates from the sea, fall over land and proceeds to the sea *via* rivers and underground pathways. This "renewable cycle" regulates itself until human activities reach critical levels; so water must be managed as a common resource (Pandey, 2004). The scope of that management depends on the nature of the connections. Where settlements pollute a river, rules are required to balance competing needs and to protect people and their environment (Pandey and Mishra, 2013). Initially, traditional custom and practice may suffice. But, as situations turn out to be more complex, they may need to be underpinned by formal knowledge, organizations, bylaws and regulations.

Integrated Water Resources Management (IWRM)

Integrated Water Resources Management is an experiential concept which was built-up from the on ground experience of practitioners. It is a process which promotes the co-ordination, development and management of water, land and related resources, in order to maximize the consequential economic and social benefit in an equitable manner without compromising the sustainability of vital ecosystems (Pandey, Bondooni and Negi, 2004).

Water is a key source of development for our financial and societal systems while it also has a vital role in maintaining the integrity of our natural habitats (Hassing *et al.*, 2009). However water is only one of a kind of vital natural resources and it is very important that water issues are not considered in isolation. Managers, whether in the government or private sectors, have to make complex decisions on water allocation.

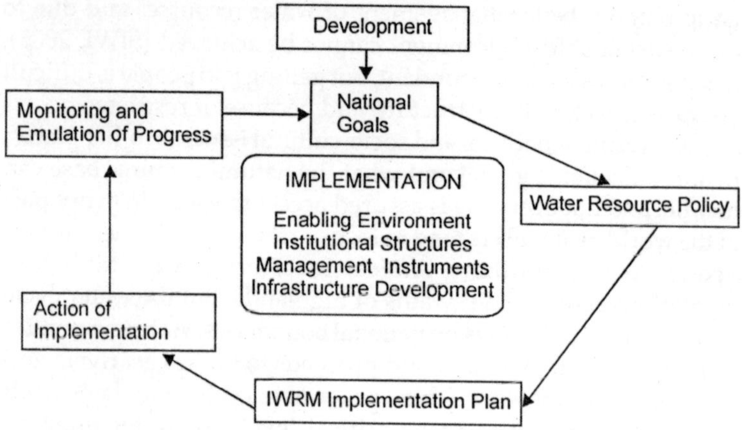

Fig. 1.5: Stages in IWRM Planning and Implementation

Source: Status Report on Integrated Water Resources Management and Water Efficiency Plans, UN-Water (2008).

This is the foundation for the Integrated Water Resources Management (IWRM) approach that has now been accepted internationally as the way to promote for well-organized, equitable and sustainable development and management of the world's limited water resources and for coping with contradictory demands. Key principles in IWRM (The Dublin Principles, 1992) —Freshwater is a limited and susceptible resource, essential to sustain life, development and the environment. Water development and execution should be based on a participatory approach involving users, planners and policy-makers at all levels.

Women play a central part in the provision, supervision and conservation of water. Water has an economic value in all its competing uses and should be recognized as a financial good. Today, the need for stronger supportive action and the role of integrated water resource management is increasing clearly (Singh and Pandey, 1996). The 1992 Rio Summit adopted Agenda 21, a broad plan of action for every area in which humans impact the environment.

Global Water Policy Project

The Global Water Policy Project was founded in 1994 by Sandra Postel, a leading authority on international freshwater issues. The project promotes the conservation and sustainable use of Earth's fresh water through mass communication to important stakeholders. It also motivates society in the management of fresh water resources and promotes various water conservation efforts.

In 2010, Sandra was selected Freshwater Fellow of the National Geographic Society, where she serves as lead water expert for the Society's freshwater efforts. By aligning her mission through the GWPP alongside the power and reach of the National Geographic Society, she seeks to build lasting positive change in the way humanity uses, manages and values fresh water. Under Sandra's leadership, National Geographic and its partners are pioneering an innovative approach to freshwater preservation and restoration called *"Change the Course"*, the initiative is being piloted in the iconic Colorado River Basin and to date has restored 2.8 billion gallons of water to depleted rivers and wetlands.

Water Policy and Strategy of the United Nations Environment Programmeme

Water has played a major role in the formation of UNEP. In fact, the Regional Seas Programme was one of its first flagship initiatives and remains these days a strong foundation programme for UNEP. Since the United Nations Conference on Environment and Development conducted in Rio de Janeiro in 1992, the problems related to freshwater resources management have taken a major function in the international arena.

The significance of freshwater issues continues to rise at various levels as elabourated upon in the Millennium Development Goals, the World Summit on Sustainable Development, the Commission on Sustainable Development and other platforms. The UNEP water policy and strategy as set out in the annex to the present statement will be in operation for a six-year period from 2007 through 2012 and will be operationalised through the UNEP dual programme of work. Execution of the policy and strategy will be monitored by the Governing Council against the projected accomplishments and indicators outlined in appendix I to the policy and strategy. Recommendations for assessment of the water policy and strategy will be made prior to 2012.

Conclusion

Fresh Water is a limited renewable natural resource so that its availability and suitability is vital for entire living things. Fresh water resources are allocated irregularly in space and time perspective and due to major population demand is in critical situation. The different options for augmentation expand the boundaries of the water resource in a conventional sense, serving to match demand and supply. All components of the hydrological cycle, and the influence of human activities on it, need to be understand and quantified efficiently and sustainable development and protect our natural water resources on the earth. Water pollution and water diversions intimidate to interrupt social and economic development in many areas as well as the health of environment.

Groundwater resources can, in many instances, increase surface water, particularly as a source of drinking water. However, in several cases, these aquifers are being tapped at an unsustainable rate or affected by pollution. More awareness should be paid to the sustainable supervision of non-renewable surface or groundwater.

Many traditional practices are being refined, while more recent advances are being developed further. More support needs to be given to policy options, such as demand execution, which stress more efficient use of water resources, as well as to technical solutions on the supply side.

References

Agarwal, A., *et al.* (2000). "Integrated Water Resources Management". *TAC Background Paper 4*. Stockholm: Global Water Partnership, p. 22 (2016, January 12) Retrieved from http://www.gwp.org/Global/GWP-CACENA_Files/en/pdf/tec04.pdf

Cosgrove, J. and Rijsberman, F. R. (2000). "World Water Vision: Making Water Everybody's Business". *Earthscan*, UK. (2016, January 14) Retrieved from http://www.worldwatercouncil.org/fileadmin/wwc/Library/WWVision/TableOfContents.pdf

FAO (2002). "Crops and Drops: Making the best use of Water for Agriculture". *Food and Agriculture Organization of the United Nations*. Rome (2016, January 14) Retrieved from ftp://ftp.fao.org/ docrep/fao/005/y3918e/y3918e00.pdf

Fry, C. (2008). *The Impact of Climate Change: the World's Greatest Challenge in the Twenty-first Century*. New Holland Publishers Ltd.

Gleick, P.H., Wolff, G., Chalecki, E. L. and Reyes, R. (2002). "Globalization and International Trade of Water". In: Gleick P.H., *et al. "The Worlds Water 2002-2003, the Report on Fresh Water Resources"*, Island Press, Washington, DC, USA, pp. 33-56. http://www.siwi.org/documents/Resources/Reports/CSD_Making_water_part_of_economic_development_2005.pdf

Hassing Jan, Niels Ipsen, Torkil Jønch Clausen, Henrik Larsen and Palle Lindgaard-Jørgensen (2009). "Integrated Water Resources Management in Action". *The United Nations World Water Assessment Programme Dialogue Paper*. Jointly prepared by DHI Water Policy and UNEP-DHI Centre for Water and Environment. United Nations Educational Scientific and Cultural Organization.

http://www.unwater.org/water-cooperation-2013/water-cooperation/facts-and-figures/en/

PAI, (1997). "Sustaining Water, Easing Scarcity: A Second Update". Revised data for the population action international report, sustaining water: Population and the Future of Renewable Water Supplies. http://www.populationaction.org/resources/publications/water/water97.pdf

PAI, (1999). Sustaining Water: Population and the Future of Renewable Water Supplies. http://www.cnie.org/pop/pai/h2o-toc.html.

Pandey, B.W. and Mishra, N. P. (2013). "Sustainable Use of Water Resources: The Need for New Management Options". In: Subhash Anand (ed.) *Progress in Environmental Management: Indian Experiences*. New Delhi: Research India Press, pp. 250-271.

Pandey, B.W. (2004). "Spatio-Temporal Dimensions of Drinking Water Supply in Cholapur Block, Varanasi". In: G. S. Chauhan and R.N. Dubey (eds.) *Water Resources Management*. New Delhi: Nataraj Publications, pp. 117-134.

Pandey, B.W., Bandooni, S.K. and Negi, V.S. (2004). "Community Participation in Water Resources Conservation and Management in Raath Region of Garhwal Himalaya". In: G.S. Chauhan and R.N. Dubey (eds.) *Water Resources Management*. New Delhi: Nataraj Publications, pp. 203-224.

Postel, S. (1999). "Pillar of Sand: Can the Irrigation Miracle Last?" New York: W. W. Norton & Co.

Serageldin, I. (1999). "Sustainable Agriculture for a Food Secure World." *Social Research: An International Quarterly*. Volume 66, No. 1 (Spring 1999): 105-115.

Shiklomanov, Igor, (1993). "Water Fresh Water Resources". In: Peter H. Gleick (Ed.). *Water in Crisis: A Guide to the Water Resources*. Oxford University Press, pp. 13-24.

Singh, R.B. and Pandey, B.W. (1996). "Environment Monitoring of Particulate Matter and Pollution in Major Rivers of India". In: K. Hartmut and Wilfried (eds.) *Advances in Limnology 47, Official Journal of the International Association for Theoretical and Applied Limnology*. E. Schweizerbat's sche Verlags Buchhandlung Publication. Stuttgart, Germany, pp. 557-561.

Singh, R.B. and Pandey, B.W. (1993). "Environmental and Human Response to Hydro Geomorphology: Micro-Level Study of Ganga Basin". *Journal of Scientific Research*. Vol. 43 (1&2), Banaras Hindu University, pp. 153-167.

Singh, R.B. and Pandey, B.W. (1996). "Perspective for Managing Rural Water Resources: A Study of Ganga-Gomati Doab". In: R.B. Singh (ed.) *Research in Geography: Land-Use Change and Sustainable Development*. Vol. 1. New Delhi: A.P.H. Publication, pp. 307-318.

Simonovic, S.P. (2000). "Tools for water management: one view of the future". *Water International*. 25: 76-88.

Solanes, M., and Gonzalez-Villarreal, F. (1999). The Dublin principles for water as reflected in a comparative assessment of institutional and legal arrangements for integrated water resources management. Sweden: Global Water Partnership, Stockholm, p. 17.

United Nations (19920. Conference on Environment & Development. AGENDA 21. Rio de Janerio, Brazil 3 to 14 June.

United Nations Environment Programme. (2002). GEO: *Global Environment Outlook 3*. London: Earthscan. pp. 150–177, http://www.unep.org/geo/geo3/english/pdf.htm.

UNEP (1999). "World day for Water". www.unep.org/unep/per/ipa/pressrel/r03-1799.001.

UNESCO (2001) Managing Risks: World Water Assessment Programme. Paris: United Nations Educational Scientific and Cultural Organization.

U.S. Environmental Protection Agency, "State Actions Banning MTBE (Statewide)" http:// www.epa.gov/mtbe/420b04009.pdf.

Weyer, P. J. (2001). "Municipal drinking water nitrate level and cancer risk in older women: The Iowa women's health study". *Epidemiology* 11:327– 338.

Ward, M. H. (1996). "Drinking water nitrate and the risk of non-Hodgkin's lymphoma". *Epidemiology* 7:465–471.

2

My City, My Delhi—Biomedical Waste

Sushma Moitra, Saloni Bahri and *Somdutta Sinha Roy*

Introduction

Health care facilities are important for human health and life. It is an irony that during medical activities, the waste that is produced is posing a threat to human health. Biomedical Waste (BMW) is "Any waste which is generated during the diagnosis, treatment or immunization of human beings or animals or in research activities pertaining thereto or in the production or testing of biological.[1] Proper handling of biomedical waste is very importance as it is infectious and hazardous.[2] Biomedical waste consists of biotechnology and microbiology wastes, human anatomical waste that includes organs, tissues and body parts, animal wastes produced during research from veterinary hospitals, waste sharps like hypodermic needles, syringes, scalpels and broken glass, discarded medicines, cytotoxic drugs, soiled waste such as dressing, bandages, plaster casts, material contaminated with blood, tubes and catheters, liquid waste from any of the infected areas, incineration ash and other chemical wastes.[3]

Types of Biomedical Waste

It is estimated that approximately 75-90 per cent of the biomedical waste generated by healthcare activities is non-hazardous. It is similar to domestic waste and is referred to as healthcare general waste (HCGW). It is made of chapter, plastic packaging, food preparation, etc. that have not been in contact with patients. The remaining 10-25 per cent is hazardous. It may be infectious, toxic or radioactive and can be injurious to humans or animals and detrimental to environment (Table 2.1). This fraction is referred to as healthcare risk waste (HCRW) It is important to understand that if both these types get mixed together then the whole waste becomes harmful.[4,5]

Table 2.1: Different Hospital Waste Categories

Category	*Type of Waste*	*Treatment and Disposal Options*
Category 1	Human Anatomical Waste (Human tissues, organs, body parts).	Incineration/Deep Burial
Category 2	Animal waste (Animal tissues, organs, body parts, carcasses, bleeding parts, blood and experimental animals used in research).	Incineration/Deep Burial
Category 3	Microbiology and biotechnology waste (waste from lab culture, specimens from microorganisms, vaccines, cell cultures, toxins, dishes, devices used to transfer cultures).	Local Autoclaving/ Microwaving/ Incineration
Category 4	Waste Sharps (Needles, Syringes, scalpels, blades, glass).	Chemical Disinfection Autoclaving/ Microwaving, Mutilation and Shredding
Category 5	Discarded medicines and cytotoxic drugs (outdated, contaminated, discarded drugs).	Incineration/Destruction and disposal in land fills
Category 6	Soiled waste (contaminated with blood and body fluids including cotton, dressings, soiled plasters, linen).	Autoclaving/ Microwaving/ Incineration
Category 7	Solid waste (tubes, catheters, IV sets).	Chemical Disinfection/Autoclaving/ Microwaving, Mutilation and Shredding
Category 8	Liquid waste (Waste generated from laboratory and washing, cleaning, disinfection).	Disinfection by chemical treatment and discharge into the drains
Category 9	Incineration ash	Land fills
Category 10	Chemical waste	Chemical disinfection and discharge into the drains

Source: http://www.medwasteind.org/random.asp

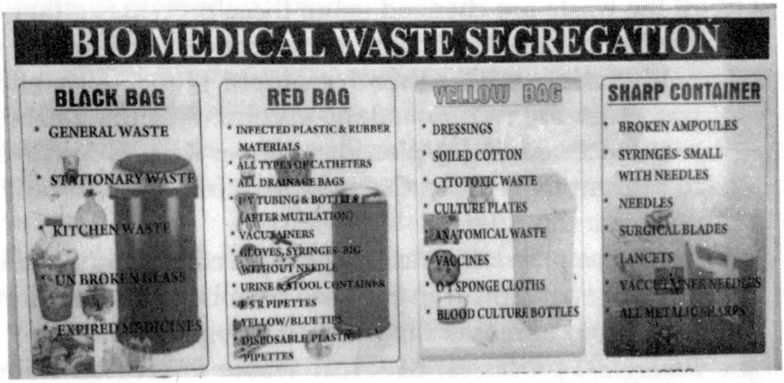

Fig. 2.1: The Colour Codes for Segregation of Biomedical Waste (Photograph by authors).

Fig. 2.2: **(A)** Autoclave set-up for sterilization of biomedical waste before disposal. **(B)** Colour coded waste collection bins lined with coloured plastic bags (photograph by authors).

Fig. 2.3: The biomedical waste is transferred to the autoclaving units through a pass-box. The pass-box shown here is with a small glass window (photograph by authors).

Need of Management of Hospitals Waste

The reasons behind proper management of BMW are the risks associated with inadequate practices followed which can lead to hazards such as[5, 6]:

- Poor infection control practices and poor waste management can cause no socomial infections in patients.
- Injuries from sharps can lead to infection to hospital personnel and waste handler.
- Outside hospital, waste handlers and scavengers are at risk of infection and also general public living in the areas close to hospitals.
- Hazardous chemicals and drugs pose a risk to health of persons handling wastes at all levels.
- Development of resistant strains of micro-organisms.
- Direct risk of air, water and soil pollution due to waste, or due to defective incineration emissions and ash.
- Disposed of drugs, and other "disposables" are repacked and sold off to unsuspecting buyers by unscrupulous elements.
- Organic portion ferments and attracts fly breeding.

Scenario of BMW in Delhi

BMW in Delhi is under the jurisdiction of Delhi Pollution Control Committee (DPCC). According to DPCC report of 2013 submitted to Central Pollution Control Board (CPCB), Delhi has a total of 3993 Health care establishments based on the applications for authorization received in DPCC and the establishments having agreement with any of the three Common Biomedical Waste Treatment Facility (CBWTFs) located in Delhi. Quantum of biomedical waste in Delhi adds up to 13.5 tons/day.[8] This is a huge number but does not include smaller health care establishments who may not be disposing there BMW according to the guidelines. Any BMW mixed with regular waste may pose greater health hazards. For a mega city like Delhi, more stringent rules and regulations with appropriate implementation protocols are required for averting any major health issues arising from improper disposal of BMW. Larger capacity incinerators are required to meet the ever increasing generation of biomedical waste. This issue is further aggravated by the fact that the jurisdiction of Delhi does not only include the city of Delhi only but also the larger NCR region which includes major, densely populated satellite cities in the adjoining states, further contributing to rapid rise in BMW.

Conclusion

Proper management of biomedical waste, i.e. collection, segregation and disposal is very important, especially for a mega-city like Delhi where a little mistake can give rise to a huge medical problem effecting millions of people. There is great need to raise awareness about issues related to biomedical waste for the protection of environment and community health. Scientific management of growing biomedical waste is a legal necessity as well as social responsibility. The practices being followed for the BMW management are inadequate. Thus, there is an urgent need to conduct training programmes for educating the people about the dire consequences of improper handling of biomedical waste.

Notes

1. Government of India, Ministry of Environment and Forests Gazette notification No. 460 dated July 27, New Delhi, 1998: 10-20.
2. http://www.preservearticles.com/2012031026176/what-does-biomedical-waste-means.html
3. http://vikaspedia.in/energy/environment/waste-management/bio-medical-waste-management/what-is-bio-medical-waste
4. http://www.who.int/mediacentre/factsheets/fs253/en/
5. Mathur, P., Patan, S. & Shobhawat, A.S. (2012). Need of Biomedical Waste Management System in Hospitals—An Emerging issue—A Review. *Curr World Environ. An International Research Journal of Environmental Science.* 7(1): 117-124. ISSN: 0973-4929, Online ISSN: 2320-8031.
6. http://www.medwasteind.org/random.asp
7. http://www.cpreec.org/pubbook-biomedical.htm
8. http://www.dpcc.delhigovt.nic.in/pdf/bmw_2013.pdf

3

Society, Religion and Bio-Diversity Conservation in India with Special Reference to Sacred Plants

Ranjana Roy Mishra

Introduction

India is a vast country having diverse religious culture and traditions. It is also famous for its rich biodiversity. Our traditions and rituals are quite helpful in conserving our diversity of plants. Many plants are worshiped or have religious values. Fear among people of cutting sacred plants leads to their conservation. Indian religious beliefs have associated many of the plants with Gods and several plants are considered Gods themselves or Gods residing over them. Our ancestors started these traditions and now in modern times these old rituals have become helpful in conserving plants (Ahirwar, 2013; Brahma *et. al.*, 2014; Sharma & Joshi, 2012). Today, when the population is increasing at an exponential rate and plants are being cut rapidly for construction of houses and agricultural land, these traditions have become a blessing in disguise to save trees from cutting. Modern man living in cities has become techno savvy and fails to identify even very common plants growing around him. These traditions then become more important to make him familiar with the plant while offering it to God. These plants not only provide fruits, fibre, drugs etc., but also reduce pollution, purify air and bring rain. They absorb carbon dioxide gas from atmosphere for photosynthesis and decrease excessive heating of earth thereby decreasing global warming.

The present chapter discusses how society and religious beliefs help in conservation of plants in India.

Unique Tradition of Tree Plantation in Some Villages

In different states of rural India, there are different ways of protecting trees. In many villages of Bihar and Rajasthan, there is a tradition of planting trees with the birth of a girl child with a belief that the planted tree will grow with the child and its fruits, wood and other products after sale will be helpful in education and marriage of the girl. In Piplantri village of southern Rajasthan's Rajsamand district there is a tradition of planting 111 trees with the birth of a girl child (Singh, 2013). In Dharhara village in Bihar's Bhagalpur district a girl child's birth is celebrated by planting at least one mango tree (Biswas, 2013).

In many tribal areas of Bihar and Odisha, before cutting a tree, permission is sought from it with a promise that five saplings will be planted in return. These age-old traditions are vanishing slowly which needs to be encouraged by the modern man even in cities to safeguard the environment.

Plant Conservation by Sacred Groves

India has a long tradition of conservation of all resources that are useful to people. Forests have been the lifeline for tribal and rural people since ages. For conservation of living creatures of forests, the concept of sacred groves is used in these areas. Sacred Groves comprise of patches of land from few trees to forests of several acres that are usually dedicated to Gods and Goddess or tree spirits. These spaces are protected by local communities because of their religious beliefs and traditional rituals that run through several generations. People believe that any kind of disturbance will offend the God, causing diseases, natural calamities or failure of crops. Sacred groves have been a traditional means of biodiversity conservation. None is permitted to cut any tree or plant, kill animals and birds, or do any harm to any form of life in this area.

The presence of sacred zones in biodiversity parks like Yamuna Biodiversity Park in Delhi is a mark of this old conservation method. Although, there has been no comprehensive study on the

Sacred Groves/Forests of the entire country, experts estimate the total number of Sacred Groves/Forests in India could be in the range of 100,000–150,000 (Sacred Plants: http://ecoheritage.cpreec.org/). In some forests even the dry leaves, stem and fallen fruits are not touched. For example, the Garo and the Khasi tribes of Meghalaya do not allow any human interference in the sacred zones (Sacred Plants: http://ecoheritage. cpreec. org/). In some zones, deadwood or dried leaves may be picked-up, but the green tree or its branches are never cut. For example, the Gond tribes of Madhya Pradesh do not allow the cutting of tree, but allow fallen parts to be used (Sacred Plants: http://ecoheritage. cpreec. org/). Sacred groves in the hills of Garhwal and Kumaon are mentioned in old Hindu scriptures like the *Puranas*. Shipin, about 12 km. from Shimla is believed to be the biggest deodar grove which consists of trees that are hundreds of years old. Villagers in this area who pass through it dust their clothes to make sure they do not carry anything belonging to the grove. Trees in the area cannot be cut or felled and all deadwood found in the forest is used only in the temple, located in the grove.

Sacred Groves/Forests are classified as two types:

(i) ***Traditional Sacred Groves***: It is the place where the village deity resides.

(ii) ***Temple Groves***: A grove is created around a temple and conserved.

Ecological Significance of Sacred Groves

1. ***Conservation of Biodiversity***: The Sacred Groves/Forests are important repositories of floral and faunal diversity that have been conserved by local communities.
2. ***Recharge of aquifers***: The groves are often associated with ponds, streams or springs, which help meet the water requirements of the local people. The vegetative cover also helps in the recharging the aquifers.
3. ***Soil conservation***: The vegetation cover of the Sacred Groves/Forests improves the soil stability of the area and also prevents soil erosion.

Sikhism and Plants

The naming of sacred shrines after species of trees is unique to the Sikh religion. Punjab's Sacred Heritage author D.S. Jaspal has compiled a pictorial documentation of 59 sacred Sikh shrines in India and Pakistan named after 19 species of trees in his book "TRYST WITH TREES". An example is Gurudwara Dukh Bhanjani Ber Sahib in Golden temple, Amritsar which is named after a *beri* tree, *Zizyphus jujube,* which is considered very sacred by Sikh community. Gurudwara Dukh Bhanjani Ber literally means "the tree of healing". It is located on the eastern side of the *sarovar* in the Golden Temple. The tree is associated with the legend of *Bibi Rajani* whose leper husband is said to have been cured of his malady by having a dip in the old pond which had existed here since ancient times. People have a strong faith that water in this portion of the tank will heal their ailments. To conserve the germ plasm of this sacred *beri,* the technique of clonal technology has been used by D.S. Jaspal to produce more number of plants from this sacred tree. (http://www.museumoftrees. org/sacred_garden.php)

Christianity and Plants

In Christianity, many flowers represent many symbols of this religion. (i) The main flower that means a lot in the Christian religion is the **passion flower**. This flower is mainly a symbol of Jesus' scourging, crowning with thorns and crucifixion. (ii) The **archetypal flower** symbolizes the purity and is associated with the Virgin Mary. (iii) The **pomegranate** is a significant symbol of hope and resurrection. (iv) **Roses** represent the prayers, wounds and sacrificial blood that Christ shed. White rose represent Christ's purity and the red rose represents Christ's sacrificial blood. The red rose also is the symbol of love. (https://plantsincivilization. wordpress.com/2009/04/16/flowers-in-christianity/

Pine and Araucaria trees are also of special significance to Christians. These plants are generally planted by Christians near churches and in their home gardens so that they can be decorated during different ceremonies and occasions like Easter and Christmas.

Islam and Plants

There are several sayings from the Prophet Muhammad that relate the importance of trees and plants in Islam. Planting trees is regarded as an act of charity and the planter receives blessings from all those who benefit from it. Trees are treated with respect and are not unnecessarily harmed in this religion. The *Qur'an* also has numerous passages that describe the lush gardens and trees in heaven, highlighting their value not only in living world but their significance after death.

Pomegranates are specially mentioned three times in the *Qur'an* as one of the fruits that will be found in paradise, as a reminder of the nutritious provision from God and as a sign of His artistry. (http://khaleafa.com/value-of-trees-in-islam/)

Nutritionally pomegranate fruit is rich in Vitamin C and iron with a calorific value of 65 (calories). It is a good source of sodium, riboflavin and calcium. Pomegranate plants also provide herbal medicines for diarrhoea, fevers, gum disorders and earaches.

Hinduism and Plants

In Hindus several Plants have been traditionally considered sacred for the following reasons:

1. ***Association with a deity***: For example, Bel tree (*Aeglemarmelos*) is associated with Lord Shiva and *Tulsi* (*Ocimum sanctum*) with Lord Krishna/Vishnu.
2. ***Trees sheltering any object of worship***: *Sthala vrikshas* are actually the trees that shelters an open-air shrine, which is later replaced by a temple.
3. Some plants are believed to have **originated from bodies or limbs of Gods**. For example, the Flame of the forest (*Bute amonosperma*) is believed to have originated from the body of Lord Brahma and the *Rudraksha* tree (*Elaeo carpus-ganitrus*) rose from the tears of Lord Shiva.
4. Plants with **socio-economic significance or a major role in the local ecology** are also considered sacred. For example, *Khejri* tree (*Prosopis cineraria*) by the *Bishnois* of Rajasthan is related to the crucial role the tree plays in the desert ecology. It provides the community with food, fodder and building material.

Sacred plants of Hindu religion are can be classified as Trees, Herbs and Grains.

Sacred Trees

1. *Ficus religiosa* (*Pipal*/Sacred Fig tree): It is the state tree of Bihar, Odisha and Haryana. This tree is considered very sacred and people are afraid of cutting it. The tree is considered as an incarnation of Lord Vishnu. The tree also symbolises the continuity of life because the tree itself lives and grows for hundreds of years. It is said that Buddha achieved *nirvana* under this tree and it is considered a holy tree by Hindus and Buddhists. Due to this, the *Pipal* tree is also called as the *Bodhi* tree or the 'tree of wisdom'. It is also said that Ghosts reside on it. This tree is worshipped during Vishnu and *Pitri puja* in almost every state of India. Science says that *Pipal* is the only tree that produces oxygen in day as well as night. It is a CAM (Crassulacean Acid Metabolism) plant and is a hemi-epiphyte, i.e. seeds germinate and grow as an epiphyte on other tree and when the host tree dies it establishes in soil. It is said that when they grow as an epiphyte they carry CAM and releases oxygen during night also but in soil switch over to C_3 pathway.

   According to the book of Ayurveda, *Pipal* leaves, fruits and bark are killers of diseases. The tree has a cooling property. Licking honey placed on its leaves is believed to cure speech irregularities. Its leaves, when heated in ghee, are applied to cure wounds. Ingesting the bark, fruit and buds with different combination of things cures diseases related with bile, inflammation swelling etc. (https://jaagruti. wordpress. com/2010/04/12/science-behind-religious-practices_3/)
2. *Ficus benghanalensis* (*Bargad*/Banyan): It is our national tree and state tree of Madhya Pradesh. The tree symbolizes the *Trimurti*: Vishnu is believed to be the bark, Brahma, the roots and *Shiva,* the branches. Banyan tree has 'aerial roots' that is, its branches drop to the ground, take root again, and send out more twisting, trailing branches. These represent matted hair of Shiva. Banyan also symbolises life and fertility in many Indian cultures. This plant is worshipped during *Vat Savitri Puja* by married women in Hindu religion in Uttar Pradesh, Bihar and Odisha.

Married women tie holy thread around *Bargad* during *puja* and believe worshipping this tree will bring long life to their husbands. This is considered a pious tree and is not cut due to these beliefs. The twigs are used as tooth brush. The tree attracts a large number of birds, squirrels, insects, flying foxes and is a home for large number of creatures. Delicate Map Butterfly lay its eggs on the tender pink leaves. The leaves also attract squirrels. *Akshaya Vata*, the 'undying' banyan tree at Allahabad, is the subject of many legends, and still attracts millions of pilgrims. A group of three sacred trees, known as *tentar*, 'triad'– a banyan, a *Pipal* and *Paakar*—planted together, is especially sacred, and is known as *Harsankari*, 'the chair of Hari'. The fruits are eaten by many birds like *bulbul*, *mynas* and animals like flying fox. Leaves and twigs are favourite snack of elephants. It is an ornamental avenue tree. Its tough and elastic wood is used for making tent poles, carrying poles and yokes for bullock carts. It provides cool, refreshing shade on a hot summer's day.

3. *Aegele marmelos* (*Bel*/Wood apple): It is the state tree of Puducherry. Leaves and fruits are offered to Lord Shiva during *Mahashivaratri*. We find the reference of this tree in *Atharvaveda*. It is considered a holy fruit and generally planted near Hindu temples.
4. *Cocos nucifera* (*Nariyal*/Coconut): Coconut is the state tree of Kerala. It is called *Kalpavriksha* or the 'wish-fulfilling tree'. The fruit is also believed to represent Lord Shiva, the three eyed God and the three black marks on the coconut shell symbolises his eyes. The fruit is considered very sacred and prayers are offered to many Gods with its fruit. It is an essential part of all the ceremonies of Hindus. Coconut water is considered pious and distributed as sacred water after *pujas*.
5. *Santalum album* (*Chandan*/Sandalwood): It is the State tree of Karnataka. The wood of this plant is considered very sacred. It is an essential part of the Hindu temples and homes. The paste of the wood is applied on forehead in most of the religious occasions in Hindus.
6. *Musa paradisiacal* (*Kela*/Banana): It is worshipped by both unmarried and married women in many States of India.

The whole plant is considered sacred. Leaves and fruits are used for many religious ceremonies like *Ganesh chaturthi, Grihpravesh, Satya Narayan puja,* weddings etc. The food is served on its leaves during many social and religious occasions. It is generally planted near Hindu temples.

7. *Mangifera indica* (*Aam*/Mango): It is the State tree of Gujarat and Maharashtra. The wood, leaves and flowering branches are believed to bring goodness and happiness to homes. Its plant parts are used in many religious ceremonies like marriages, *Grihpravesh* etc. throughout in India. It is grown for goodness and prosperity. In Gujarat, on the night of the seventh of the month of *Savan* (July-August), a young mango tree is planted near the house and worshipped by women to protect children from disease.
8. *Neolamarckia cadamba* (*Kadamb*/Kadam): The plant is considered very sacred because it is believed that Lord Krishna played flute under it. We find its reference in *Kalidasa* literature. In Southern India it is referred as *Parvati* tree. The tree is worshipped for wealth and children. It is also sacred for *Jain* community. So, it is not cut out of religious belief or fear. The fruit juice is given to children to treat gastric irritability. A decoction of the leaves is good for ulcers and wounds. The fruits are edible. The timber is used for making pulp and paper, boxes, crates and furniture. The wood is also used as fuel.
9. *Nyctanthesarbortristis* (*Harsringar*/Night Jasmine/Queen of Night): Its flowers are offered to Lord Shiva. It is said that it brings happiness and prosperity. So, people plant it near their house all over India.
10. *Bambusa bambos* (*Baans*/Bamboo): The plant is considered very sacred and its stem is used for making *mandaps* for Hindu weddings and religious ceremonies. Bamboo flute is associated with Lord Krishna.
11. *Elaeo carpusganitrus* (*Rudraksha*/Utrasum Bead tree): According to the old mythological epic "*Shiv Purana*", *Rudraksha* was the favourite tree of Lord Shiva. Its seeds are traditionally used as prayer beads by Hindus. Usually, the beads of this tree are strung together as a garland. It is

considered a very holy tree by Hindus and they conserve it. *Rudraksha* beads are the seeds of the fruit obtained from *Rudraksha* trees. *Rudraksha* beads are covered by an outer shell of blue colour on fully ripening, so they are also called blueberry beads and the sweet tasting fruit flesh can be used for treatment of various diseases. It is kept in water for a number of days and then *Rudraksha* is taken out after peeling off the pulp and brushing it clean. It is believed that the seed of *Rudraksha* contains the secrets of the entire evolution of the cosmos within it. Each seed also possesses from 1 to 38 vertical lines running down its surface, like the longitude lines on a globe. These lines are known as *mukhi*, or faces, and are natural formations of the seed. Seeds with one vertical line are known as *Eka-mukhi* (one facet), which are very rare; those with two lines are *Dvi-mukhi* (two facets), and so on. No other bead is considered to be as auspicious and powerful as a *Rudraksha*.

12. *Bixaorellana* (*Sindoor*/Vermilion): *Sindoor* is traditionally applied along the parting-line of a woman's hair as mark of a married woman in Hindus. It is a dye extracted from the fruits of this plant. This is also considered a sacred plant in many states of India like Assam.
13. *Thevetiaperuvianum* (*Kanair*/Temple flower): The yellow coloured flowers are used in worshipping Gods and Goddesses and it is generally planted in home gardens to fetch flowers.
14. *Hibiscus rosasinensis* (*Gurhal*/China rose): The red coloured flowers of this plant are offered to Goddess Parvati during *Gauri Puja* in Bihar, Uttar Pradesh and Bengal. Women grow this plant for its flowers.
15. *Areca catechu* (*Supari*/Betalnut): It is required during marriage ceremonies of Hindus and various religious rituals in Assam, Bihar, Odisha and Bengal. It is a tradition in Assam, Bihar and Bengal to greet guests by offering *paan* and *supari*.
16. *Zizyphus nummularia* (*Ber*/Chinee apple/Indian Jujuba): The tree is associated with Lord Shiva. The fruits are offered to Lord Shiva during *Shivaratri*. The *ber* fruit is also associated with Sabari, an old woman who is mentioned in the Hindu epic *Ramayana*. The tree is also

considered sacred by the Sikh community. The Golden temple in Amritsar has a *'Ber'* tree called the *'Beri Sahib'* in its central courtyard. The tree is also worshipped. The ripe fruit is very nutritious and is consumed raw. It is also used for making candies, pickles and used in desserts. The powdered raw fruit is eaten to cure ulcers, swellings in mouth, diarrhoea. The fruit juice is used to treat venereal disorders. The leaves of the tree are used as fodder for the cattle. A paste of the bark helps to cure boils and tumours. The wood is used for construction and for making agricultural implements. The thorny tree makes good fencing. The tree is also used as a host for the lac insect, *Kerrialacca* in India.

17. *Phoenix dactyilefera* (*Khajoor*/Dates): The fruits are offered to rising Sun during *Chatha puja* in Bihar and Uttar Pradesh. It is offered to Lord Shiva on *Mahashivaratri.*
18. *Azadhiracta indica* (*Neem*/Margosa): It is the state tree of Andhra Pradesh. It is worshipped in many States of India. In some parts, the tree is worshipped as Goddess *Neemari Devi.* The Gujjar tribes of Rajasthan worship it as *'Neem Narayan'*. *Neem* is also associated with Goddess *Sitala Devi* in north India the deity who can cause or cure small-pox.
19. *Tamarindus indica* (*Imli*/Tamarind): It is believed to be a seat of ghosts in southern India. So people do not cut it and thereby conserve it.
20. *Bauhinia variegata* (*Kachnar*/Orchid tree/Camel foot tree): It is the state flower of Bihar. The flowers are offered to Lord Shiva.
21. *Butea frondosa* (*Palash*/*Dhak*/*Tesu*/Flame of forest): It is the national flower of Jharkhand. The tree is worshipped by ladies on *Akshyatritya* in many parts of India. The flowers are offered to Devi Saraswati on *Saraswati Puja* in Bengal and *Devi Kali* on *Kali Puja* in Bengal. The dried flowers are used as a diuretic. The gum obtained from the tree is called Bengal Kino. It contains tannin and is used in the treatment of diarrhoea. The seeds have anti-helminthic properties and are used in the treatment of worms. The wood is soft and durable and is used for making boats. A yellow dye, obtained from the fresh *Palash* flowers is used during the festival of Holi.

22. *Madhuca longifolia* (*Mahua*/Indian butter tree): The flowers are offered to worship Lord Shiva in many tribal parts of Bihar and Odisha. It is considered a sacred tree for carrying out many ceremonies like marriage and worshipped on almost every auspicious occasion in tribal areas of Odisha.
23. *Citrus sinensis* (*Neemboo*/Lemon): Lemons along with green chillies are hanged on doors and shops to ward off evil eyes. Lemon is an emblem of *Devi Shakti* in Southern India. Prayers are also offered with a garland made of lemons to Lord Shiva in many states of India.
24. *Cassia fistula* (*Amaltas*/Golden flower): It is believed in some regions that rain comes 45 days after flowering of this tree. In southern India its flowers are used during *Onam* festival.
25. *Phyllanthu semblica* (*Amla*/Indian Gooseberry): The *Amla* tree is one of the most sacred plants in India. It is widely believed that *Amla* tree rose from the tears of Lord Brahma. The fruit is also associated with Goddess Lakshmi. It is offered to Lord Shiva in *Mahashivaratri*.
26. *Syzgium cumini (Jamun*): It is considered a fruit of Gods in Gujarat. It is believed that Lord Rama thrived on it during his *vanvaas* period. It is also offered to Lord Shiva on *Mahashivaratri*.
27. *Saraca indica* (*Ashoka*/Sorrowless tree): The tree is sacred to Hindus. There are numerous legends associated with the tree. It is associated with Devi Sita in the epic *Ramayana* as *Ashoka vatika*. It is believed that Sita spent her sorrowful days under an *Ashoka* tree.

Sacred Herbs

1. *Cynodon dactylon* (*Doob*/Bermuda grass): It is a necessary part of any religious ceremony in Hindus. The leaves are offered during *Ganesh puja* and *Satya Narayan puja*. It is planted in gardens and pots for its leaves.
2. *Ocimum Sanctum* (*Tulsi*/Basil): This is considered to be most sacred plant among Hindus. The plant is worshipped as Goddess *Tulsi*. There are two varieties of Tulsi that are venerated—*Rama Tulsi* and *Krishna*/*Shyama Tulsi* (the dark-

coloured) *Tulsi* leaves are offered to Lords Rama, Krishna and Vishnu. It is believed to purify the homes and ward off evils. Every house has at least one plant. *Tulsi* leaves dipped in water are distributed as sacred water after *pujas* in temples. Tulsi is a herbal remedy for various common ailments. The juice extracted from the leaf is given to cure fever, dysentery, skin infections, intestinal worms and to reduce vomiting. The stem is made into beads and used as rosaries by the Hindus.

3. *Curcuma longa* (*Haldi*/Turmeric): The plant is considered very pious. It is an essential part of wedding ceremonies throughout the India. Turmeric paste is applied to would be brides to bring glow on their face in Bihar, Uttar Pradesh, Punjab and several other States of India.
4. *Nelumbo nucifera* (*Kamal*/Lotus): It is our national flower and State flower of Haryana, Jammu & Kashmir and Karnataka. It is believed that Goddess Lakshmi resides on its leaves. The flowers are offered to Lakshmiji during *Deepawali* and *Lakshmi puja*. The flower is also associated with Lord Brahma and Vishnu. In Buddhism, the lotus represents purity of body, speech and mind, floating above the muddy waters of attachment and desire. The *Bahai* community adopted the lotus symbol in the design of the *Bahai*, Lotus temple at New Delhi.
5. *Tagetes* (*Gainda*/Marigold): The flowers and garland made of flowers are an essential part of all the religious ceremonies of Hindus. The flowers are offered to several Gods and specially to Goddess Saraswati during *Saraswati puja* in Bihar, Bengal and Uttar Pradesh.
6. *Calotropisprocera* (*Ark*/Rubber bush): It is a weed which is generally found growing on the roadsides. Its leaves and flowers are offered to Lord Shiva during *Mahashivaratri* in many states of India. Although, it is a weed but due to its sacred nature people conserve it and holds a good example where we find a plant being conserved for religious purposes.
7. *Datura stramonium* (*Datura*/Jimson weed): Devotees offer the fruits of this plant to Lord Shiva on Mahashivaratri. Although this grows as a weed throughout India, but during *Mahashivaratri* fruit sellers sell this thorny fruit like

hot cakes. This is a very good example where we find weeds being conserved for religion.

8. *Cannabis sativa* (*Bhang*/Hemp): Leaves, fruits and flowers are offered to Lord Shiva on *Mahashivaratri* in many states of India like Bihar, Uttar Pradesh, Himachal Pradesh and Uttarakhand.
9. *Piper betel (Paan*/Betal leaf): The leaves are used in many religious ceremonies in Assam, Bihar and Bengal. They are specially used during weddings in Bihar and Bengal.
10. *Lawsonia alba* (*Mehendi*/Henna): It is the most essential component of Hindu marriages. The paste of the leaves is applied on the hands of bride during weddings and also used on other festivals like *Rakshabandhan, Teej, Karvachauth* etc.
11. *Trapabispinosa* (*Singhara*/water caltrop): The fruit of the plant is eaten during *Navratras* by fasting devotees and it is widely sold in markets during this time.
12. *Ipomeabatatas* (*Sakarkandi*/Sweet potato): Boiled tuberous roots are eaten during *Ganesh Chaturthi* in several parts of India.
13. *Amaranthuspaniculatus* (*Ramdana/lalsaag/chaulai*): The *ladoos* made out of the seeds are eaten by devotees fasting during *Navratras.*
14. *Saccharumofficinarum* (*Ganna*/Sugarcane): Sugarcane is used for offering prayers to rising sun during *Chhath puja* in Uttar Pradesh and Bihar.
15. *Clitoriaternatea* (*Aparajita* flower): God is worshipped with this sacred flower in various states of India.
16. *Epipremnumaureum* (Money plant): It is planted outside homes throughout India to bring prosperity and wealth in home.
17. *Capsicum annum* (Chilly/*Mirchi*): Chillies along with lemons are hanged at doors of houses to ward off evil spirits. It is also put in fire along with mustard seeds by old ladies in villages as to protect new born child from evil eyes.
18. *Rosa damascena* (*Gulab*/Rose): *Phoolon ki chadar* made from the flowers is offered by Muslims during prayers in mosque and offered by Hindus to their Lords in temples. Christians require it for their marriage ceremonies.

Sacred Grains/Seeds

1. *Oryzasativa* (*Dhan*/Rice): Rice is a symbol of prosperity in India. Rice grains are associated with Goddess *Annapoorna* by Hindus. There are many festivals associated with the sowing, planting and harvesting of rice like *Pongal* and *Onam* in South and *Bihu* in Assam. *Akshata* made of rice mixed with turmericis used in many religious ceremonies of Hindus like *Rakshabandhan*, weddings etc.
2. *Hordeumvulgare* (*Jau*/Barley): It is one of the important components of *hawan samagri*. It is used at the time of *Navratras* to produce small seedlings which is considered very sacred.
3. *Cicerarietinum* (*Chana*/Gram): Prayers are offered with its grains during *Chatth Puja* and *Vat Savitri Puja* celebrated in Uttar Pradesh and Bihar.
4. *Sesamum indicum* (Sesame/*Til*): Ceremomies are done with *til* on *Makarsamkranti*. *Til ladoos* are eaten during *Makarsamkranti* and *Lohri*. It is also a part of *havan samagri*.
5. *Arachis hypogea* (*Mungaphali*/Grounnut): Groundnut seeds are an essential ingredient of the festival *Lohri* celebrated in Punjab.
6. *Zea mays* (*Makka*/Corn): The festival of *Lohri* is celebrated by offering pop corns and groundnut in fire to mark the start of harvest season in Punjab, Haryana and Delhi.
7. *Brassica campestris* (Mustard/*Sarson*): Old ladies in villages mix its grains with chillies and put them in fire to ward off evil eyes.

Conclusion

The culture of India is so beautiful and diverse. The presence of so many states and so many religions makes it more beautiful. Every state has made one plant as its state tree because of the sacred reason or other reason. People living on hills and villages consider plants as a source of their livelihood. Rural people get their food, fuel, fibre and fodder from these plants. They utilise the plants in their fullest manner. They make their houses with them, get fruits and food from them and use dried branches as their fuel. Villagers have associated one plant or other with some religion to save them from cutting.

There are several stories in the history of Indian culture where people have sacrificed their lives in protest of cutting of trees. One the most famous stories are of sacrifice of a *Bishnoi* woman Amrita Devi in Rajasthan over 300 years ago in protest of felling of *Khejri* (*Prosopis cineraria*) trees. This was followed in Uttarakhand hills where tribal people led by famous environmentalist Sunderlal Bahuguna hugged trees to save them from cutting in Chipko Andolan.

In cities, the modern man is so busy with the daily routine that he has no time to look around and take care of the environment. These old traditions help in conserving the plants. In the modern times if a plant is used as a part of ritual or ceremony, in a way it is conserved. The religious beliefs are a beautiful method of plant conservation. We follow our customs and traditions and in turn enrich our environment with greenery and diversity of plants. Traditions and biodiversity conservation go hand in hand this way.

These beautiful and unique traditions make our country different from others. These traditions teach modern man that there are very simple methods through which we can conserve our biodiversity. The lists of the plants discussed above are very few in number compared to the vast biodiversity we have in India. There are endless rituals and ceremonies and endless list of plants associated with each one of them in India. We should preserve and encourage these rituals for the benefit of our better and a green future!

References

Ahirwar, J.R. (2013). Socio-Religious Importance of plants in Bundelkhand region of India. *Research Journal of Recent Sciences,* 2:1-4.

Biswas, A. (2013). Bihar village sets example by planting trees on birth of girls. *Hindustan Times,* June 5.

Brahma, S., Narzary, H., Brahma, J. (2014). Socio-cultural and religious plants used by BODO tribes of BTC, Assam, India. *International Journal of Scientific and Research Publications,* 4 (1): 1-11.

Flowers in Christianity:https://plantsincivilization. wordpress. com/2009/04/16/flowers-in-christianity/ April 16, 2009.

Sacred Plants: http://ecoheritage. cpreec. org/CPR Environmental Education Centre: Conservation off ecological and heritage sites of India.

Sacred Gardens: http://www. museumoftrees. org/sacred_garden. php.
Sacred Groves of India: deoxy. org/gaia/index_forests. htm
Science behind the religious practices:https://jaagruti. wordpress. com/2010/04/12/science-behind-religious-practices_3/. April 12, 2010.
Sharma, V. & Joshi, B.D. (2012). Role of sacred plants in religion and healthcare system in Almora district of Uttarakhand State (India). *Academia Arena* (2) 6: 19-22.
Singh, M.P. (2013). A village that plants 111 trees for every girl born in Rajasthan. *The Hindu*, April 11.
The Value of Trees in Islam: http://khaleafa. com/value-of-trees-in-islam/
Ruskin Bond, (1975). *The World of Trees*, New Delhi: National Book Trust, India.

4

Iconic Saree Weaving Clusters of India

A Case Study of Saree Weaving Settlements of Banaras

Shahid Jamal and *Anjan Sen*

Introduction

Craftsmanship means more than technical virtuosity. It is not only a profound understanding of materials, and of the tools with which materials are fashioned, but most importantly it involves a genuine pride which drives an individual to craft and weave as well as can be done, beyond what is required, beyond economic considerations of reward. An excellent example of such craftsmanship is Saree weaving is India. Traced to the Vedic civilization, evolving with cross-cultural influences of trade, confluences of techniques and patterns, the sari still has innovations in its production processes. As an unstitched garment for women, it has no parallels in terms of versatility, richness of colour, texture, and variety of weaving techniques using different kinds of yarn, including cotton, silk, gold and silver thread. The important sites under UNESCO are from five Indian states: Madhya Pradesh, Uttar Pradesh, Maharashtra, Andhra Pradesh and Assam. It focuses on the tangible elements of sari weaving clusters irrespective of the popularity of the sari.

Firstly, Chanderi in Madhya Pradesh (24. 4312° N, 78. 748° E):

The town of Chanderi is divided into *mohallas* or residential neighbourhoods. The *mohallas* of the different communities of the weavers are important part of the urban morphology. The thirteenth century Moroccan visitor Ibn Batuta remarked: "it is a big city with thronged market places" like sadar bazaar.

Secondly, Banaras (25.2820° N, 82.9563° E) and Mubarakpur (26.0900° N, 83.2900° E) in Uttar Pradesh:

Banaras is home to the iconic brocade sari. Built heritage of Banaras sari weaving settlement is intact to a large extent, with a large number of weavers still in their original homes and active looms. Designs and motifs are sourced from architecture. Cotton weaving started in Mubarakpur during fourteenth century. During Sultan Muhammad Bin Tughlaq's era there were 4000 silk sari weavers in Mubarakpur. Mubarakpur is known for making pure silk Banarasi saris with zari work.

Thirdly, Paithan (19.4800° N, 75.3800° E) and Yeola (20.0420° N, 74.4890° E) in Maharashtra:

Paithan is comprise pure gold threads and yarns of silk spun in the 2000-year old traditional method. This form of weaving was developed in Paithan (Aurangabad district), historically called Pratishthana. This art form soon spread to the other places in Maharashtra namely Yeola, Pune, Malegaon and Nashik. One can even see motifs from Ajanta cave paintings.

Fourthly, Koyyalagudem (17.1167°N 81.3000°E) and Pochampalli (17.3861° N, 78.6433° E) in Andhra Pradesh:

The Plan of a weaver's house developed from the livelihood needs of the inhabitants. Every member of the family is involved in the process of weaving and most of the time is spent in the weaving room, the largest of all the rooms.The latter city is popularly known as the silk city of India. Weaver's house contains both semi-open and enclosed spaces for sari weaving.

Finally, Sualkuchi in Assam (26.1700° N, 91.5700° E):

Sualkuchi has a glorious history in production of muga and mulberry silk since at least fourth century B.C. and finds a mention in Kautilya's *Arthashastra* (referred to as Suvarnakunda of ancient Kamrupa). Of a naturally rich, golden colour, muga is the finest of India's wild silks. The loom is a prized possession in every Assamese home. Weaving has been a way of life in the state since time immemorial. Assam tribal weaver clusters: The Karbi, Mishing, Rabha, Singpho and Tai-phake tribes have a strong textile tradition. The Mech tribe is silk-weavers in profession. The Dimasa tribes are renowned for their expertise in silk-culture and weaving-prowess and are the producers of Endi. Weaving among the tribal societies of Assam is a home craft using the back-strap loom or loin loom, which is simple and portable.

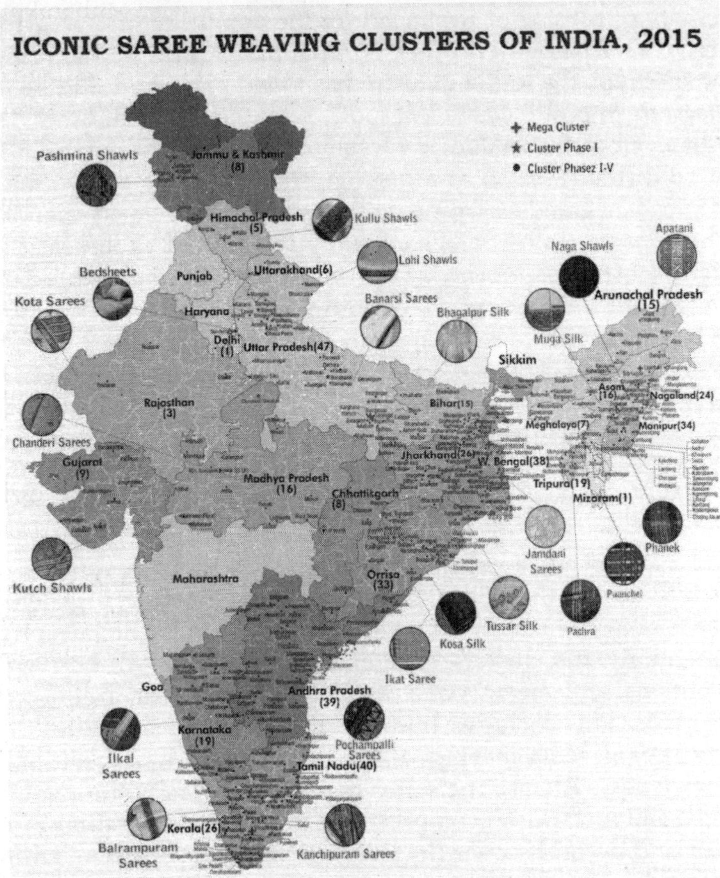

Map 4.1: Iconic Saree Weaving Clusters of India

The Contextual Background

Banaras is famous for its socio-economic and religious importance all over the World. The city is equally important as a brocade-weaving centre throughout the country. The weaving industry, which flourished during the Vedic period and touched its peak at the time of Mughal period, explains how the act of weaving was a part and parcel of the life of the Banaras people. Whether, it is the religious activity or earning of livelihood for the population, the weaving activity surpassed all other occupations. From the historical perspectives, the textile industry has found place from Rig Vedic literature to post-independent India. Since the Rig Vedic times, we hear about several kinds of textiles among which figures out the cloth of gold (the *Hiranya*) as a distinguished type, the god in their resplendent grandeur wear it, as they drive in their stately chariots. The *Hiranya* cloth has been usually interpreted as the earliest equivalent for the present day zari work or the **kimkhab** (brocades). During the Mughal period, around fourteenth century, weaving of brocades with complex designs using gold and silver threads became the domain of Banaras. Through the movement of silk weavers from Gujarat during the famine of 1603, it is likely that silk brocade weaving started in Banaras in the seventeenth century and developed in excellence during the eighteenth and nineteenth century.

Architecture of a region is shaped by many influencing factors such as climate, locally available material, construction techniques and needs of the inhabitants. This serial exemplifies vernacular architecture of the several regions of India where occupational needs of inhabitants is the major factor influencing architecture. Essentially, the clusters have existent tangible built heritage/ traditional settlement, as well as active traditional weaving practice in place. This includes traditional looms and technological advances in loom-making within the framework of traditional knowledge systems. The series highlights diversity throughout India and each cluster comprising at least one of the attributes as outstanding on its own (In terms of settlement pattern, scale, category, loom types, woven fabric, process, community knowledge systems, continuity, etc.).

In addition to these extraordinary skillsets, sari weavers also carry in their memories and hands centuries-old traditions of motifs, colours and design, linked to the art and aesthetics of the past—corresponding to the regional architecture and artefacts of each region. The serial bears a unique testimony to a cultural tradition of Saree weaving which influences the regional architecture. The serial is an outstanding example of traditional human settlements that developed in accordance with the occupational needs of the weavers. The vernacular form reflects the way of life and caters to the various functions of the artisan communities engaged in weaving and pre/post-loom activities.

Over the times, the Banarasi silk handloom industry has been incurring huge losses because of competition from mechanized units producing the Banarasi silk saris at a faster rate and at cheaper cost, another source of competition has been saris made of cheaper synthetic alternatives to silk. In 2009, next two years of gap, weaver associations in Uttar Pradesh, secured Geographical Indication (GI) rights for the 'Banaras Brocades and Sarees'. GI is an intellectual property right, which pinpoints a good as patenting in a certain region where a given quality, reputation or other characteristic of the product is essentially attributable to its geographical origin. According to GI certificate, Banarasi products fall under four classes (23–26), namely:

1. Silk brocades
2. Textile goods
3. Silk sari
4. Dress material and silk embroidery.

Furthermost notably this means that no sari or brocade made outside the six identified districts of Uttar Pradesh, that is Varanasi, Mirzapur, Chandauli, Bhadohi, Jaunpur and Azamgarh districts, can be legally sold under the name of Banaras sari and brocade. In 2009, weaver associations in Uttar Pradesh, secured Geographical Indication (GI) tag for the 'Banaras Sarees and Brocades'; while in 2014, UNESCO included the built heritage of sari weaving settlements in its tentative list as "Iconic Weaving Clusters".

Objectives

1. To evaluate the importance of "Geographical Indications" tag to the various products under umbrella term 'Banaras Sarees and Brocades'.
2. To appraise the role and significance of "Iconic Weaving Clusters" in the weaving of 'Banaras Sarees and Brocades'.

Research Methodology and Database

In order to access the sari weaving cluster Banaras following method of acquiring information have been used. Purposely

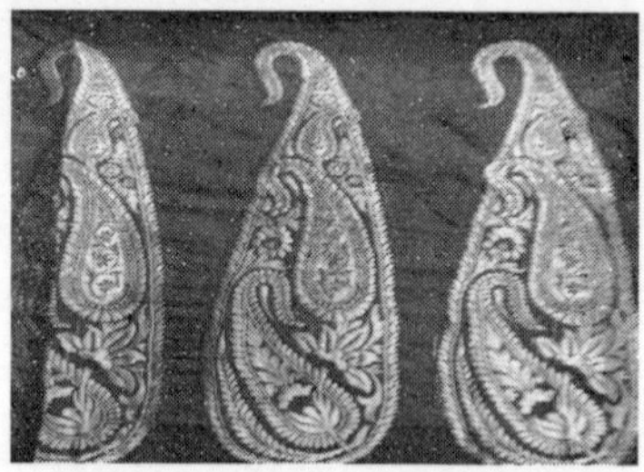

Logos

Handloom Mark

Silk Mark

participatory survey was conducted in Banaras/Varanasi district of Uttar Pradesh on August, 2015, comprised 100 weavers from Varanasi city with three hub viz. Madanpura, Lallapura and Saraiya. Fifteen weavers from each hub and fifty five from city were randomly selected. People perception was taken into consideration and ground reality of weaving clusters were also analyzed.

The secondary data has been collected from the Trade Facilitation Centre and Crafts Museum at Varanasi, Department of Handloom, Ministry of Textiles, Banaras Bunkar Samiti, Banarasi

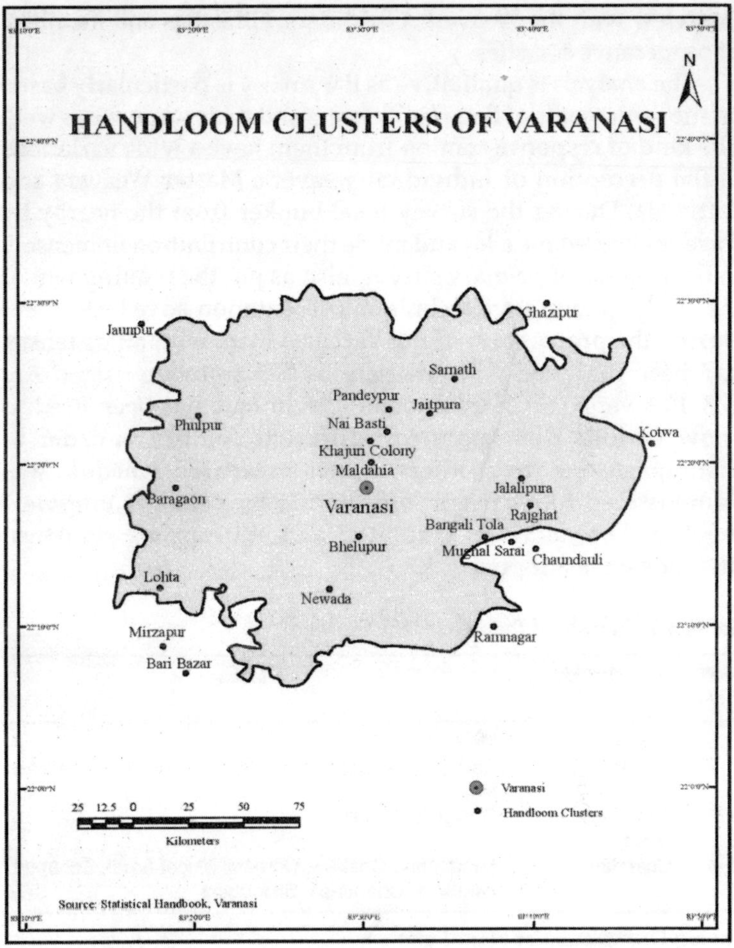

Map 4.2: Handloom Clusters of Varanasi

Vastra Udyog Sangh, Banaras Hath Kargha Vikas Samiti, Adarsh Silk Bunkar Sahkari Samiti, different literary works in the form of articles, journals, Gazetters, books, magazines and different other information have been used for the analysis.

In order to identify the sari weaving settlement of Banaras and to identify its iconic characteristics, researchers have tried to use qualitative techniques in-depth using the structured personal interview with the Weavers, Gaddidars, Girasthas and members of cooperative societies.

The analysis is qualitative as the survey is particularly based on the settlements of Banaras weavers and their response as well. The kind of response coming from them have a wide variations in the perception of Individual weavers, Master Weavers and Sattiwala. During the survey local bunker from the nearby by societies helped me a lot and made their contribution immensely in the process of primary survey, also as per the requirement of the study quantitative technique presentation have been used. During the preparation of the Varanasi map, with all its tehsils had been digitized with the help of GIS software named Arc GIS 10.1 version. Chorochromatic technique has been used to show various districts using different colours in order to distinguish one from others. A self-structured schedule was administered to elicit the information by personal interview method. The data was tabulated and appropriate statistical methods were adopted.

Table 4.1: Sample of the Secondary Survey

Sl. No.	*District*	*Places*
1.	Azamgarh	Mubarakpur
2.	Mirzapur	Rajgadh, Chetgunj, Narayanpur, jamalpur, Seekhad, Majua
3.	Sant Ravidas Nagar	Gopigunj, Sewapur
4.	Chandauli	Sahabgunj, Chakiya, Barhani, Mugal Sarai, Sahupuri, Fatehpur, Chandauli, Shikargunj

Source: Department of Handloom.

Table 4.2: Sample of Primary Survey

Source of Procurement	*Silk*	*Zari*
Master weavers	28	28
Local dealers	46	46
Co-operative societies	26	26

Sources: Collected Through Survey.

Study Area

The latitude of Varanasi, is 25.32, and the longitude is 82.98. Varanasi, is situated in Uttar Pradesh province, in the north of India. The city lies within the Indo-Gangetic Plain and has two effluents: Varuna in the north and Assi in the south. The brocade weaving of the Banaras is cluster based and scattered all over the Banaras district and some adjacent districts. The Banaras city is the main centre of weaving. The maximum weavers of the product belong to the city only. Yet the other production centres of the districts cannot be over looked so far as the production and the employment is concerned. The main centres of the brocade weavings are at Varanasi, Azamgarh, Mirzapur, Bhadohi (Sant Ravidas Nagar), Chandoli, Chunar and Chakia. Among all, Varanasi city is the most important centre of brocade weaving and more than 80 per cent weavers belong to the Varanasi city and its adjacent area only. Out of the different *Mohallas* (areas) of the Varanasi, Madanpura and Ahaipur are two most important areas of the brocade weaving. It is believed that the brocade weaving in the city initially started in these two areas and subsequently adopted by the other families.

The **reason for choosing this study** area is that I am itself a weaver so I can bring some inner as well as unique information for the sari weaving settlement of Banaras and that will become my responsibility to educate them about various schemes as well as various aspects of it.

Organization of the Study

Loom

It is a device used to weave cloth. The basic purpose of any loom is to hold the warp threads under tension to facilitate the interweaving of the threads. The precise shape of the loom and its mechanics may vary, but the basic purpose is the same.

Weaving

Weaving is completed by intersecting the longitudinal threads, the warp, *i.e.* "that which is thrown across", with the transverse threads, the weft, i.e. "that which is woven".

The key constituents of the loom are the warp beam, heddles, harnesses or shafts, shuttle, reed and take-up roll. In the loom, yarn handling includes shedding, picking, battening and taking-up operations. These are the major nods. This is the most significant process in the chain. The weaving process used in the cluster is called as Take-up motion method. In this process weights are used at the end of the warp to maintain uniform tension.

In the cluster, a weaver is either a job worker receiving a dyed yarn, design and hands over a woven product and receives wages or a businessman in his own right. In the latter case he invests in buying yarn, produce according to the design bought by him. The weavers who operate one or two looms are mainly job workers and form 50 per cent of the population in Banaras cluster.

Shedding

Shedding is the rising of part of the warp yarn to form a shed (the vertical space between the raised and unraised warp yarns), through which the filling yarn, carried by the shuttle, can be inserted. On the recent loom, simple and difficult shedding operations are performed automatically by the heddle or heald frame, also identified as a harness.

This is a rectangular frame to which a series of wires, called heddles or healds, are attached. The yarns are passed through the eye holes of the heddles, which hang vertically from the harnesses. The weave pattern determines which harness controls which warp yarns, and the number of harnesses used depends on the complexity of the weave. Two collective procedures of controlling the heddles are as follows:

- Dobbies-set on the top of machine made-up of kanti soil, for the purpose of design.
- Jacquard Head.

Picking

By way the harnesses raise the heddles or healds, which raise the warp yarns, the shed is created. The substantial yarn is inserted through the shed by a small carrier device called a shuttle. The shuttle is pointed at each culmination to allow passage through

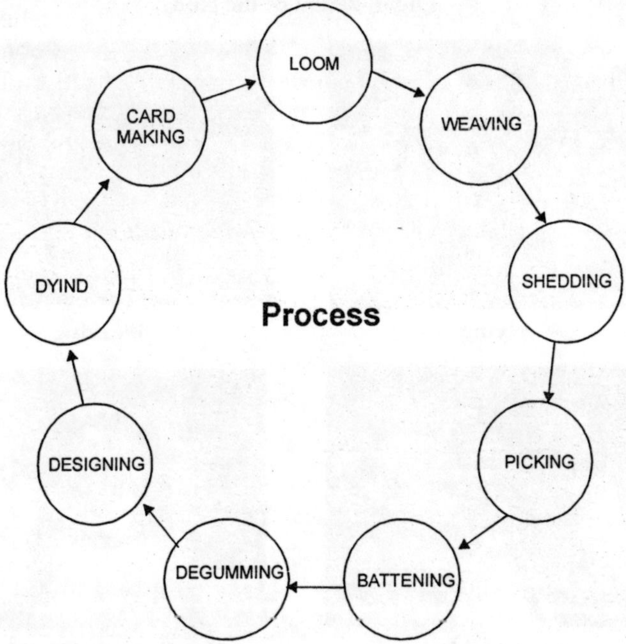

the shed. In a traditional shuttle loom, the filling yarn is wound onto a quill, which in turn is mounted in the shuttle. The filling yarn emerges through a hole in the shuttle as it moves across the loom. A single crossing of the shuttle from one side of the loom to the other is known as a **pick**. As the shuttle moves back and forth across the shed, it weaves an edge, on each side of the fabric to stop the fabric from twisting.

Battening

Amid the heddles and the take-up roll, the warp threads pass through another frame called the reed (which resembles a comb). The percentage of the fabric that has already been formed, but not yet rolled-up on the take-up roll is called the fell. After the shuttle moves across the loom laying down the fill yarn, the weaver uses the reed to press (or batten) each filling yarn against the fell. Conventional shuttle looms can operate at speeds of about 150 to 160 picks per minute.

Organization of the study

Dying

Weaving

Card Making

Handloom bebin (Nari)

Picking

Colouring

Here be present two secondary motions, because with each weaving operation the newly constructed fabric must be looped on a cloth beam. This method is called taking-up. At the same time, the warp yarns must be let off or released from the warp beams. On the way to grow into fully automatic, a loom needs a tertiary motion, the filling stop motion. This will brake the loom, if the weft thread breaks. An automatic loom requires 0.125 hp to 0.5 hp to operate.

De-gumming

It is an important operation for silk yarn to remove the waste material. The operation is done manually. The yarn will be boiled in water at optimal temperature of 80° to 90°C. The peculiarity of the Banaras Cluster is usage of caustic soda for de-gumming, moreover, there is no scientific method for controlling and measurement of temperature.

Designing

Designing is entirely done at cluster level by local designers. There are around 200 designers in the cluster. Most of the designers are on full time basis since childhood as such their literacy level is very low.

Most of the times the designer develops designs on his own than getting input from Master Weaver/ Cooperative Societies. He generates designs in anticipation of demand thus incurring the risk of not being paid at all. On an average the designer takes one week to produce a graph and produces 60 to 48 graph per year. The price he gets per design varies from Rs. 600-800 according to the chowke. The buyer may simply buy the design and makes the payment or ask him to make a graph as well.

Graph making is routine task but takes a minimum of two days to make it. Most of the times the designer will perform both designing and graph making at a package price.

The exposure of designers to books or to Computer is very negligible. His exposure to external design fraternity is completely absent. His earnings are much better than other actors in the cluster and with the changing times his demand is increasing as the average life of most of the designs is not more than six months. However, the share of design development in production cost is insignificant and does not have major impact on profitability.

Dyeing

Most of the Dyers operate from their house. Very few Master Weavers (*Grihasthas*) are having dye house of their own. A typical Dyeing unit occupies 8-10 sq. Number of furnace varies from 1 to 3. Yarn in batch as such it can produce depend on their capacity.

But it has been found in most of the dyeing houses that the capacity utilization is not more than 50 to 60 per cent. This is mainly because of variation in batch size and decline in production levels. The normal dyeing order quantity in the cluster is 1 to 2 kgs, which is the main hindrance for starting of Common Dye House Facility, as mechanized dyeing is also profitable below 5 kgs.

Card Making

It is the most mechanical and simple operation in the chain. Cards are hung from top of the loom, which guides the thread and thus weaving. A design generally involves a few hundred cards. A card cutter cuts and punches with small non-electric implements. He makes 200 cards per day and charges Rs. 5-10 per card. The raw material cost is Rs. 3-5 per card. He thus earns almost Rs. 200 per day.

The card-maker's mat extend credit-up to one month and accepts only cash payment. The raw-material cost has gone up by 100 per cent in last 5 years, while selling price of the card has not been changed, causing decline in wage earnings. However, a card cutter is significantly better off than a weaver.

In the cluster, a weaver is either a job worker receiving a dyed yarn, design and hands over a woven product and receives wages or a businessman in his own right. In the latter case he invests in buying yarn, produce according to the design bought by him. The weavers who operate one or two looms are mainly job workers and form 90 per cent of the population in Banaras cluster.

The master-weavers may have looms of his own or enter in to wage payment relationship with small weavers.

Results and Discussion

Essentially each identified sari weaving cluster has existent built heritage, as well as active traditional weaving practice in place. Authenticity and integrity for the tangible element identified with weaving is assessed for—

- The vernacular architecture of the weavers' settlements
- The modes of production (such as traditional looms)

This includes traditional looms and technological advances in loom-making within the framework of traditional knowledge systems. Authenticity of the weaving practice lies in the continuity of traditions and techniques. **The traditional weaving practices are inherited from one generation to the next**. The skill comes naturally by virtue of families carrying out the ancillary activities along with the weaver, leading to learning traditional techniques. These settlements are intact and authenticity is maintained.

During the medieval period, along with Mughals, skilled Muslim weavers from the West Asian countries came to India. These weavers found Varanasi complementing to their art of intricate pattern of weaving and settled there under the patronage of the then Muslim rulers. The fusion of Hindu design pattern with Muslim ones had put Varanasi at the helm of silk weaving activities.

Ralph Fitch (1583–1591) describes Banaras as a prosperous sector of the cotton textile industry. The most primitive mention of the brocade and Zari textiles of Banaras is found in the nineteenth century. Through the movement of silk weavers from Gujarat during the famine of 1603, it is likely that silk brocade weaving started in Banaras in the seventeenth century and developed in excellence during the eighteenth and nineteenth century. During the Mughal period, around fourteenth century, weaving of brocades with complex designs using gold and silver threads became the domain of Banaras. The traditional Banarasi sari is done with lot of inflexible effort and skill full work using the silk. The sari making is a cottage industry for about 12 lakh people associated directly or indirectly with the handloom silk industry of the region around Varanasi encompassing Gorakhpur, Chandauli, Bhadohi, Jaunpur and Azamgarh districts.

Table 4.3: Modifications and Variations in Traditional Sarees N = 100

Sl. No.	*Changes Made*	*Percentage of Respondents*
1.	Motifs	100
2.	Zari	63
3.	Yarn type	54
4.	Saree length	48
5.	Reed count	14

Source: Collected Through Field Observation.

Their special characteristics are Mughal inspired designs such as intricate intertwining flowered and foliate motifs, *kalga* and *bel*, a string of upright leaves called *jhallar* at the outer, edge of border is a characteristic of these saris. Other features are gold work, compact weaving, figures with small details, metallic visual effects, pallus, *jal* (a net like pattern), and *mina* work. The saris are frequently chunk of an Indian bride's bridal goods. Depending on the intricacy of its designs and patterns, a sari can take from 15 days to a month and sometimes up to six months to complete. *Banarasi saris are mostly worn by Indian women on important occasions such as when attending a wedding and are expected to be complemented by the woman's best jewellery.*

The main centres of the brocade weavings are at Varanasi, Azamgarh, Mirzapur, Bhadohi (Sant Ravidas Nagar), Chandoli, Chunar and Chakia. Banaras is one of the rich weaving craft centre of India, famous for Brocade *Saris* and dress material. One unique and intricate silk brocades and saris of Banaras has made it world famous. Among the different varieties of *saris* produced in the centres, some exclusive varieties of the *saris* are Jangla, Tanchoi, Vaskat, Cutwork, Tissue and Butidar which are made of silk warp and silk weft, on Plain/satin ground base, brocaded with extra weft patterns in different layouts introducing Buties, Bells, Creepers, Buttas in ground, border and anchal for getting glamourous appearance.

With the change in time and consumer preference, the weavers of the cluster are also undertaking changes in the design and pattern of the product along with product diversification. In order to cater to the need of the overseas and domestic buyers, the weavers of the cluster are also producing home furnishing, silk dhotis, stole, scarf, muffler, mats, dress material, wall hanging, made ups like curtain, cushion cover, table cover, napkins, runners, etc.

Table 4.4: The *Sari* Segment Typically Consists of Two Sub-Segments

Segment	*Area*
Satin-based work (largely Karnataka yarn)	Badi Bazar, Alaypura, and Pilikothi
Organza type work (largely Chinese yarn)	Madanpura

Source: Collected through Interview.

In general, *sari* weaving involved all communities but share of Muslims were high. *In early days weaving was monopolized by the Hindus (Khatri Hindus, a sub-caste)*, who helped the migrant Muslim weavers to establish their craft. The woven products made by the Muslim weavers were marketed by the Hindus. Thus, weaving was completely monopolized by the Muslims, while the *Hindus became traders. Therefore, at a present mainly Muslims (73%) are involved in hand weaving which is inherited in the religion compared to Hindus.* The similar results are also record by the Zahir (1996) and Ahiwasi (1975) who stated that Muslims were involved in Banaras silk sari weaving. During data collection, it was found that resource availability, market and transportation facilities forced the weavers to reside in the city. The similar report is also made in Ministry of Textiles (2005) who indicated that about 70 per cent of the weavers in Banaras districts are living in city.

Conclusion

Architecture of a region is shaped by many influencing factors such as climate, locally available material, construction techniques and needs of the inhabitants. This serial exemplifies vernacular architecture of the several regions of India where occuputational needs of inhabitants is the major factor influencing architecture. Essentially, the clusters have existent tangible built heritage/ traditional settlement, as well as active traditional weaving practice in place. This includes traditional looms and technological advances in loom-making within the framework of traditional knowledge systems. The series highlights diversity throughout India and each cluster comprising at least one of the attributes as outstanding on its own w.r.t. the other cluster (in terms of settlement pattern, scale, category, loom types, woven fabric, process, community knowledge systems, continuity etc.).

In addition to these extraordinary skillsets, sari weavers also carry in their memories and hands centuries-old traditions of motifs, colours and design, linked to the art and aesthetics of the past—corresponding to the regional architecture and artefacts of each region.

Criterion (iii): The serial bears a unique testimony to a cultural tradition of *Sari* weaving which influences the regional architecture.

Criterion (v): The serial is an outstanding example of traditional human settlements that developed in accordance with the occupational needs of the weavers. The vernacular form reflects the way of life and caters to the various functions of the artisan communities engaged in weaving and pre/post-loom activities.

References

Baliga, B.S., 1960, *History of Handloom Industry*. Madras: Government of Madras, p. 15.

Binu, S. Thomas, 1986, *Time to Grasp the Nuttle Business World*. Bombay, Vol. VI, No.1.

Dev, Nirendra, 2008, *A Major Attraction for Festival Season*. Mumbai: Handloom Bonanza.

Dev, Nirendra, www.bestofindiarestofindia.blogspot.com (*Source*: PIB Features)

Dwivedi, R.C., 1987, *Glimpses of Cooperative through Press*. New Delhi: Cooperative Times, p. 70.

Government of India, 1980, *Report of the Sub Group on Handlooms*. New Delhi: Ministry of Commerce, p. S3.

Government of India, 1942, Report of the Fact Finding Committee (Handloom & Mills). p. 180.

Government of India. VIII Plan Report of the Sub Group on Handlooms. New Delhi: Ministry of Textiles, 1989, p. 171.

Government of Tamil Nadu, 1959, *A Survey of Handloom Industry*, p. 139.

Harlapur, S.F., *et al.*, 2015, *Styles of Weaving and Wearing*.

Madhuri, G. V. and Tejaswani, K. (2012), Role of SME'S in Internationalisation of Andhra Pradesh Handloom Industry. *Hyderabad*: Volume 2, Issue 6.

National Skill Development. Human Resource and Skill Requirements in the Handlooms and Handicrafts Sector. New Delhi: Transforming the Skill Landscape.

Nayak, P., *Tradition and Pride of Odisha*. Odisha: Khandua Sarees & Fabrics.

Nehru, Jawaharlal, 1982, *The Discovery of India*. New Delhi: Jawaharlal Nehru Memorial Fund, Oxford University Press, p. 298.

Patil, Vimla, 2012, *The Origin of the Saree*.

Planning Commission. *Handlooms Export Promotion Council*. Ministry of Textiles, 2004–05.

Reserve Bank of India, 1955, All India Rural Credit Survey Committee, The *General Report*, p. 4 0.

Seemanthini, Niranjana, 2001, Report on Growth and Prospects of the Handloom Industry. *Dastkar Andhra*.

"Statistics and Observation". *Journal of Textile Association*, Bombay: Vol.51, No.5, (1991): 183-186.

5

Conservation of Endangered and Economically Important Medicinal Plants of India: A Review

Neeti Yadav

Introduction

India is rich in all the three levels of biodiversity such as species diversity, genetic diversity, and habitat diversity of medicinal plants (Mukherjee and Wahile, 2006). The present demand for medicinal plants is approximately US $14 billion per year estimated by World Health Organization (WHO). The demand for medicinal plants is likely to increase more than US $5 trillion in 2050. The medicinal plant-related trade in India is estimated to be approximately US $1 billion per year (Kala *et al.*, 2006). International Union for Conservation of Nature and Natural Resources (IUCN) has placed 560 species of India under the Red List of Threatened species, out of which 247 species are in the threatened category. IUCN recognises the following categories: extinct, extinct in the wild, critically endangered, endangered, vulnerable, near threatened, least concern, data deficient and not evaluated. Species with small populations that are not at present endangered or vulnerable, but are at risk are called rare (Singh, *et al.*, 2006). The genetic diversity of medicinal plants in the world is getting endangered at alarming rate because of ruinous harvesting practices, over-harvesting, forest degradation, agricultural encroachment, urbanization etc. (Gupta, *et al.*, 1998). Therefore, it is a matter of urgency to manage and conserve the traditional medicinal plant resources. Although species conservation is achieved most effectively through the management of wild populations and natural habitats (*in situ* conservation), but most of the medicinal plants either do not produce seeds or seeds are too small to germinate in soils and if the seeds are able to germinate then the raised plants are highly heterozygous. Therefore, mass multiplication of uniform disease free planting material becomes a general problem. In order to overcome these barriers, *ex situ* techniques can be used to complement *in situ* methods and, in some instances, may be the only option for some species (Sarasan, *et al.*, 2006; Negash, *et al.*, 2001). Tissue culture has greatly enhanced the scope and potential of mass propagation by exploiting the regenerative behaviour in a wide range of selected medicinal plants. Many important medicinal herbs throughout the world have been successfully propagated *in vitro*, either by organogenesis or by callus formation. The present study was therefore undertaken with a view to establishing efficient protocols for *in vitro* rapid propagation of the above endangered and economically important medicinal plants.

Medicinal Plants and Conservation Protocols

Tinospora cordifolia (willd.) Miers Ex Hook. F. & Thoms commonly known as *Guduchi* belonging to the family Menispermaceae is a large, glabrous, succulent, perennial deciduous twiner with succulent stems and papery bark, climbing shrub. The aerial roots that arise from the stem are thread like. The leaf is heart shaped and smooth. The flowers are yellowish in colour emerges in bunch in rainy season. The fruits are pea like which are seen in winter in India. It is distributed throughout the tropical Indian subcontinent. It has been used in Ayurvedic preparation for the treatment of various ailments throughout the centuries. Ancient Hindu physicians prescribed it for gonorrhoea. The plant is used in Ayurvedic, "*Rasayanas*" to improve the immune system and the resistance against infections. The whole plant is used medicinally; however, the stem is approved for use in medicine as listed by the Ayurvedic Pharmacopoeia of India (Sinha, *et al.*, 2004). In folk and tribal medicine the whole plant, powdered root and stem bark, decoction of root and stem, juice of the root and paste or juice of leaves or stem are used to treat various ailments such as fever, jaundice, general debility, cough, asthma, leucorrhoea, skin diseases, bits of poisonous insects and venomous snakes and eye disorders (Singh, *et al.*, 2003). It acts as a memory booster, develops intelligence, and promotes mental clarity. It is described as one of the *Medhya Rasayana* (mental rejuvenative) in the *Charak Samhita* (The oldest and most potent book of Ayurvedic medicine). It is regarded as a liver protector.

In vitro micro-propagation protocol for *T.cordifolia* (Sivakumar, *et al.*, 2014.). The healthy plants of *Tinospora cordifolia* were collected and raised in pots containing soil and farmyard manure (1:1) in greenhouse condition. The explants were prepared from the nodal portion of the stems, internodes and shoot tip, which were first washed thoroughly in running tap water for about half an hour to remove soil and other superficial contamination, and then allowed to stay for 3–4 hrs. in double distilled water to facilitate the phenolics and a characteristic gummy substance of polysaccharide leaching out of explants. The disinfected explants were surface sterilized under aseptic conditions in a laminar flow chamber. Later the explants (1 cm each) with upper portion were washed with 1 per cent sodium hypochlorite solution (v/v) for 5 min followed by thorough washing under running tap water for 15 min. Then single bud explants (1 cm each) with upper portion were washed with 1 per cent Bavistin (w/v) for 5 min followed by 3 times washing with sterile distilled water. The explants were surface sterilized with 0.1 per cent (w/v) mercuric chloride for 6 min. and later rinsed 4 or 5 times with sterile distilled water. Later the edges of the explants were trimmed with a sterile blade to eliminate possible residue of sterilant and the explants were then used for culturing. For, *in vitro* shoot initiation from various explants of *Tinospora cordifolia,* the surface sterilized explants such as nodes, internodes and shoot tips were cultured on full strength MS medium supplemented with various concentrations of Cytokinins BA (N6-benzyladenine) (0.44–13.31 μM), KIN (Kinetin) (0.46–13.94 μM) and 2ip (N6-2-isopentenyl adenine) (0.49–14.76 μM) were tested individually for shoot induction. The cultures were incubated under a 16 hours photoperiod (50 $\mu m.m^2/sec.$ provided by cool-white daylight Sylvania fluorescent lamps) at 25°C and 55 per cent relative humidity in sterile environment condition. Different experiments were conducted to find out an optimum culture conditions for the maximum shoot initiation (budding) from the cultured explants. And use the different type of Phenolic exudation controlling substances such as polyvinyl pyrollidone, activated charcoal, silver nitrate and ascorbic acid were used at the time of initiation. Shoot proliferation and elongations were cultured on MS medium supplemented witl various concentrations of Cytokinins BA (4.22–12.64 μM), KIN (6.23–12.44 μM) and 2ip (2.11–13.32 μM) were tested individually and combine with Auxins like NAA (α-naphthyl acetic acid) (4.22–12.88 μM) and IAA (Indole-3-acetic acid) (1.32–11.86 μM). After 20 days the culture was used to rooting, 1 to 2 cm long shoots were transferred to half strength of MS medium amended with 3 per cent sucrose with Auxins IAA (1.76–17.13 μM), IBA (Indole-3-butyric acid) (1.32–14.70 μM) and NAA (1.34–16.11 μM) tested individually. All the experiments were done in six cultures with ten replicated experiments. The *in vitro* rooted shoots were carefully removed from the culture vessel and they were gently washed with sterile distilled water to remove every trace of media. Thereafter, plantlets were dipped in 0.05 per cent Bavistin (systemic fungicide) for 10 seconds to minimize the microbial infection. Again a second wash was given with sterile distilled water. The treated plantlets were then transferred aseptically to small earthen pots containing mixture of vermiculite, sterilized red soil and farmyard manure at 1:1:1 ratio in growth chamber with controlled temperature, light and humidity to acclimatize with the outside environment. Half strength liquid medium was added periodically. The plantlets were covered with polythene bags to ensure a relative humidity of 70 to 80 per cent. The acclimatized complete plantlets were then transferred to the field.

Pterocarpus santalinus **L.** popularly known as Red Sanders belonging to family Fabaceae is an endemic species confined to Southern parts of Eastern Ghats of India especially in Andhra Pradesh. It is a small to medium sized deciduous tree having a dense, round crown reaching a height of 10 to 15 m with a girth of about 90 to 160 cm. The bark is typically dark brown in colour with rectangular plates and deeply fissured when matured. When blazed, it exudes a red colour gum with numerous pink streaks. The leaves are pinnately compound which are generally shed during January and March. With the onset of summer, new flush of leaves are produced along with large yellow coloured raceme flowers. Heartwood of Red Sanders has high demand in domestic as well as international market and the wavy grained wood is valued. Along with its extensive use in furniture, the red dye obtained from the wood is used as colouring agent for textile, medicine and food. The heartwood can accumulate various elements and rare earth elements like strontium cadmium, zinc, copper and uranium. The wood has different uses in traditional and folklore medicines and is used for the treatment of diabetes, prickly heat, skin diseases and for various other ailments. Yerukula and Irula tribes of Chittoor district in Andhra Pradesh use whole plant of *P. santalinus* for ulcer treatment (Vedavathy, *et al.*, 1997). Considering the wood demand, restricted distribution, slow regeneration, illegal harvest, trade and habitat destruction, the species has been categorized as endangered by IUCN.

In vitro propagation protocol of *Pterocarpus santalinus* L. (Red Sandalwood) through tissue culture (Warakagoda, and Subasinghe, 2013). Pods were picked directly from mature red sandalwood trees (over 25 years old) at the green to brownish stage. Seeds were surface sterilized using 10 per cent clorox for 20 min followed by 70 per cent ethanol for 2 min and cultured on Gamberg (B5) medium (Gamborg, *et al.*, 1968). Six different explant types were used for the study. *In vitro* germinated seedlings were excised after 20 day to derive mesocotyl segments, cotyledonatory nodal segments and shoot tips. Mother plants were maintained under plant-house conditions to excise stem cuttings. Fresh and immature terminal shoot cuttings and subsequent nodal shoot segments (semi-hard wood, 3-5 cm in length with dormant auxiliary buds) were collected during the early hours of the day at 2 week intervals. *In vitro* germinated 20 day old seedlings were used as the control. As a rejuvenation procedure, decapitation and spraying of 10.0 ppm 6-benzyle amino purine (BAP) solution was done for the mother plants, at 2 week intervals. Plants were maintained under plant-house conditions free from pests and diseases and watered when necessary. Overhead watering was avoided. A 100.0 ppm solution of thiophanate methyl 70 per cent (topsin) was sprayed 24 h before collecting the buds for culturing to prevent fungal infections. Plants were treated with 200.0 ppm Albert's solution (complete fertilizer mixture) at 2 week intervals. Cultures were kept aseptically in a growth room (23 ± 2 °C temperature, 60 per cent Rh) and cool photoperiod under 1220 lx of light intensity. All media contained 3.0 per cent sucrose and 0.01 per cent myo-inositol. The *p*H of the medium was adjusted to 5.8. Prepared media were autoclaved at 121 ^{0}C and 1.05 kg cm^{-2} pressure for 20 min. Experiments were designed according to complete randomized design with 20 replicates in each treatment and all parametric data were analyzed using SAS statistical software. Mean separations were carried parametric data were analyzed using the Chi Square test.

***Stevia rebaudiana* Bertoni.** Belonging to the family of Asteraceae is a perennial herb. This plant is a natural sweetener and famously known as "Sweet Weed", "Sweet Leaf', "Sweet Herbs" and "Honey Leaf', which is estimated to be 300 times sweeter than cane sugar. It naturally grows in low lying areas on poor sandy acidic soils adjacent to swamps, and so is adapted to and requires constantly wet feet or shallow water tables. It grows up to 1 m tall and has leaves 2-3 cm long. The leaves are the source of diterpene glycosides, stevioside and rebaudioside (Yoshida, 1986.). Stevioside is regarded as a valuable natural sweetening agent because of its relatively good taste and chemical stability. Stevioside is of special interest to diabetic persons with hyperglycemia and the diet conscious (Arpita, *et al.*, 2011). Natural sweeteners that can substitute for sucrose have caught great attention due to the growing incidence of obesity and diabetes.

The rapid micropropagation protocol developed (Tiwari, *et al.*, 2013). Different parts of the plant were used as explants for the *in-vitro* regeneration of *Stevia rebaudiana* Bertoni. The seeds of the plant were obtained from J.N.K.V.V. Jabalpur, M.P. For *in vitro* regeneration of *Stevia rebaudiana* Bertoni Murashige and Skoog's medium was used with various concentrations of plant growth regulators (Murashige, and Skoog, 1962). General aseptic techniques concerning *in vitro* culture of the explants were followed in the present experiment. After surface sterilization the explants were cut into very small pieces (about 1 cm) and inoculated on to shoot induction and proliferation media. When the shoot was fully growth (for 1 month) the shoots were taken out from the test tube a laminar flow hood and were cut (about) 1 cm. Then the micro-cuttings were sub cultured on root induction medium. All inoculations and aseptic manipulations were carried out in a laminar air flow cabinet. Before use the working surface of the cabinet was cleaned by swabbing with 90 per cent ethyl alcohol and UV light (for 20 minutes) to reduce the chances of contamination. The instruments like scalpels, forceps, needles etc.

were sterilized by an alcoholic dip followed by flaming inside the laminar air flow cabinet. Other requirements like Petri dishes, bottles, conical flasks, cotton, distilled water etc. were sterilized by steam sterilization method. Before the onset of inoculations hands were washed thoroughly by soap and then swabbing with 70 per cent ethyl alcohol. Cutting and transfer of the explants were carried out taking all possible care to ensure contaminations free inoculations. The rooted plantlets were first transferred to plastic pots containing garden soil, sand and peat moss (1:1:1), covered with transparent polythene bags and placed in acclimatization room at 28 ± 2°C with 70-90 per cent relative humidity, after five days temperature was increased from 28 to 32°C. After two weeks, transparent bags were removed from pots for proper hardening. After four weeks, the plants were then shifted in greenhouse and in field under low light intensity. The data for various growth attributes were recorded such as per cent explants regeneration, multiple shoot formation, shoot length, per cent plantlets rooted, number of roots per plantlet, and survival of plants during acclimatization and in the field was recorded.

After the initiation of explant plantlet is a generated. In this experiment for the multiplication of plantlet, it is transferred to the multiplication MS medium supplemented with BAP (Cytokinin) at different concentrations *viz.* 0.5, 1.0, 2.0, 3.0, 4.0, 5.0 mg/l and 0.00 mg/l were used as control. The concentrations of BAP used found to be not significant differences for all parametres. Frequencies of bud break and bud elongation and mean number of regenerated shoots and shoot length were observed at 5 mg/l BAP, i.e. frequency of bud break is 82 per cent and bud elongation is 88 per cent while mean shoot number is (14.83) and mean shoot length is (4.51). While at concentration lower then 5.0 mg/l treatment resulted decline in all parametres. After bud break of explant plantlet is a generated. In this experiment for the multiplication of plantlet, it is transferred to the multiplication MS medium supplemented with KIN (Cytokinin) at different concentrations viz. 0.5, 1.0, 2.0, 3.0, 4.0, 5.0 mg/l and 0.00 mg/l were used as control. The concentrations of KIN used found to be not significant differences for all parametres. Frequencies of bud break and bud elongation and mean number of regenerated shoots and shoot length were observed at 5 mg/l KIN, i.e. frequency of bud break is 72 per cent and bud elongation is 88 per cent while mean shoot number is (9.25) and mean shoot length is (5.51). While at concentration lower than 5.0 mg/l treatment resulted decline in all parametres. After multiplication of plants the plantlets clumps were dissected and plantlets were transferred in to rooting medium. The one way factorial design was carried to study the effect of IBA (auxins) and their interaction on frequency of Root number (FRN) and frequency of Root length (FRL) at different concentrations. IBA is a plant growth regulator play important role in the rooting of plants. No significant differences in rooting were observed by various concentration of IBA, i.e. 0.5, 1.0, 1.5, 2.0, 2.5 mg/l. Frequencies of Root No. observed in 2.0 mg/l IBA (3.62) and frequencies of Root length observed in 2.0 mg/l IBA (3.71). While at concentration lower then 2.0 mg/l treatment resulted decline in all parametres. In this study experiments were conducted to standardize the explant source and culture media for multiple proliferation of shoot and result in mass propagation of homogenous elite plantlets of *S. rebaudiana*. The result of the experiment and other earlier research report clearly support the possibility of propagating *S. rebaudiana* by adopting *in vitro* techniques.

Tylophora indica (Burm.F.) Merill. commonly known as *"Antmool"* or *"Dama Bel"* belonging to family Asclepiadaceae is an important endangered medicinal plant. It is a perennial branched climber having cylindrical, twinning stem with long fleshy roots. Leaves are ovate oblong to elliptic oblong and acute at tip. Flowers are bisexual, minute and grow in umbellate cymes. Corolla is greenish yellow outside and purplish within. It is found in the plains, forests, hilly slopes and outskirts of forests. It forms dense patches in moist and humid conditions and the plant shows stunted growth in the areas with lesser rainfall. It is indigenous to India native to the plains and hill forests of Eastern and Southern India. It is used as folk remedy for the treatment of number of diseases and ailments particularly bronchial asthma, bronchitis, allergies, rheumatism and dermatitis (Shivpuri, *et al.*, 1968). The roots and leaves of this plant contain pharmacologically active alkaloids tylophorine, tylophorinine and anticancerous tylophorinidine.

An efficient protocol for large scale multiplication of this endangered species developed (Sharma, *et al.*, 2011). In the present study, *de novo* adventitious shoot formation occurred on MS medium supplemented with different concentrations of BAP alone or in conjunction with adenine sulphate. However, the best results were observed on MS medium supplemented with BAP (22 μM) and adenine sulphate (1.35 μM) where optimum growth of meristemoids occurred on the leaf segments. These meristemoids when cut into small groups and subcultured on fresh inductive medium multiplied further resulting in an exponential increase in number and eventually developed into green leafy shoots in nearly 85 per cent of the cultures. Multiple shoot formation directly from leaf explants on MS supplemented with BAP (5 mg/l) and adenine sulphate (0.5 mg/l). The shoots thus formed were excised and transferred for rooting on half strength MS and MS medium supplemented with different concentrations of IAA, IBA and NAA. Among the various auxins used IBA proved to be the best. However, excellent root induction occurred on half strength MS medium alone. The rooted plants were first hardened under *in vitro* and green house conditions for 4 weeks before final transfer to the field. During the period of hardening, proliferation of roots and emergence of new leaves was observed and there was substantial improvement in the survival rate which was nearly 90 per cent. Large numbers of uniform clones for commercial production were obtained.

Conclusion

Medicinal plants occupy a vital sector of health care system in India and represent a major national resource. The above mentioned endangered medicinal plants are used by various tribals and local people to cure different ailments. Hence, there is an immense need for conservation of diversity of medicinal plant wealth for the present and fore coming generations, by adapting the suitable strategy with most appropriate method of conservation. The development of efficient *in vitro* tissue culture protocols would help to save the endangered status of the above medicinal plants.

References

Mukherjee, P. K. and Wahile, A., 2006. Integrated approaches towards drug development from Ayurveda and other Indian system of medicines. *J. Ethnopharmacology*, 103:25–35.

Kala, C. P., Dhyani, P.P. and Sajwan, B. S., 2006. Developing the medicinal plants sector in northern India: Challenges and Opportunities. *J. Ethnobiology Ethnomedicine*, p.32.

Singh, J.S., Singh, S.P. and Guota, S.R., 2006. *Ecology, Environment and Resource Conservation*. New Delhi, India: Anamaya Publishers.

Gupta, A., Vats, S.K. and Lal, B., 1998. How cheap can a medicinal plant species be? *Curr. Sci.*, 74: 555-56.

Sarasan, V., Cripps, R. and Ramsay, M.M., 2006. Conservation *in vitro* of threatened plants-progress in the past decade. *In vitro Cellular Dev. Biol. Pl.*, 42:206–14.

Negash, A., Krens, F., Schaart, J. and Visser, B. 2001. *In vitro* conservation of enset under slow-growth conditions. *Pl. Cell, Tissue Organ Cult.*, 66: 107–11.

Sinha, K., Mishra, N.P., Singh, J. and Khanuja, S.P.S., 2004. *Tinospora cordifolia* (*Guduchi*), a reservoir plant for therapeutic application: a Review. *Indian Journal of Traditional Knowledge*, 13:257–270.

Singh, S.S., Pandey, S.C., Srivastava, S., Gupta, K.S., Patro, B. and Ghosh, A.C., 2003. Chemistry and medicinal properties of *Tinospora cordifolia. Indian J. Pharmacol*, 35:83-91.

Vedavathy, S., Sudhakar, A. and Mrudula, V., 1997. Tribal medicinal plants of Chittoor Ancient. *Science of Life*, 26: 307-331.

Yoshida, S. 1986. Studies on the production of sweet substances in *Stevia rebaudiana:* I. Simple determination of sweet glucoside in Stevia plant by thin layer chromate-scanner and their accumulation patterns with plant growth. *Jap. J. Crop. Sci.*, 55(2):189-195.

Arpita, D., Gantait, S. and Mandal, N., 2011. Micropropagation of an elite medicinal plant: *Stevia rebaudiana, Bert. Int. J. Agric. Resech.*, 6(1):40-48.

Shivpuri, D.N., Singhal, S.C. and Prakash, D., 1968. Preliminary studies in *Tylophora indica* in tthe treatment of asthma and allergic rhinitis. *J. Add. Phys. India.*, 15910: 9-15.

Sivakumar, V., Dhana Rajan, M.S., Mohamed Sadiq A. and Jayanthi, M. 2014. *In vitro* Micropropagation of *Tinospora cordifolia* (Willd.) Miers ex Hook. F. & Thoms — An Important Medicinal Plant. *Journal of Pharmacognosy and Phytochemistry*, 3 (2):5-10

Warakagoda, P.S. and Subasinghe, S., 2013. *In vitro* propagation of *Pterocarpus santalinus* L. (Red Sandalwood) through tissue culture, *J. Natn.Sci. Foundation Sri Lanka*, 41 (1): 53-63.

Murashige, T. and Skoog, F., 1962. A revised medium for rapid growth and bioassays with tobacco tissue cultures. *Physiol. Plant*, 15:473-497.

Tiwari, S., Arnold, R., Saxena, A., Mishra, R.M, Singh, A., Tiwari, A., Rajak and Singh, P., 2013. Studies on rapid micropropagation of Stevia rebaudiana Bertoni:A natural sweetener. *Int. J. of Pharm. & Life Sci. (IJPLS)*, 4(5):2667-2671

Sharma, S., 2011. A micro-propagation system for *Tylophora indica* and extraction of tylophorine from cultured and *in vitro* raised plants. M.Sc Thesis.

Gamborg, O.L., Millar, R.A. and Ojima, K., 1968. Nutrient requirements of suspension cultures of soyabean root cells. *Experimental Cell Research*, 50: 151-158.

6

Economic Development in Bihar and Conventional Fuel Use

Ganita Bhupal

Introduction

Economic development and environmental upkeep have been said to be related in a very interesting way in the environmental economics literature. The theory predicts that with increase in rate of growth and development, the environmental degradation first gets aggravated on account of a number of factors. The production process and the industrial sector gets a boost, the consumption drive is underway which promotes excessive use of resources at the cost of environmental sustainability, the government policies favour development and growth over the concerns of envrionment and so on. With rise in per capita incomes and GDP, the picture then starts to reverse. With more incomes, people can afford better education and lifestyles and hence are more able to care about the environment, governmental policies also turn towards stabilizing the economy and protecting the environment, industrial process get improved on account of technological innovation and thus, there is increased focus on environmental sustainability. This relationship between environmental indicators and economic development is summarized in the environmental economics literature as the Environmental Kuznets Curve or EKC.

When plotted in a curve, the EKC is drawn as a an inverted U shaped curve with environmental scenario plotted on the Y axis and the income per capita for the economy plotted on the X axis. The EKC hypothesis therefore shows that for some level of income per capita, the environmental scenario should worsen and then improve after a threshold per capita income is met. This result has been in applicability since the early 1990s when Grossman (1991) first proposed the concept. It was taken-up by World Bank and UN thereafter and a number of research papers have appeared in various journals acclaiming this theory to be true/false. A comprehensive review of literature suggests that the empirical evidence on the existence of EKC is inconclusive. The studies which have looked at the empirical evidence supporting EKC are mostly based on the cross country evidence and have not looked at the household data for evidence regarding EKC. The contributions of this chapter to the existing literature are many: its the first empirical study to analyze the impact of economic development on the household fuel consumption, I analyze the impact of economic development on household level data, perhaps the first study to do so and when I choose to focus on a specific state, I try to see whether the results which have been found controversial on the large scale carry any mettle on the micro-level data.

Bihar has emerged as the frontrunner of economic development in India in the past-decade or so. Apart from an increase in the state domestic product, the state has shown a tremendous performance in terms of indicators of social and economic change. Bihar has performed outstandingly in increasing the rates of female school enrollment and participation, in terms of decreasing the economic inequality and increase of female political participation. All of these changes can be attributed to various factors and the inclusive governance polices and massive efforts towards improving the situation remain crucial to such changes.

The rest of the chapter is organized as follows : the next section discusses the literature review, section 3 discusses the data, section 4 discusses the results and analysis and section 5 concludes.

Literature Review

The literature on EKC is relatively new and came into existence after the landmark paper by Grossman and Krueger (1991). Since then a number of empirical studies have been conducted to check the validity of EKC hypothesis. A number of indicators have been used to mark environmental quality. These include sulphur dioxide, nitrogen dioxide, carbon dioxide, level of water quality, and concentration of pollutants in water, deforestation etc. Studies which use country level data have identified various patterns about the behaviour of pollutant level with the per capita income and various results have been found to be econometrically consistent with the data. For example, Stern and Common (2001) find that there exists a monotonic relationship between sulphur concentration and income per capita when they include the entire panel of countries and an inverted U relationship exists only when they focus on the high income countries. Harbaugh *et al.* (2002) find no evidence of the inverted U relationship between the ambient air pollution and the national income. Cole *et al.* (1997), on the other hand, assess the relationship using a number of indicators and find that the meaningful EKC relationships exist only for local air pollutants and the same does not apply to global pollutants, which exhibit a monotonic relationship between the pollutants and the income.

In the context of Indian economy too, a number of studies have been undertaken to verify the EKC. The study by Managi and Jena (2007) discusses the relationship between sulphur dioxide, nitrogen dioxide and suspended particulate matter and SDP per capita and find an EKC like relationship. Another study by Tiwari *et al.* (2013) discusses the relationship between coal consumption and economic growth and they show the presence of EKC in the long as well as the short run.

All of the above studies have been undertaken with the state or country level data and none of these studies try to check for the response of household behaviour to the process of growth and development. In this sense, this chapter becomes the first paper to analyze the response of the households to the economic development and changes in the development indicators around them. I identify the response in terms of the household use of the firewood as a fuel. The main hypothesis is that firewood is considered an unclean fuel and if the households respond to economic development, then over a period of time, the consumption of firewood should either decline per household or the number of households using firewood should decrease.

Data

The data for this study have been taken from the India Human

Development Survey which is panel dataset and covers two rounds—2005-06 and 2011-12. The data proves to be appropriate for the study because the economic development in Bihar is said to have taken place around 2006. So, the panel study of same rural households in Bihar proves to be an effective measure of how the household behaviour changes in response to the economic and social development. The study covers about 15 districts in Bihar and I use data from around 1500 households to undertake the simple analysis. Out of the total 1547 households, about 1085 are rural and the rest of the 442 households are urban.

Results

The variable for conventional fuel use is the use of firewood in each rural household. I conduct separate analysis for rural and urban households. The analysis has been conducted for the following seventeen districts of Bihar : Purbi Champaran, Madhubani, Purnia, Supaul, Saharsa, Muzaffarpur, Siwan, Saran, Bhagalpur, Banka, Sheikhpura, Nalanda, Buxar, Kaimur, Rohtas, Patna and Gaya.

Table 6.1: Proportion of Households using Firewood as Fuel in Urban Areas

Districts	*Proportion of Households*	
	2005-06	*2011-12*
Purnia	68.89	58.70
Saran	40	70.73
Sheikhpura	11.11	25
Nalanda	0	0
Patna	23.33	34.5
Buxar	42.89	42.86
Rohtas	4.44	45.05
Gaya	55.56	72.22
Bhagalpur	40	20.51

Source: Author's Study Area.

Out of the seventeen districts in Bihar, nine had urban sample households—Purnia, Saran, Bhagalpur, Sheikhpura, Nalanda, Patna, Buxar, Rohtas and Gaya. The rest of the districts had only rural sample households. The three districts of Bhagalpur, Gaya and Rohtas had samples from both rural and urban areas. The main variable that I use to analyze the question at hand is whether the household uses firewood as a fuel in their kitchen and/or other purposes. I analyze the number of households using the firewood in 2006 and 2011-12 round and compare whether the number of households using this fuel has increased or decreased in the time period in between the two rounds.

The overall proportion of households in urban areas.

The main results from this exercise have been presented in Tables 6.1 and 6.2. I display the results district wise and year-wise.

The proportion of households in each district who use firewood as the main fuel in the household is the main variable under analysis. I find that only in certain districts does the proportion of households using fuel wood show a decline.

The main districts where the urban households show a decline in the amount of fuel Purnia and Bhagalpur. The proportion of households declined from 68.9 to 58.7 per cent and from 40 to 20.51 per cent respectively in both these districts. The rest of the districts show either a constant rate of fuel using households (Nalanda and Buxar) or show an increasing trend. In the rest of the districts, the proportion of urban households using firewood as the main fuel has increased and in huge proportions. In some cases (e.g. Gaya) the increase was very large and went-up to 40 per cent in the proportion of households. The increase in urban centres is a particularly worrying trend because urban areas are traditionally less dependent on firewood and polluting fuels.

Table 6.2: Proportion of Households using Firewood as Fuel in Rural Areas

Districts	*Proportion of Households*	
	2005-06	*2011-12*
Purbi Champaran	99.24	93.83
Madhubani	90.37	92.73
Supaul	100	97.22
Saharsa	67.86	98.39
Muzzaffarpur	80	98.8
Sivan	96	97.5
Bhabua	10.26	50
Rohtas	57.14	82.02
Bhagalpur	40	20.51
Nalanda	54.3	66.25
Banka	85	86.36

Source: Author's Study Area.

Turning the discussion to rural areas, I find that the same trend of urban areas applies here too. Majority of the districts show an increase in the proportion of households which use firewood. There are only two districts which show a decline: Purbi Champaran and Supaul. The rest of the districts show an increase and in most of the cases, the increase registered is a very large increase. The data thus only point towards an increase in the proportion of households using firewood.

Conclusion

This study tries to analyze the roe of household behaviour in terms of firewood consumption as a response to the economic development in various districts of Bihar. I check for the proportion of households in urban and rural areas of Bihar using firewood as a fuel in 2005-06 and 2011-12. I find that in majority of rural and urban areas, the per cent of households using firewood has incased by a large amount. The results, thus, do not point towards the existence of an EKC in the time period under consideration.

References

Cole, M., Rayner A. and Bates, J. (1997) The Environmental Kuznets Curve: An Empirical Analysis. *Environment and Development Economics* 2(4):401-416.

Grossman, G. and Krueger, A. (1991) Environmental Impact of a North American Free Trade Agreement. *National Bureau of Economic Review* working paper no. 3194.

Harbaugh, W., Levinson, A. and Wilson, D.M. (2002) Reexamining the Evidence for an Environmental Kuznets Curve. *The Review of Economics and Statistics,* 84(3):541-551.

Managi, S. and Jena, P. (2007) Productivity and Environment in India. *Economics Bulletin,* 17(1):1-14.

Stern, D. and Common, M. (2001) Is there an Environmental Kuznets Curve for sulphur? *Journal of Environmental Economics and Management,* 41(2):162-178.

Tiwari, A., Shahbaz, M. and Hye, Q. (2013). The Environmental Kuznets Curve and coal consumption in India: Cointegration and causality analysis in an open economy. *Renewable and Sustainable Energy Reviews,* 18:519:527.

7

Allied Activities and Agricultural Patterns of Malda District, West Bengal

Pankaj Kumar, Saidur Rahaman and *V. Madha Suresh*

Introduction

Mango production is one of the major economic activity in the district. Mango orchards in the district cover a total of 26,500 hectares land in 2009 (*District Statistical Handbook*, 2010). It provides employment to a large numbers of people and helps rejuvenate the district economy through generation of crores of rupees in main and ancillary activities. It deserves to a special mention here that the district has been identified as an agricultural export zone for Mango and Litchi. Litchi is produced in 950 hectares land spreading over 13 blocks in the district, where the production during 2007-2008 was about 9000 Metric ton (*District Statistical Handbook*, 2009). Dairy development plays a vital role in the rural economy and there is anabundant scope for dairy development. Out of the total reporting area of Malda district (3,70,862 hectares), about 20 per cent area (70,076 hectares) in current fallow that can be utilized for fodder rising. The total area under forest cover in the district is 1,680 hectares comprising only 0.45 per cent. About 60 hectares area will be taken-up for plantation during next three year from 2009, 2010 and 2011 (*District Statistical Handbook*, 2010, 2011 and 2012). But there may not be much potential for development of forestry and wasteland in the district due to high pressure of population.

Malda ranks at the top in terms of wetlands of area less than 10 hectares and more than 109 hectares. In fact, out of the recorded 23 major wetlands in West Bengal 11 wetlands are situated in

Malda district. Malda district has 25,000 hectares of water area of which also included with tank and pond cover of 5,869 hectares. Out of this only about 10,000 hectares is utilized for fisheries purpose. In the district there are 29,661 hectares ponds, Dighis like Bara Sagardighi, Beels, Kharis, (Dighis, Beels, Kharis—these are all water bodies) and rivers. The major rivers in the district are the Ganga, the Mahananda, the Purnabhaba, the Tangon, the Kalindri, the Pagla, the Bhagirathi and the Phoolahar. The annual production of fish in the district is about 29,288 tons against an estimated demand of 48,000 tons leaving a gap of 18,712 tons (*District Statistical Handbook*, 2009 and Agriculture and Horticulture Department, Malda, 2014).

The district is divided into three physiographic regions, namely Tal, Barind and Diara (Table 7.1). The Tal is mostly composed of bog lands formed in many marshy pockets around vestigial inland drainages. Most of Tal track remains submerged under considerable depth of water during the monsoon rains and comprises of Ratua 1, Ratua 2, Chanchal 1, Chanchal 2, Harishchandrapur 1 and Harishchandrapur 2 development Blocks of Malda (*District Gazetteer*, 2004). The Barindregion is generally dry and is covered by abundant natural vegetation excepting the sandy beds of rivers. Some portions of Barindarea are covered by jungles, which consist chiefly of thorny scrub bush jungles mixed with bamboos and common Indian trees like *Pipal, Vat* etc. However, with time, the jungle region has been gradually shrinking. Malda also has areas consisting of old river beds, ponds, marshy land and other watery regions. The Rivers Ganga, Mahananda, Phoolahar and Kalindri flow through the district. As such, some areas of the district are subject to frequent inundations. Agriculture is the main occupation of the populace, the main crops being are Paddy, Wheat, Jute and *Rabi* crops. Diara is a relatively well drained flat land formed by the alluvial deposition of newer alluvium in the transitional zone between the upland and the marshy Tal track. Malda is famous for its Silk and Mangoes, both of which are produced in the western region of the district, due to the favourable soil conditions for the growth of Mango and Mulberry trees (*District Gazetteer*, 2004).

SWOT Analysis for Agriculture and Allied Sectors

The soil of Malda is more fertile among the others district of West

Table 7.1: Crop and Topographical Characteristics of Different Regions

Region	Chararteristics	Block Covered	Area (In Ha.)
TAL	Low Lying areas subject to inundation in every rainy season. It gradually slopes down towards the south and west. Soil is of clay-to-clay loam type with heavy texture. Main crop grown are paddy, Jute, Pulses, Wheat and Oilseeds. Textural classes of this zone are sandy 2-3%, sandy loam 8-9% loam 35-36%, clay loam 42-43% siltloam 4-5% and Clay 5-6%	Ratua 1 Ratua 2 Chanchal 1 Chanchal2 Harishchandrapur 1 Harishchandrapur 2	1,14,099
DIARA	Flat land on the western side of Mahananda. Light soils of new alluvium type. Water level high and within the reach of STW even in summer. Main crops are Jute, Aus, Wheat, Pulses and Oil seeds.Textural classes of this zone are sandy 7-8%, sandy loam 15-16% loam 45-47%, clay loam13-156%, silt loam 11-12% and clay 5-6%	Englishbazar, Manikchak, Kaliachak 1 Kaliachak 2 & Kaliachak 3	1,32,851
BARIND	Comparatively high lands on the east of the Mahananda River (highest altitude 69.7 m in Gazole) Wide undulation with successive ridges and depression with small water sources and no shade. Ground is hard, ground water level is very low except inrainy season. Main crops are *Kharif* rice, Jute, Autumn Rice. Soilis old alluvium, heavy. Textural classes of soil of this zone aresandy loam 0-5%, loam 10-12%, Clay loam 30-35% and clay 55-57%	Gazole, Bamongola, Habibpur& Old Malda	1,32,851

Source: *District Gazetteers of Malda*, 2004 and *Statistical Hand Book*, 2005.

Bengal, especially in the Tal and Diara regions. There are various crops and plantation farming practices in the district i.e., rice, wheat, jute, potato, sugarcane, oilseeds, maize, mica, pulses etc. Now study focus on strength, weakness, opportunities and threats for the agriculture, farmers as well as the effects of local peoples, agricultural market, soil and climate (Table 7.2).

Table 7.2: Strength, Weakness, Opportunities and Threats on Agriculture

Strength	• District receives a good amount of rainfall every year. • Diversified topography offers the potential for the production of a wide variety of agricultural, horticultural and sericulture produces. • Conducive condition for rain fed crops like legumes, Kharif Maise, short duration Mustard (Toria variety), Pulses like Kalai, *Moong*, Lentill etc. • Cropping intensity of the district is about 196%. • Existing farming communities and ongoing innovations. • Wide scope of public and private partnership.
Weakness	• Traditional crop cultivation practices due to less extension inputs to farmers. • Lack of technical-up gradation facilities. • Dependence on underground water and mechanized water lifting facilities. • Poor knowledge among farmers to harness rain water harvesting and usage of existing water harvesting structures. • Presence of major clay components in soil and thereby results in compactness. • Depletion of nutrient capacity of soil. • Regular water logging in Tal area of the district. • Dependency on paddy cultivation and less attention towards cultivation of millets and legumes. • Poor financial condition of the farmers. • Lack of adequate, timely credit from financial institutions.
Opportunities	• Scope for surface water harvesting based irrigation. • Scope of developing more diversified farming system. • Scope of public private partnership based innovative extension activities. • Scope of '0' tillage legume cultivation. • Scope of introduction of more increased productive variety of Maize. • Provision and implementation of better post-harvest management system. • Better marketing through regulated market network • Involvement of Self-Help Group (SHGs) Farmers' Clubs and NGO's in information dissemination. • Technical inputs on production of organic manure.
Threats	• Use of imbalanced fertilizers and pesticides without any soil test. • Increased population pressure over cultivable land. • Increasing intensity of climate change and absence of adaptation mechanism.

Source: Primary Survey, February 2015.

Horticulture

Mango production is one of the major economic activity in the district. Mango-orchards in the district cover a total of 25,250 hectors land in 2005-2006 (Table 7.3). It provides employment to a large numbers of people and helps rejuvenate the district economy. The varieties like Fazli, Langra, Himsagar, Laxmanbhog, Gopalbhog, Bambai, Krishanbhog, Zardalu, Ashwina, Amrapali, Malika etc. are commercially cultivated. About 250 varieties of mango are found in the district in comparison to 1100-1200 varieties of the country. The estimated production of Mango during 2005-2006 was 15,000 metric tons having average yield at 6.5 metric tons per hectare (Agriculture and Horticulture Department, Malda,

Table: 7.3: Area Under Fruits and Vegetables Production

Crops	*Year*	*Area ('000 hector)*				*Production ('000MT)*			
		02-03	*03-04*	*04-05*	*05-06*	*02-03*	*03-04*	*04-05*	*05-06*
Fruits	Mango	24.50	24.85	25.00	25.25	63.68	86.00	145.00	150.00
	Banana	0.70	0.70	0.72	0.74	12.53	12.70	12.84	13.15
	Pineapple		0.10	0.15	0.16		2.70	3.30	3.80
	Papaya	0.20	0.20	0.20	0.22	6.48	6.66	6.76	6.85
	Guava	0.30	0.30	0.31	0.32	4.92	4.90	5.06	5.31
	Jackfruit	0.30	0.33	0.33	0.34	3.46	3.71	4.06	4.31
	Litchi	0.61	0.62	0.85	0.9	6.45	6.51	6.99	7.37
	Other Citrus	0.18	0.18	0.19	0.22	1.54	1.62	1.64	1.72
	Sapota	0.22	0.22	0.23	0.23	2.59	2.54	2.66	2.71
	Others	0.22	0.20	0.20	0.21	1.00	1.19	1.23	1.29
	Total	**27.23**	**27.70**	**28.18**	**28.59**	**102.65**	**128.53**	**189.54**	**196.51**
Vegetable	Tomato	2.41	2.42	2.42	2.43	32.54	33.18	33.80	35.60
	Cabbage	3.85	3.87	3.89	3.94	112.81	106.67	107.25	112.56
	Cauliflower	3.23	3.24	3.24	3.25	93.35	93.45	94.69	96.13
	Peas	0.70	0.70	0.72	0.73	3.36	3.37	3.42	3.43
	Brinjal	11.06	11.13	11.19	0.96	102.20	192.07	195.19	192.89
	Onion	1.24	1.26	1.28	1.31	13.89	14.18	15.96	17.61
	Cacurbits	8.31	8.63	8.64	8.61	78.84	75.88	67.43	66.35
	Ladies Finger	2.88	2.69	2.74	2.75	31.38	29.51	31.57	32.91
	Radish	1.96	1.97	1.98	2.07	20.77	22.29	24.03	26.73
	Others	14.24	14.44	13.60	14.48	41.14	53.22	52.00	51.25
Total		**49.88**	**50.35**	**50.70**	**50.70**	**620.36**	**623.82**	**625.34**	**635.46**

Source: Directorate of Food Processing Industries and Horticulture, Government of West Bengal, 2008.

2014).The next major horticultural crops in the district are; litchi and banana. While the average production of banana is 13,150 metric tons and litchi production was 7370 metric tons spreading over 13 blocks of the district in 2005-2006 (Table 7.3). Other minor fruits grown in Malda include; Papaya, Pine apple, Guava, Sapota etc. (Directorate of Food Processing Industries and Horticulture).

Table 7.4: Strength, Weakness, Opportunities and Threats on Horticulture

Strength	• Malda is famous for fruits especially Mango in all three regions and Litchi in Diararegion. • Production of Bamboos is high in Barind and Tal region. • Diversification of farming fruits taking place. • Mango research station with nurseries run by Government. • Malda has been covered under two Agri Export Zone (AEZ) one for Mango and other for Litchi. • Food park in Malda established.
Weakness	• Lack of thrust for production of organic mango. • Marketing information of horticultural product price is very limited. • Age old orchards with very low fruiting condition. • Absence of business development information providers for export marketing. • Lack of adequate credit flow from the financial institution of the district. • Refrigerated vans, gradings, packaging and transportation are limited. • Less availability of quality vegetable seeds. • Lack of area-based problem specific training.
Opportunities	• Growing trend of organic mango production. • Fruit merchants are now searching options for other possible markets. • National bamboo mission is active in the district. • Fruit processing industry in Malda running well. • Post-harvesting knowledge and information on fruits and vegetables is expected to support growth. • Establishment of post-harvest technology centre will help in management of Products.
Threats	• Flood, drought and soil erosion occurs every year. • Establishing Marketing information and other infrastructure for promoting marketing are limited. • Over use of chemicals in fruit trees. • Production of sulphur dioxide and carbon mono-oxide from growing number of brick kilns, affecting the crop productivity.

Source: Primary Survey, February 2015.

On the other hand the major vegetables crops are Brinjal, Cabbage, Cauliflower, Cacurbits and Tomato. The total production of Brinjal during 2005-2006 was 19,289 metric tons followed by Cabbage production was 11,256 metric tons, Cauliflower production was 9,613 metric tons, Cacurbits production was 6,635 metric tons and the average production of Tomato was 3,560 metric tons in the Malda district (Table 7.3).

The district can be categorized as a major horticulture producer with a gross area of over 80,378 ha. This includes 28,386 hectares under fruit crops and 51,992 hectares under seasonal vegetables (Agriculture and Horticulture Department, Malda, 2014). Vegetable production is predominant in almost all the blocks and during all the seasons under intensive cultivation. Predominant vegetables grown are; Brinjal, Ladies finger, Tomato, Cucurbits, Yamand winter vegetables. Non-traditional vegetables like Broccoli, Capsicum, red Cabbage are being explored. A major part of the area under vegetable production is high yielding/hybrid varieties and the productivity/quality of vegetables is high due to intensive production practices.

Animal Husbandry

Animal Husbandry is the third largest livelihood activity in the district, next only to agriculture and horticulture in the district. Consumption of milk, egg and meat are very high in the district. District offers suitable climatic condition for poultry and dairy farming. Dairy farming on a small scale provides supplementary source of income to the rural population especially to the small and marginal farmers and agricultural labourers. Despite huge potentiality, Malda district still remains seriously deficit in requirement of live-stock products.The requirement of milk per capita per day is 210 grams against a supply of nearly 56.66 grams in the district (Agriculture and Livestock Census, 2008).

Most of the animals are of indigenous, non-descript variety and the average milk yield is 1-1.5 litre per day. The mortality rate is 8 per cent for the male population and 3-4 per cent in respect of female population. The farmer's choice pattern in most part of the district is cows. However in Old Malda and Manikchak block the choice is of buffaloes [Agriculture and Rural Development (ARD), Malda, 2010].

Table 7.5: Livestock Information

District	Area Under Fodders (ha)		Cattle (Nos.)			Buffaloes (Nos.)			Sheep (Nos.)			Goat (Nos.)			Poultry (Nos.)			Total
	Fodder Crop	Grazing Land	Cross Bred	Indigenous	Total	Improved	Indigenous	Total	Improved	Indigenous	Total	Improved	Indigenous	Total	Fowl	Duck	Total	Pig
Malda	1046 ha	10500 ha	66432	665206	731638	N.A.	N.A.	50830	N.A.	N.A.	56208	N.A.	N.A.	975506	2876016	392330	N.A.	60793

Source: Agriculture and Rural Development (ARD), Malda, 2010.

Fisheries

In Malda, there is very good scope for development of commercial fish farming on account of around 10,000 hectors of water logged areas. The Beels (large water bodies) also can bereclaimed and made suitable for fish farming. The climatic condition is highly suitable for fish culture. Also, fish farmers of this district are enriched with fish farming knowledge by tradition and heritage. All these have made these districts highly potential for fisheries development. The potential under fisheries is depicted in the following (Table 7.6) (Plate 7.1).

Table 7.6: Fisheries Potential

Sl. No.	*Potential Under Fisheries*		
1.	Impounded Water Area (Tanks and Ponds)		10773 hectors
2.	River		6,497.60 hectors
3.	Canel		2511.42 hectors
4.	Beel & Baors		4551.55 hectors
5.	Water Logged Water Bodies		10000 hectors
6.	Number of Fishermen	Male	88674
		Female	46347
		Total	135021
7.	Number of Fishermen Co-operative Society		86
8.	Central Fishermen Co-operative Society		01
9.	Fish Seed Hatchery		07
10.	Fishery Laboratory		01
11.	Number of Whole Sale Market		02
12..	Ice Plant		04
13.	Demand and Production		101
14.	Requirement of Fish		37362.28 MT

Source: Fisheries Department, Malda, 2009.

Sericulture

Sericulture is an agro-based cottage industry. It is highly labour intensive and employed 60 per cent of the labour from the women members of the family. Cultivator/ farmers produces cocoons as raw-materials for the reeling industry and the product (Raw silk yarn) of the reeling industry are the raw material for silk weaving industry. Malda is the major silk producing district, having acreage of mulberry 19,692 Acres (2005-06) that constitute 56.43 per cent of state acreage (i.e. 34,892 acres). Nearly 62,000 numbers of farmer's families are engaged in farm activity and they produce 10,790 metric tons in 2005-06 reeling cocoons.

Table 7.7: Production of Sericulture Industry in the District

Year	*Cocoons Production ('000 Kahan)*	*Value of Production ('000 Rupees)*
2002-03	7035 (Kg)	5,19,767
2003-04	10599 (Kg)	8,49,644
2004-05	9457 (Kg)	7,92,438
2005-06	7632 (Kg)	8,62,400

Source: Deputy Director of Sericulture, Malda, 2008.

The average production of cocoons was highest in 10.59 kilograms Kahan in 2003-04. Consequently, the cocoons production was decrease from 10.59 kilograms Kahan to 7.63 kilograms Kahan from 2003-04 to 2005-06. Thus, the value of production reversely increased from 5,19,767 to 8,62,400 in 2002-03 to 2005-06 (Table 7.7).

Agricultural Marketing

Malda district has two Agriculture Marketing Sub-Division viz. Malda Sadarand Chanchal. The department of Agriculture Marketing has been trying its level best with its limited resources and manpower to provide following infrastructural facilities for better agricultural marketing service (Table 7.8).

As already discussed, Malda is a prominent trade centre for products like Mango, Jute, Paddy etc. gives product-wise, location-wise details of markets in the district where such trading is done. It can be seen from the table that Mango and Sericulture fetch maximum trade in monetory terms. The most prominent centre for Mango trading is situated at English bazar, while the maximum trading of Silk Cocoons is done in Kaliachak-I block. The following table depicts the position of regulated markets in the study area (Table 7.8).

Land-Use Pattern

It reveals from an analysis of the data that of the total geographical

Region 1: Manikchak Ghat. (Diara Region) Region 2:MathurapurARC, Manikchak,

Region 1: This is the region where agricultural land converted into the flooded regions of Ganga. But this land is high fertile, and suitable for the seasonal agriculture. During the rainy season this land completely submerged under the water.

Region 2: Mango plantation land is con verted into agricultural land. Because lesser amount production of Mango. There are various crops practice in this are, like Rice, Wheat, Jute, Potato, Oilseeds, Maize, Mica, Pulses etc. Wheat is the Potato is the main crop.

Region 3: Kaliachak 2

Region 4:Ratua 1

Region 3: The climatic condition is highly suitable for fish culture in this region. There are commercial fish cultivation practices in this region. Farmer's traditionally practicing pisciculture, and his livelihood patterns is completely dependent on this culture.

Region 4: This is the region where agr icultu-ral land converted into the Mango plantation land. And crops rotation is also changed. This change brings impacts on livelihood patterns of the farmers. Besides in this region some of the other farmer practicing rice and wheat.

Photo 7.1: A Synaptic overview of different agricultural activities of the Study Area, Primary Survey, February 2015.

area, only 1.26 per cent is considered degraded land in the district of Malda. It is also a fact that Malda ranks at the top both in terms of wetlands in West Bengal. Out of total cultivable area of 2,80,000 hectares. The land-use pattern in the district is as given in table 7.9.

Table 7.8: Coverage and Commodity-wise Deatails of Market Centres

Sl. No.	Blocks	Name of the Market Centre	Periodicity	Important Commodities Handled	Commodity-Wise Quantity Handled (Annual)	Area Covered	No. of Farm Families Covered
1.	Harishchandrapur 1	Kushida Hat	Weekly	Cattle, Paddy, Wheat	N/A	5-10 Km	1600
2.	Harishchandrapur 2	Talgram Hat Tulshihata	Weekly	Paddy, Wheat, Vegetables, Cattle	N/A	2-15 Km	1800
3.	Chanchal 1	Chanchal Hat	Weekly	Paddy, Wheat, Vegetables, Cattle	N/A	5-15 Km	2100
4.	Chanchal 2	Maoltipur Hat	Weekly	Vegetables, Paddy, Wheat, Pulses	N/A	2-20 Km	750
5.	Ratua 1	Samsi Regulated Market & Balupur Hat	Weekly	Oilseeds and Vegetables	Total Value Rs. 1.554 Crores	2-50 Km	3500
6.	Ratua 2	—	—	—	N/A	—	—
7.	Gazole	Gazole Hat Alampur Hat	Weekly	Musterd, Paddy, Vegetables	N/A	5-20 Km	1250
8.	Habibpur	Aiho Hat Bulbulchandi Hat	Weekly	Cocoon, Paddy, Wheat, Vegetables	N/A	5-25 Km	850
9.	Bamangola	Pakuaa Hat	Weekly	Paddy, Wheat Vegetables	N/A	5-25 Km	1300

(Contd.)

Source: Directorate of Agricultural Marketing, Government of West Bengal.

Table 7.8 (*Contd.*)

Sl. No.	*Blocks*	*Name of the Market Centre*	*Periodicity*	*Important Commodities Handled*	*Commodity-Wise Quantity Handled (Annual)*	*Area Covered*	*No. of Farm Families Covered*
10.	Old Malda	Nababganj Hat 8 Mile Hat Ballatali Hat Sanibari Hat	All Weekly	Jute, Wheat, Goat, Cattle	N/A	5-15 Km	1300
11.	English bazar	English bazar Regulated Market	Daily during Mango Season for 3 Months	Mango	3360 MT	1-65 Km	3000
12.	Manikchak	Mathurapur, Champanagar Hat	Weekly	Paddy, Wheat, Vegetables	N/A	1-15 Km	500
13.	Kaliachak 1	Babur Hat	Weekly	Cocoon, Paddy, Wheat	N/A	1-25 Km	1100
14.	Kaliachak 2	Gosai Hat	Weekly	Rice	N/A	1-15 Km	600
15.	Kaliachak 3	Sahabajpur & Golapganj Hat	Weekly	Cattle	N/A	1-30 Km	500

Source: Directorate of Agricultural Marketing, Government of West Bengal.

Table 7.9: Agro-Ecological Situation (AES) of the District

High Land	*Medium Land*	*Low Land*	*Total*	*Special Area*	
				Drought Prone	*Flood Prone*
41918	190709	47373	280000	112481	21145
Light		Medium		Heavy	
Sandy	*Sandy Loam*	*Loam*	*Sandy Clay Loam*	*Clay Loam*	*Clay*
11988	23875	73222	38780	60572	71563

Source: Principal Account Officer (PAO), 2008, Malda.

There is requirement of intervention from the State Government for excavation/cleaning up of the large water bodies present in the district. This will enable the adjacent area of the water bodies to utilize the water for cultivation as also use the structure for inland fish (Table 7.9).

Major Crops and Varieties

Major crops grown are Paddy, Wheat, Maize, Pulses, Oil seeds, Sugarcane and vegetables in the district. As far as Horticulture is concern, it provides employment to a large numbers of people and helps rejuvenate the district economy through generation of crores of rupees in main and ancillary activities.

Paddy or Wheat crops are the predominant, followed by Jute and some plantation. Among the jute plantation, classified into three categories, Mango plantation, Sal plantation, and Segun plantation. Among the plantation categories Mango plantation is predominatns especially Manikchak, Ratua 1, Ratua 2, Old Malda, and some part of Harishchandrapur 1 and Harishchandrapur 2 (Figure 7.1). English bazar is an urban region of the district. So, agriculture is not practicing in this region. During the primary survey there were are only 2 respondents are asked, they are practicing only fisheries. Fisheries also predominats role play in Kaliachak 2, Manikchak, and Ratua 2, because in this region there are lack of availability of swamp, beels, ponds etc. (Figure 7.1).

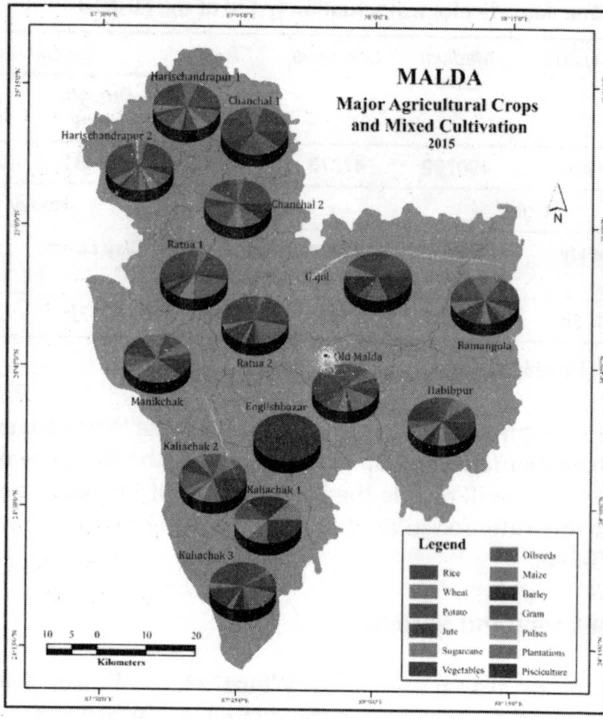

Fig. 7.1: Major Agricultural Crops, Fisheries, and Plantation Farming

Source: Primary Survey, February 2015.

Agricultural Land-Use Changes from Earlier to Present

Most of the people are dependent on agriculture. So, there is less variation changes of agricultural activity in some pockets of the district, like English bazar, Chanchal 1, Gajol, and most of the part of Kaliachak 1. Because there region is highly developed comparison to the others blocks of the district. In these region most of the land are use only commercial activities, like small scale industry, manufacturing industry etc. (Figure 7.1). On the other hand, others pockets of the district like, Ratua 1, Ratua 2, Manichak, Old Malda, Kaliachak 2 and Kaliachak 3 are agricultural blocks of the district. In above blocks are most of the agricultural land are less changes comparison to the English bazar, Chanchal 1, Gajol, and most of the part of Kaliachak 1 blocks. There are vast transformation of land from one activity to another activity, and also transf)rmation of land from one agricultural activity to another agricultural activities in the especially Harishchandrapur 1 and Harishchandrapur 2 blocks, like agriculture to plantation and bricks manufacturing/small scale industry. Crop rotation also changed in this region. Due to the high productivity of soil, the farmers/cultivators are continuously practicing agriculture.

Agricultural Land-Use Change

If we talk about the plantation land Manikchak, Ratua 1, Ratua 2 are highly developed, especially mango plantation. There are lack of transformation of land from agricultural land to plantation land. Manikchak, Ratua 1 and Kaliachak 3 are highly influenced by the flood hazard condition of Ganga. There are lack of land transformation from agricultural to become flooded regions of Ganga River, this region is known as the Diara region.

According to the respondents, the study classified into five categories of the transformation of agricultural activity to another activity. Those five categories are: 1. Crop rotation change; 2. Agricultural land converted into a plantation land; 3. Conversion in to pond due to less production of agricultural products; 4. Plantation or agricultural land to residential/ built-up area; and 5. Agricultural land were flooded regions of river (Figure 7.2).

Crop rotation is changed almost every blocks of the district. As far as agricultural land converted into plantation land is concerned, Harischandrapur 1, Ratua 1, Ratua 2, Habibpur, Old Malda, Kaliachak 3 are the good example of converted from agricultural land into plantation land. There is a category classification of agricultural land-use transformed from agricultural land to flooded region of river, (Figure 7.2). Especially, Manikachak (Manikchak Ghat) region. Most of the respondents are told that they had more than 3 *bigha* land, but now this land is under the flooded region of Ganga River.

Positive and Negative Impacts of Agricultural Land-Use Change

Under this content, this study try to focus what are the positive and negative impacts of agricultural land-use changes from one to another activity. Under this positive category the study tries to maintain the

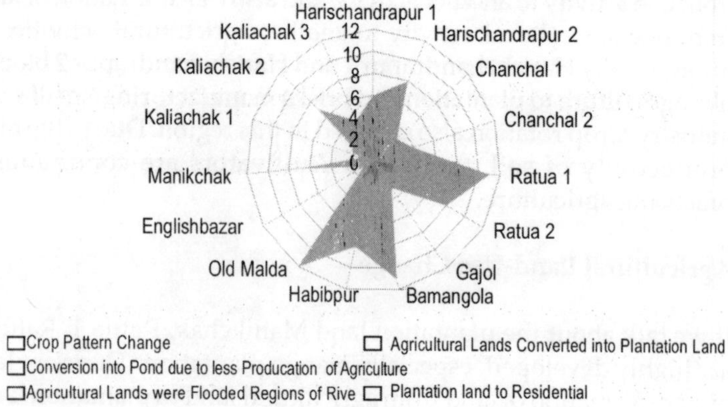

Fig. 7.2: Agricultural Land-Use Change

Source: Primary Survey, February 2015.

actual observation of the respondents. According to them, the positive impacts are: 1. Raising the level of income; 2. Way of better livelihood patterns of his/her own; 3. Commercial purposes; and 4. Some of the other impacts are directly and indirectly related to the rural people's life. On the other hand we can not deny the negative impacts. These negative impacts are: 1. Less availability of food production; 2. Less availability of the income sources of the local labours; 3. Reduced agricultural land, and the last one is very rare change; and 4. Reduced plantation land.

In this above maintain the study deal with the positive and negative impacts of land-use changes on livelihood patterns of the people. Now, try to deal block-wise discussion what they are said. Negative impacts are tremendously highlighted in Harishchandrapur 1, Chanchal 1, Ratua 2, and especially Manikchak, Kaliachal 2, Kaliachak 3, caused by the flood (Figure 7.3).

Cropping Pattern

Cropping pattern of the district is showing increasing in cropping intensity. With an average cropping intensity at 196 per cent, the district can be considered having fairly good cropping intensity. However, a point to be noted here that the size of small and marginal farmers are maximum and their average land holding size is only around 0.76 hectares per farmer (*District Statistical Handbook*, 2009).

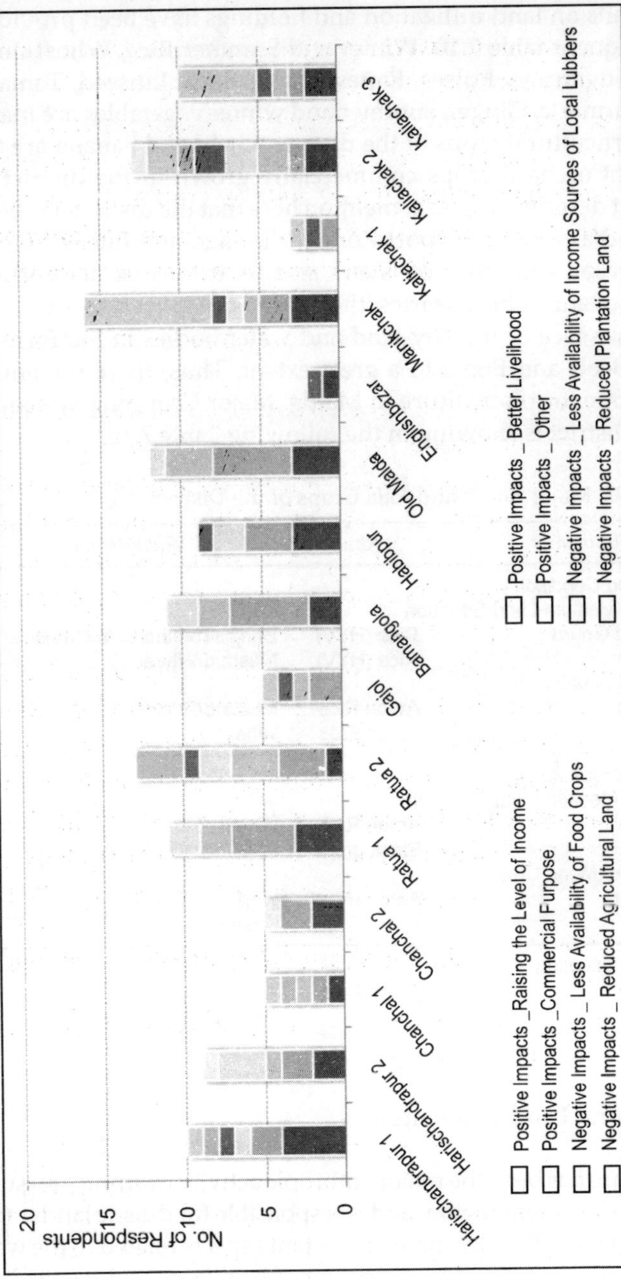

Fig. 7.3: Positive and Negative Impacts due to Agricultural Land-Use Change

Source: Primary Survey, February 2015.

Details on land utilization and holdings have been provided in subsequent table 7.10. Winter and Summer Rice, Wheat, Jute, Maize, Sugarcane, Pulses, Rapeseed, Mustard, Linseed, Tomato, Chili, Turmeric, Ginger, summer and winter vegetables are major Agri-horticultural crops of the district. Litchi and banana are the dominant orchard crops commercially grown in the district of Malda. It deserves a special mention here that the district has been identified as an Agri-Export Zone for Mango and Litchi. Due to existence of a number of rivers and its extensive network of tributaries and subtributaries, the district of Malda also gives rise to the presence of marshy land and water bodies in the form of Ponds, Beels and Boars to a great extent. Thus, there remains a good scope for pisciculture in Malda. Major Cropping system of Malda District is showing in the following Table 7.10:

Table 7.10: Major *Kharif* and *Rabi* Crops of the District

Pre-Kharif/Summer	*Kharif*	*Rabi/Winter*
A. Irrigated Condition		
Upland & Medium Land Situation		
1. Pointed Gourd	Rice (HYV)	Brinjal/Tomato/Cole Crops
2. Fallow	Rice (HYV)	Mustard/Wheat
Low Land Situation		
Boro Rice	Amon Rice	Mustard/Brinjal
Jute	Amon Rice	Wheat
B. Rainfed Condition		
Upland & Medium Land Situation		
Jute	Amon Rice	Wheat
Maize	Black gram	Chilli
Sugarcane (Mono Crop)		
Black Gram	Amon Rice	Lentil
Turmeric		Linseed
Low Land Situation		
Maize	Amon Rice	Wheat/Tomato
Aus Rice	Fallow	Lentil/Mustard/Vegetable

Source: *District Statistical Handbook*, 2009.

Agricultural Land-Use Pattern

Agriculture has been the major anthropic activity exerting pressure on the environment region, and is responsible for drastic landscape transformation. Besides many important aspects related to the way agriculture is practiced (e.g. amount of fertilizers and pesticides, till age practices). Agricultural land-use patterns and area under the principal crops from 2004 to 2014 has been shown in the following Table 7.11.

Issues Related to Agricultural Development

Increase in the production of cereals and non-cereal agricultural commodities will have to be essentially achieved through increase in productivity, as the possibilities of expansion of area and livestock population are minimal (e.g. Kaliachak, Harishchandrapur 1 and Bamangola region). The burning issues that are important in a nationwide context are detailed herein:

1. Increase in population;
2. High pressure on Agricultural lands;
3. Environment degradation;
4. Globalization;
5. Degradation of Soil Health;
6. Resource based degradation and water scarcity;
7. Loss of bio-diversity;
8. Inadequate investment in agricultural sector;
9. Lack of adequate infrastructure;
10. Lack of co-coordinated approach;
11. Gender-related issues; and
12. Rural employment generation.

With increase in population and inadequate employment generation, the pressure on land has increased considerably leading to fragmentation of holding. The number of small and marginal farmers has increased considerably in over the years. As the pressure on land increased, the farmers are forced to over-exploit their land for livelihood support which again leads to environmental degradation, degradation of soil health and such related issues. This clearly indicates that all these issues are inter-related and solving one of these will be of no use; an integrated approach involving policy-decision, adoption of new emerging technologies, infrastructural support and development of human resource base is the key to address these issues in an effective manner. A more focused, coordinated and determined approach is needed to get an evergreen revolution.

Table 7.11: Area under Principal Crops in the district of Malda, (2004 to 2012)

(thousand hectares)

Crops	*2004-05*	*2005-06*	*2006-07*	*2007-08*	*2008-09*	*2009-10*	*2010-11*	*2011-12*
Food Grains:								
1. Rice	217.3	218.6	154.2	147.3	221.7	216.8	200.8	204.9
Aus	8.1	6.9	6.6	6.2	5.9	5.8	3.4	3.7
Aman	144.5	144.2	80.0	73.1	143.0	143.0	132.8	144.5
Boro	64.7	67.5	67.6	68.0	72.8	68.0	64.6	56.7
2. Wheat	54.1	45.9	42.9	46.9	44.4	44.1	47.6	43.5
3. Barley	1.5	1.3	1.2	1.2	1.1	1.2	1.5	1.3
4. Maize	10.9	11.2	13.7	11.1	9.5	8.6	8.8	13.6
5. Other Cereals	0.2	0.1	0.1	0.1	–	–	–	–
Total Cereals	**284**	**277.1**	**212.1**	**206.6**	**276.7**	**270.7**	**258.7**	**263.3**
6. Gram	7.8	6.1	4.7	3.9	3.4	3.3	2.3	3.4
7. Tur	0.1	@	@	@	@	0.1	0.1	@
8. Other Pulses	21.9	19.3	21.4	20.4	17.2	17.3	14.1	15.8
Total Pulses	**29.8**	**25.4**	**26.1**	**24.3**	**20.6**	**20.7**	**16.5**	**19.2**
Total Food Grains	**313.8**	**302.5**	**238.2**	**230.9**	**297.3**	**291.4**	**275.2**	**282.5**
Oil Seeds:								
1. Rapeseed & Mustarc	38.3	38.0	38.9	36.4	32.7	32.7	30.4	32.4
2. Linseed	0.3	0.3	0.3	0.3	0.1	0.1	0.1	0.1
3. Other Oil seeds	0.7	0.8	1.1	1.0	0.5	0.4	0.7	0.4
Total Oil seeds	**39.3**	**39.1**	**40.3**	**37.7**	**33.3**	**33.2**	**31.2**	**32.9**

(Contd.)

Table 7.11 (*Contd.*)

Crops	*2004-05*	*2005-06*	*2006-07*	*2007-08*	*2008-09*	*2009-10*	*2010-11*	*2011-12*
Fibres:								
1. Jute	23.7	22.2	23.2	22.5	21.7	18.2	18.0	21.5
2. Mesta	0.6	0.6	0.6	0.4	0.3	0.2	0.4	0.6
3. Other Fibres	–	–	–	–	–	–	–	–
Total Fibres	**24.3**	**22.8**	**23.8**	**22.9**	**22.0**	**18.4**	**18.4**	**22.1**
Miscellaneous Crops:								
1. Sugarcane	3.1	2.6	2.4	2.3	2.3	2.2	2.2	2.2
2. Potato	2.5	2.5	2.8	2.9	3.6	4.4	5.0	3.9
3. Tobacco	0.4	0.2	0.2	0.2	0.2	0.2	0.2	0.1
4. Tea	–	–	–	–	–	–	–	–
5. Chillies (dry)	2.1	1.8	2.0	2.4	2.5	2.5	2.6	2.6
6. Ginger	0.2	0.2	0.1	0.2	0.2	0.2	0.3	0.3
Total Miscellaneous Crops	**8.3**	**7.3**	**7.5**	**8.0**	**8.8**	**9.5**	**10.3**	**9.1**

@ less than 50 hectors

Sources: 1. Directorate of Agriculture, Government of West Bengal; and 2. B.A.E.& S., Government of West Bengal.

Conclusion

The land-use and land cover pattern of a region is an outcome of natural and socio-economic factors and their utilization by man in time and space. Land is becoming a scarce resource due to immense agricultural and demographic pressure. Hence, information on land-use and land cover and possibilities for their optimal use is essential for the selection, planning and implementation of land-use schemes to meet the increasing demands for basic human needs and welfare. As the district of Malda is an important agricultural region in West Bengal, the economic well-being of its population bears a close relation to the current state of agriculture in the district.

It has consequently been observed that cropping patterns vary considerably across the district. In several well irrigated regions that are also prone to inundation, long-duration crops like sugarcane are generally grown, which reduce cropping intensity since they occupy the land for the better part of the year. Cropping intensity is visibly higher, on the other hand, in agricultural regions where short-duration *Kharif* and *Rabi* crops are the main crops sown and grown.

Given the width of such inter-block variations in the availability of arable land and irrigation and incropping intensity and crop yields, the ability of the rural workforce to subsist through agricultural livelihoods within each agro-ecological regions would depend very strongly on the cropping intensities and the dominant cropping patterns followed within each region. Consequently, a significant degree of association generally exists between block-wise agricultural conditions in each block in Malda district. Only Kaliachak 1 offers a major exception to this, because of the remarkable shift that has occurred in its dominant rural livelihood patterns from agricultural to non-agricultural work. Lastly, the study should not forget to mention that there is a regional variation of agricultural patterns among the different blocks. For example, Paddy cultivation are more predominant in Ratua 1, Harischandrapur, and Chanchal region on the other hand Mango plantation play predominant role in Manikchak and Old Malda region.

References

Agricultural Census. 2000-2001. Department of Agriculture and Cooperation. Ministry of Agriculture. Government of West Bengal.

Agricultural Census. 2005-2006. Department of Agriculture and Cooperation. Ministry of Agriculture. Government of West Bengal.

Agricultural Census. 2010-2011. Department of Agriculture and Cooperation. Ministry of Agriculture. Government of West Bengal.

Agriculture and Horticulture Department. 2014. National Horticulture Board. Ministry of Agriculture. Government of West Bengal.

Agriculture and Livestock Census. 2008. Department of Animal Husbandry, Dairying and Fisheries. Ministry of Agriculture. Government of West Bengal.

Agriculture and Rural Development. 2010. Ministry of Rural Development. Government of West Bengal.

Deputy Director of Sericulture. 2008. Malda. Government of West Bengal.

Director of Agriculture (Evolution). 2010. Ministry of Agriculture. Government of West Bengal.

Director of Agriculture. 2006-07. Ministry of Agriculture. Government of West Bengal.

Directorate of Agricultural Marketing. 2006. Government of West Bengal.

Directorate of Food Processing Industries and Horticulture. 2008. Government of West Bengal.

District Gazetteers of Malda. 2004. West Bengal. Malda District. Government of West Bengal. Malda.

District Gazetteers of Malda. 2008. West Bengal. Malda District. Government of West Bengal. Malda.

District Land and Revenue Office. 2011. Applied and Economics. Malda District. Government of West Bengal. Malda.

District Statistical Handbook. 2005. Bureau of Applied Economics and Statistics. Department of Statistics & Programme Implementation. Government of West Bengal. Parts 5.1-5.4c.

District Statistical Handbook. 2006. Bureau of Applied Economics and Statistics. Department of Statistics & Programme Implementation. Government of West Bengal. Parts 5.1-5.8.

District Statistical Handbook. 2007. Bureau of Applied Economics and Statistics. Department of Statistics & Programme Implementation. Government of West Bengal. Parts 5.1-5.4c.

District Statistical Handbook. 2008. Bureau of Applied Economics and Statistics. Department of Statistics & Programme Implementation. Government of West Bengal. Parts 5.1-5.8.

District Statistical Handbook. 2009. Bureau of Applied Economics and Statistics. Department of Statistics & Programme Implementation. Government of West Bengal. Parts 5.1-5.8.

District Statistical Handbook. 2010. Bureau of Applied Economics and Statistics. Department of Statistics & Programme Implementation. Government of West Bengal. Parts 5.1-5.8.

District Statistical Handbook. 2011. Bureau of Applied Economics and Statistics. Department of Statistics & Programme Implementation. Government of West Bengal. Parts 5.1-5.8.

Land and Land Reform Department. Malda. Government of West Bengal.

Principal Account Officer (PAO). 2008. Ministry of Agriculture. Government of West Bengal. Malda.

8

Impact of Quarrying on the Public Health in the Southern Bihar

Ashok Kumar, Haseena Hashia, Sandesh Yadav, and *Tariq Ahmad Ganaie*

Introduction

Earth is endowed with infinite resources and these resources are exploited by human beings for their advancement and development. Exploitation of these natural resources by human beings have altered the elements of natural system and consequently, degraded the quality of environmental surroundings. One such activity is "Quarrying", which is done in order to extract the various valuable stones either from the surface or great depth of the earth.

The increased rate of development resulted in increased rate of quarrying and due to which the impact of quarrying activity grew in scope and strength. For quite a long time, no thought was given to the possible consequences of quarrying and its related activities. But the consequences were significant and pervasive. Only recently, people have come to realize the necessity for assessment of quarrying on environmental conditions and the human beings living in the neighbouring region. The fast rate of quarrying has damaged environment by degrading the quality of air, creating noise and vibrations, large scale deforestation, habitat fragmentation, loss of biodiversity, landscape degradation and many more.

Quarries are generally localized in Gaya, Rohtas and Nawada districts of Bihar. In Gaya the mines are distributed in Manpur, Wazirganj, Dumri and Fatehpur blocks. Most of the rocks in the areas are highly weathered and are not of good quality. In some areas top rocks are weathered and quarrying is taking place only where stones of good quality are found, especially granites and amphibolites.

Bihar was leading producer in the industry of stone quarrying and crushing till the year 2000. In this year, a new state has been created as Jharkhand from Bihar. A large area of natural resources has been parted in this division. Most of the large quarrying and crushing industries came in the account of Jharkhand. After 2000, in southern Bihar there was boom in the quarrying and crushing industries due to boom in the building construction industry. There is a huge demand for stones of different sizes by the construction sector for buildings, roads, bridges etc.

Objectives

The present research study aims to achieve the following major objectives:

1. To examine the quarry sites and their extent in the study area.
2. To assess the impacts of quarrying on the surrounding environment of the study area.

Database and Methodology

Quarrying is the important activity in the Southern Bihar. Most of quarrying and crushing industries are legal, but illegal quarrying industries are also operating in the study area. Quarrying and stone crushing industry is causing several environmental and social problems. The present study is designed to assess the environmental impact of quarrying and stone crushing industry in Southern Bihar.

In this regard Primary and Secondary data has been collected. Secondary data has been collected from various government and non-government sources with vital line of information.

The primary data regarding the topic has been collected through a well-designed questionnaire. Purposive Random Sampling Technique has been used. Group discussions with government officials and community heads have been carried out to assess the ground realities and actual scenario in the area. The six quarrying sites in the study area have been sampled. Three villages and one town within a radius of 5 km from each of six major quarries have been selected. So in all there are 18 villages and 6 towns for the research study and 10 households have been surveyed in each. Hence, total 240 households have been surveyed.

Geographical Appraisal of the Study Area

The southernmost section of the State is known as South Bihar and lies south of the Gangetic Plain in the eastern part of Vindhyan Range. The geographical extent of South Bihar lies between 24° 20′10′′ N-25° 29′ 15′′ and 83° 19′ 50′′E-86°42′ 20′′E in the eastern part of the country and its height above 149.73 m. (MSL). This region is most important from the ecological point of view and is drained by the River Sone. Kaimur Hills, Rajgir Hills and Kharagpur Hills are known for the forest street in this region.

Our study area is comprised of six major quarrying sites namely Manpur and Gere, Karjara, Rajauli, Karbandiya, Pachna Baui, Nauagarhi. In the neighbourhood of these major quarrying sites, there exist 18 villages as our study area.

Land-Use and Land Cover Change (2005-12) in the Study Area

The rapidly expanding built-up area increases the demand for stones of different sizes in abandoned quantity. As these stones are weighty and incurs heavy transportation costs, a major portion of stones demand in area met locally by extracting stones from the earth. A relative comparison of Land-Use data for the year 2005-06 and 2011-12 portrays the rate of urbanization and its influence on local Land-Use. In Gaya, the urban built-up area has rapidly expanded from 38.48 km^{2}to 41.01 km^2 within a span of just five years. Consequently, the built-up mining in the districts have jumped from just 0.03 km^2 to about 2.24 km^2 during the same period. Similarly, in Rohtas districts the urban built-up area has expended rapidly from 14.36 km^2 to 20.36 km^2 during the period 2005-06 to 2011-12. The demand for stones sky-rocked and therefore, the built-up mining area though remained constant largely because of local regulations, nevertheless, the ever expanding demand was somewhat met from the neighbouring regions resulting into expansion of this category of Land-Use. For example, the built-up mining area reported to be about 3.00 km^2 and 0.15 km^2 in Aurangabad and Bhabhua district.

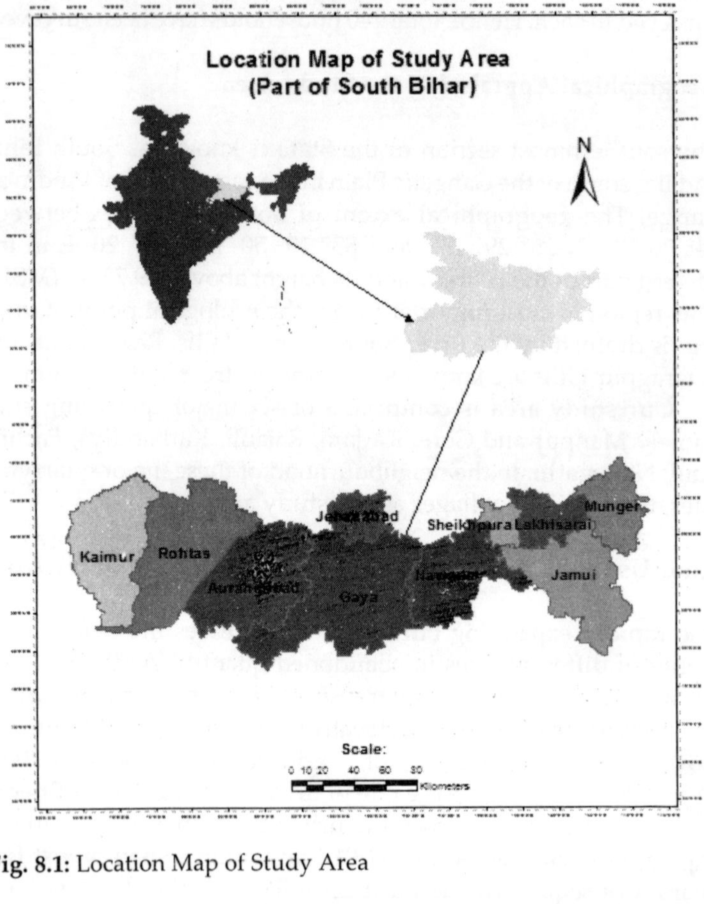

Fig. 8.1: Location Map of Study Area

The greedy miners, with an intention to indiscriminately exploit the land, resorted to both primitive and semi-primitive technology to maximize their benefits. This has rendered a vast area of land as degraded. In 2012, as per primary data obtained from local sources, about 411 crushers were being employed by miners in the district of Sasaram to extract the stone from an area of about 420 acres. Similarly, in Gaya and Sheikhpura, about 144

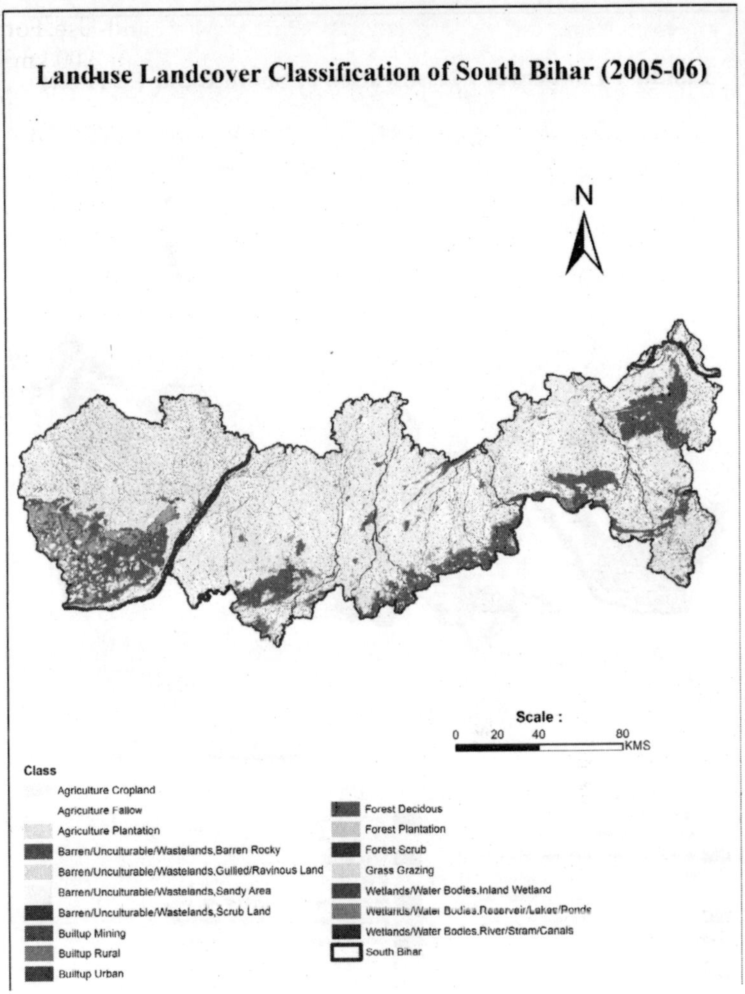

Fig. 8.2: Land-use and landcover Classification of South Bihar (2005-06)

and 120 stone crushers were employed to extract stones. In Munger and Nawada, though about 55 and 42 primitive crushers were employed, but historically, the earth is being ravaged from a long time. Area-wise, Sheikhpura has suffered most with an area of about 900 acres being harvested for stone with an average quarrying sites of about 1 to 1.5 hectares. Similarly, in Sasaram

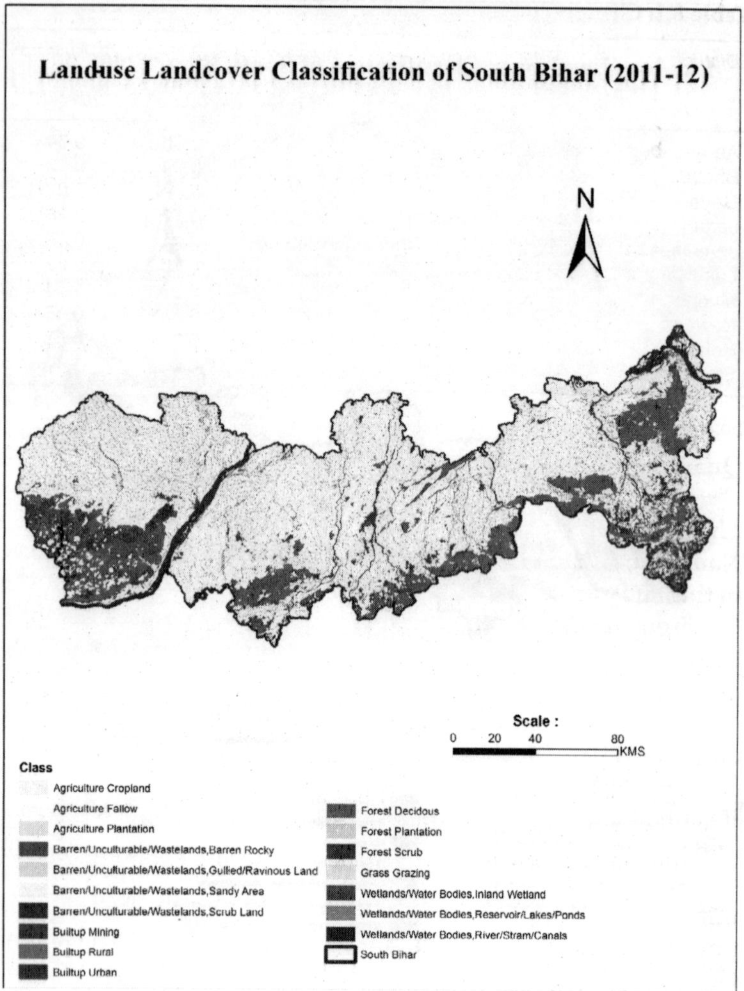

Fig. 8.3: Land-Use Land Cover Classification of South Bihar (2011-12)

and Nawada more than 400 acres land area has witnessed stone quarrying. In Munger and Gaya, the stone quarrying area is relatively smaller with each quarrying site averaging about 2 hectares.

Table 8.1: Changes in Built-up Area in the Study Area, 2005-2012

District	*Total Area*	*Built-up Urban 2005-06*	*Built-up Urban 2011-12*	*% Built-up Urban 2005-06*	*% Built-up Urban 2011-12*
Aurangabad	3305.00	4.99	11.13	0.15	0.34
Bhabua	3369.00	3.11	4.12	0.09	0.12
Gaya	4976.00	38.48	41.01	0.77	0.82
Jamui	3143.00	3.76	8.22	0.12	0.26
Jehanabadh	1569.00	3.30	4.60	0.21	0.29
Lakhisarai	1342.00	9.38	11.71	0.70	0.87
Munger	1397.00	12.81	22.91	0.92	1.64
Nawada	2494.00	4.54	11.37	0.18	0.46
Rohtas	3844.00	14.36	20.46	0.37	0.53
Sheikhpura	540.00	0.00	7.65	0.00	1.42

Source: National Remote Sensing Centre, Hyderabad.

Quarrying Sites in the Study Area

The six quarrying sites namely Manpur and Gere, Karjara, Naugarhi, Rajauli, Pachna Baui, Karbandiya are of major concern in the study area.

From the above mentioned list of the quarrying sites, Manpur and Gere along with Karjara come under the administrative control of Gaya district and also share similarity in terms of stone deposits. Naugarhi, Rajauli, Karbandiya and Pachna Baui falls under the administrative control of Munger district, Nawada district, Sasaram district and Sheikhpura district respectively. Further, Rajauli and Pachna Baui share the similar charateristics in terms of deposits.

Manpur, Gere and Karjara is characterized by the open cast mining with 0.836 ha of area in use and 4.223 ha of area are still unused. This area is surrounded by the several villages namely Gere, Mirjapur, Lodhipur Harijan Tola, Bhikampur Harijan Tola, Lohjara Harijan Tola and Belve. The rocks, in general, form a part of the Unclassified Metasedimentaries comprising mainly of Quartzite and Phyllites in the central part of the area. Archean Chotanagpur Granite-Gneiss occurs further south outside the Manpur and Gere area. Only a small outcrop of Mica Schist and Granite Gneiss occurs at Eru on the west of Wazirganj. Further, Muscovite Schist, Granitic rocks, Pyrites, Phyllites, Pegmatite, Jasper and Mylonite are also found in this belt.

Naugarhi area is characterized by the quartzite and mica

Schist. Mica Schist is highly weathered and converted into soil. Quartzite is exposed all along the hill range from Munger to Jamui with general north-south trend. Within the area only the quartzite are exposed. No, prominent Mica Schist exposure is exposed within the entire area. Due to prolonged weathering effect mica schist has been converted into soil, which has been inferred through field observations. Hence quartzite is the only one formation as exposed represents the Dharwar within the area.

Karbandiya is known for the largest quarrying activity and generally, sandstone is mined here. The granite intruding the unclassified Metasedimentary sequence is a medium-grained, saccaroidal and of leucocratic variety. It occurs as isolated hills in the northern alluvial tract around Gaya and Nimchawk. Thin veins of quartz and jasper occur at several places within the Quartzites. The pegmatite veins are of restricted occurrence and seen at a few places in the lower Phyllite. These are highly crushed and brecciated rocks composed chiefly of quartz with subordinate jasper, feldspar and epidote. Their proportion becoming so high, that the quartzite is rendered brownish altogether. Rehula, Jethian, Bandhna and Tetua are some of the localities where such fault rocks are seem to be extensively developed.

How Quarrying Degrading the Environmental Conditions of Quarrying Sites and Neighbouring Regions?

Quarrying activity leads to environmental degradation not only at quarrying sites but also in the neighbouring region of the sites. Though several indicators can be taken to prove the environmental degradation caused by quarrying activity but here, we will take only two indicators:

- Air Quality
- Noise Levels

Air Pollution Due to Quarrying

Dust emitted from the quarry sites is a major source of air pollution, although the severity will depend on factors like the local micro-climatic conditions, the concentration of dust particles in the ambient air, the size of the dust particles and their chemistry, for example limestone quarries produce highly alkaline and reactive dusts, whereas coal mines produce acidic dust.

Dust is considered to be any solid matter emanating from a quarry or a surface mineral working, or from vehicles serving it, which is borne by the air. Dust is particle of matter in the size range of 1-75 μm in diameter, with particles less than 1 μm being classified as smoke or fumes. The finest particles of between 1 and 10 μm in diameter are respirable and are associated with health effects. Particles greater than 10 μm are associated with public perception and nuisance. Nuisance dust may be described as the coarse fraction of airborne particulates, typically greater than about 20 μm.

Dust particles are dispersed by their suspension and entrainment in airflow. Dispersal is affected by the particle size shape and density, as well as wind speed and other climatic effects. Smaller dust particles remain airborne for longer, dispersing widely and depositing more slowly over a wider area. Large dust particles (greater than 30 μm), that make-upthe greatest proportion of dust emitted from mineral workings largely deposit within 100 μm of sources. Intermediate sized particles (10-30 μm) are likely to travel-up to 200-500 μm. Tiny particles (less than 10 μm) which make-up a small proportion of the dust emitted from most mineral workings are only deposited slowly. Concentrations decrease rapidly on moving away from the source, due to dispersion and dilution.

Noise Pollution Due to Quarrying

The initial source of noise on a new mine or quarry is the preparatory works for the site. This normally entails the provision of a road access, site offices and compound, and usually some mineral processing facilities. On some of the larger sites, there may be the construction of a rail access and sidings or the diversion of an existing road or river. Most of these activities are similar to the activities carried out for other large scale developments, and usually last for a limited duration.

The next activity is the exposure of the mineral for extraction. This involves the removal of soils and sometimes the removal of overburden. Soils and other soft materials are sometimes removed by scrapers, large items of plant that are either self-powered (usually assisted by dozers in the scraping stage) or towed by dozers. These machines literally scrape-up the soils and move them to another area to be deposited. This enables the soils to be stored and reused in future. Another common method is by hydraulic excavators and dump trucks.

The extraction process for any material contains a number of noise generating processes. Processing plant on site can often include the use of crushing and grading plant, prior to the mineral being transported off site by road or rail vehicles. On some sites, there will also be noise generated from the blasting of rock. In most cases, advantage is taken of the removal of the soils to provide baffle mounds. These are soil storage mounds that are generally located on the boundary of the site. The baffle mounds often provide visual and acoustic screening of the activities taking place on site. As these activities take place on the boundary of the site, the noise levels generated by the formation and removal are the highest experienced during the life of the site. The highest levels generally occur for a matter of days at each location. The next stage depends on the type of site being operated. For opencast coal sites and some quarries, a thick layer of overburden may need to be removed before exposing the deposit. For most quarries, the soil and overburden to be removed is likely to be relatively thin.

Once the material is exposed, it can then be extracted. Some minerals such as sands, gravels, clays and coal can be extracted by direct use of an excavating shovel on the mineral. Other materials such as sandstone and limestone need to be broken-up by blasting or ripping before they can be excavated. Blasting may also occur where overburden is too strong to be excavated directly by shovel. The mineral is removed for initial processing or direct removal off site. Often, the mineral is loaded on to dump trucks, but sometimes field conveyors can be used. The noise impact of this activity is that there is normally a number of large diesel engine machines working in the extraction area of the mine or quarry, and a number of dump trucks carrying material from the extraction area to the processing or dispatch area. The noise varies in level from each item of plant and includes the noise of material being deposited into dump trucks by excavators. Sometimes audible reversing warning devices on trucks create nuisance which are noticeable at considerable distances and become a source of frequent complaints.

Once the mineral has been extracted and removed from the working area, there is normally some processing carried out on the sites. This may be screening the material to separate it into different sizes. Some materials may need to be crushed to reduce the size of individual pieces to a manageable size. Crushing plant can be noisy, and for hard rock there is sometimes a need to use a pecker on the largest rocks before loading onto the dump truck, or a hydraulic breaker at the crush feed. Finally, the material is ready to be transported off site. This usually is carried out by heavy good's vehicles, although on some larger sites, the mineral may be transported by other means such as rail or barge.

Scenario of Air Quality (2012)

Before discussing the impact of air pollution on the environmental visibility, it is better to understand the levels of various components viz. Respirable Suspended Particulate Material (RSPM), Suspended Particulate Material (SPM), Sulphur Dioxide (SO_2) and Oxides of Nitrogen (NO_x) in the air of the study area. To understand the current status of various components like RSPM, SPM, SO_2, NO_x, an analysis of the secondary data obtained from the Bihar State Pollution Control Board, Government of Bihar, regarding the air quality of the six quarrying sites of the study area namely, Manpur and Gere, Karjara, Rajauli, Karbandiya, Pachna Baui, Naugarhi is necessary.

Table 8.2 shows the figures related to air quality of these six quarrying sites which will be discussed in the light of indicators namely Respirable Suspended Particulate Matter (RSPM),

Table 8.2: Concentration (μg/m³) of RSPM, SPM, SO_2, NO_x, and Pb in the Study Area

Sl. No.	Quarrying Sites	RSPM 24 hr	SPM 24 hr	SO_2	NO_x	Pb 24 hr
1.	Manpur & Gere	117	590	23.0	25.2	0.023
2.	Karjara	130	610	21.4	26.9	0.036
3.	Rajauli	113	630	30.2	32.0	0.034
4.	Karbandiya	177	720	30.3	37.4	0.169
5.	Pachna Baui	146	630	22.5	35.3	0.024
6.	Naugarhi	136	604	36.2	33.2	0.024

Source: Bihar State Pollution Control Board, Bihar, 2012.

Suspended Particulate Matter (SPM), Sulphur Dioxide (SO_2), Oxides of Nitrogen (NO_x), Lead (Pb) particles in the air.

The first two, i.e. RSPM and SPM determine the suffocating nature and the choky quality of the available air while the other three (SO_2, NO_x, Pb) determine the poisonous nature of air.

The 24 hour monitoring of RSPM and SPM shows that among all the six Quarrying sites, Karbandiya is characterized by the highest values of 177 $\mu g/m^3$ and 720 $\mu g/m^3$ for RSPM and SPM respectively. Next to Karbandiya, stands Pachna Baui with higher values of 146 $\mu g/m^3$ and 630 $\mu g/m^3$ for RSPM and SPM respectively. The next two towns namely Naugarhi (RSPM-136 $\mu g/m^3$ and SPM-604 $\mu g/m^3$) and Karjara (RSPM-130 $\mu g/m^3$ and SPM-610 $\mu g/m^3$) have suffocating and low grade air available for breathing. Lastly, towns namely Manpur and Gere (RSPM-117 $\mu g/m^3$ and SPM-590 $\mu g/m^3$) and Rajauli (RSPM-113 $\mu g/m^3$ and SPM-630 $\mu g/m^3$) too have suffocating and low grade air to breath with slight variations in values of RSPM and SPM in comparison to other towns.

The monitoring of Sulphur Dioxide (SO_2) and Oxides of Nitrogen (NO_x) have been done at an interval of 8 hrs and thus values of SO_2 and NO_x are recorded at 06-14 hr. (Morning to Noon), 14-22 hr. (Noon to Night), 22-06 hr. (Night to Morning).

Table 8.2 reveals that levels of SO_2 and NO_x acquire minimum values during 06-14 hrs., i.e. morning to noon and 22-06 hrs., i.e. night to morning. The reason behind acquiring minimum values is the less use of vehicles for transportation purposes and less use of machinery for drilling, digging, loading and unloading of stones due to off working hours and consequently, less vehicular smoke is released which in turn lowers the value of SO_2 and NO_x during these specific time periods. On the other hand, during 14-22 hrs., i.e. noon to night, the values of SO_2 and NO_x attain maximum values because use of machines, vehicles, and other related activities like blasting etc. increase which in turn add more smoke to air and consequently, SO_2 and NO_x acquire maximum values.

Again, the data related to SO_2 levels of six quarrying sites shows that Naugarhi on an average acquires the highest value of SO_2 (36.3 $\mu g/m^3$). Naugarhi is followed by the Karbandiya (30.3 $\mu g/m^3$), Rajauli (30.2 $\mu g/m^3$), Manpur & Gere (23.0 $\mu g/m^3$), Pachna Baui (22.5 $\mu g/m^3$) and lastly, Karjara (21.04 $\mu g/m^3$). This means that Naugarhi has highly poisonous gases which can result in various diseases related to respiratory tract. Moreover, this poisonous nature of air is least in Karjara in comparison to other towns.

Naugarhi with highest value of NO_x (42.1 μg/m³) has highly toxic gases and is followed by Pachna Baui (41.8 μg/m³), Rajauli (38.7 μg/m³), Karbandiya (31.0 μg/m³), Karjara (30.7 μg/m³) and Manpur & Gere (29.8 μg/m³).

The last indicator is Lead (Pb) particles suspended in the air which if inhaled for longer period of time causes Asthama, Bronchitis and Pnuemoconiosis (Lung Diseases). The highest value of lead particles is present in the air of Karbandiya (0.169 μg/m³) and is followed by the Karjara (0.036 μg/m³), Rajauli (0.034 μg/m³), Pachna Baui (0.024 μg/m³), Naugarhi (0.024 μg/m³) and Manpur & Gere (0.023 μg/m³).

It is evident from the above analysis that the air available for breathing in the study area is full of dust particles and poisonous gases.

What is the Nature of Impact of Quarrying on Environmental Conditions and the Public Health of the Neighbouring Regions?

Impact on the Air Quality

The air quality in the study area is mainly degraded by the addition of Dust Emissions and Poisonous Gases. The dust emissions are the result of quarry related activities like drilling and blasting, overburden removal, haul roads, transportation and also erosion from dumps. Moreover, these dust particles are carried over by the wind action to the nearby areas and thus having adverse impact on the health of communities living in these areas. Secondly, poisonous gases are added by the exhaust from Heavy Earth Moving Machinery (HEMM) and other transport vehicles. Dust emissions and poisonous gases collectively degrade air quality and make it unfit for breathing and if inhaled, this unhealthy air results in various sorts of respiratory diseases and infections.

The impact of air pollution caused by the quarrying activities can be summed-up under the following two major heads:

- Impact on the Environmental Visibility.
- Impact on the Health of communities living in the nearby areas.

Impact on the Environmental Visibility

Now, on the basis of above analysis and the field survey environmental visibility will be analyzed keeping in view the following points:

- Extent of Reduction in Environmental Visibility by the Dust Emissions.
- Time Period of the Day When Environmental Visibility is either High, Moderate or Low.

Table 8.3 reveals the data regarding the environmental visibility during different time periods of the day. An analysis of the data shows that environmental visibility is moderate during 06-14 hrs (Morning to Noon) and 22-06 hrs (Night to Morning) while it is low during 14-22 hrs (Noon to Night). These facts are further supplemented by Table 8.4.

An examination of Table 8.4 shows that out of total surveyed inhabitants, 55 per cent expressed their views regarding the environmental visibility during 06-14 hrs., i.e. (Morning to Noon) and confirmed the moderate status of visibility in the study area. Further, 57.5 per cent inhabitants confirmed the low status of visibility during 14-22 hrs., i.e. noon to night along with 62.8 per cent inhabitants confirming the moderate states of visibility during 22-06 hrs., i.e. night to morning.

Health Impacts

Some environmental pollution can cause acute illness and are even fatal. Others may be harmful, but the disease may take years to appear. Air pollution mainly affects the respiratory system. Bronchitis, Emphysema, Asthama and Lung Cancer are some of the chronic diseases caused due to polluted air. It is feared that lung cancer is caused mainly due to polluted air because carcinogens are found in the polluted air. Its mortality rate is higher in urban areas.

The above figure shows the various effects of air pollution on the human body. Sulphur dioxide is the most serious and widespread air pollutant. Its low concentrations cause spasms in Bronchioles and its high concentrations induce increased mucus production. Sulphur dioxide is also considered to cause cough,

Table 8.3: Impact of air pollution caused by Quarrying on the Environmental Visibility of the Study Area

Sl. No.	*Village/Quarrying Sites (Location)*	*Environmental Visibility*		
		Time Period of The Day		
		06-14 hrs	*14-22 hrs*	*22-06 hrs*
1.	Manpur & Gere	Moderate	Low	Moderate
2.	Karjara	Moderate	Low	Moderate
3.	Rajauli	Moderate	Low	Moderate
4.	Karbandiya	Moderate	Low	Moderate
5.	Pachna Baui	Moderate	Low	Moderate
6.	Naugarhi	Moderate	Low	Moderate
7.	Gere Harijan Tola	Moderate	Low	Moderate
8.	Mirjapur Harijan Tola	Moderate	Low	Moderate
9.	Lodhipur Harijan Tola	Moderate	Low	Moderate
10.	Bhikampur Harijan Tola	Moderate	Low	Moderate
11.	Lohjara Harijan Tola	Moderate	Low	Moderate
12.	Belve	Moderate	Low	Moderate
13.	Dhaurhi	Moderate	Low	Moderate
14.	Majhla	Moderate	Low	Moderate
15.	Hadiya	Moderate	Low	Moderate
16.	Gopibigha	Moderate	Low	Moderate
17.	Hadilpur	Moderate	Low	Moderate
18.	Gayaghat	Moderate	Low	Moderate
19.	Kare Paein	Moderate	Low	Moderate
20.	Paigambarpur Hathiawa	Moderate	Low	Moderate
21.	Chakandra	Moderate	Low	Moderate
22.	Ramdiri	Moderate	Low	Moderate
23.	Pattan	Moderate	Low	Moderate
24.	Teliya	Moderate	Low	Moderate

Source: Bihar State Pollution Control Board, Bihar.

breathlessness, spasm of the larynx and acute irritation to the eye membranes. SO_2 also acts as an allergenic agent. Carbon monoxide (CO) often affects the oxygen carrying capacity of blood. Nitric Oxide is reported to be a pulmonary irritant and its excess concentrations may cause Pulmonary Haemorrhage. Hydrogen Sulphide is highly toxic. Lead emitted from automobiles is a cumulative poison and is dangerous particularly to children and may cause brain damage.

Table 8.4: Impact of Air Pollution caused due to Quarrying on the Environmental Visibility in the Study Area

Sl. No.	*Villages/Quarrying Sites*	*Surveyed Population*	*Environmental visibility*		
			Time period of the day		
			% of Population confirming Moderate Visibility	*% of Population confirming Low Visibility*	*% of Population confirming Moderate Visibility*
1.	Manpur & Gere	76	64.47	51.31	55.26
2.	Karjara	94	53.19	52.12	55.31
3.	Rajauli	85	54.11	51.76	57.64
4.	Karbandiya	79	59.49	62.02	64.55
5.	Pachna Baui	79	54.43	59.49	62.02
6.	Naugarhi	80	51.25	61.25	57.50
7.	Gere Harijan Tola	65	56.92	60.00	64.61
8.	MirjapurHarijan Tola	69	56.52	59.42	66.66
9.	LodhipurHarijan Tola	62	53.22	58.06	62.90
10.	BhikampurHarijan Tola	71	54.92	59.15	64.78
11.	LohjaraHarijan Tola	66	56.06	59.09	65.15
12.	Belve	62	58.06	62.90	59.67
13.	Dhaurhi	73	57.53	58.90	97.12
14.	Majhla	71	54.92	59.15	69.01
15.	Hadiya	66	56.06	59.09	62.12
16.	Gopibigha	79	54.43	58.22	60.02
17.	Hadilpur	65	56.92	55.38	60.00
18.	Gayaghat	75	48.00	56.92	56.00
19.	Kare Paein	76	51.31	53.94	53.94
20.	Paigambarpur Hathiawa	72	50.00	51.38	65.77
21.	Chakandra	74	52.70	56.75	66.21
22.	Ramdiri	73	53.42	58.90	72.60
23.	Pattan	80	57.50	58.75	70.00
24.	Teliya	78	62.82	66.66	71.79
	Total	**1770**	**55.31**	**57.51**	**62.88**

Source: Field Work by the Scholar, 2012.

The particulate pollutants such as asbestos, silica, carbon, beryllium etc., are capable of exerting a noxious (fibrotic) local action in the interstitial areas of the lungs. Radio-active elements are also harmful to man and other living organisms. The impact of air pollution on animals is more or less similar to that of a man. Chronic poisoning results from the ingestion of forage contaminated with atmospheric pollutants. Among the metallic contaminants arsenic, lead and molybdenum are important. Fluoride is another pollutant which causes fluorosis.

An analysis of Table 8.5 shows the impact of air pollution on the inhabitants of surveyed areas. The affected inhabitants are suffering from various ailments like Cough, Breathlessness, Chest Pain, Pneumoconiosis, Asthama. Hadilpur is highly affected by the air pollution in which 63 per cent inhabitants are suffering from respiratory diseases and other ailments related to air pollution.

Table 8.5: Population Affected by the Air Pollution in the Study Area

Sl. No.	*Village/Quarrying Sites (Location)*	*Total Population of Surveyed Households*	*Population Affected by Air Pollution*	*Percentage of Population Affected by Air Pollution*
1.	Manpur & Gere	76	21	27.63
2.	Karjara	94	31	32.97
3.	Rajauli	85	22	25.88
4.	Karbandiya	79	41	51.89
5.	Pachna Baui	79	20	25.31
6.	Naugarhi	80	31	38.75
7.	Gere Harijan Tola	65	27	41.53
8.	Mirjapur Harijan Tola	69	32	46.37
9.	Lodhipur Harijan Tola	62	33	53.22
10.	Bhikampur Harijan Tola	71	36	50.70
11.	Lohjara Harijan Tola	66	26	39.39
12.	Bolve	62	23	37.09
13.	Dhaurhi	73	21	28.76
14.	Majhla	71	30	42.22
15.	Hadiya	66	28	42.42
16.	Gopibigha	79	29	36.70
17.	Hadilpur	65	41	63.07
18.	Gayaghat	75	37	49.33
19.	Kare Paein	76	26	34.21
20.	Paigambarpur Hathiawa	72	22	30.55
21.	Chakandra	74	38	51.35
22.	Ramdiri	73	21	28.76
23.	Pattan	80	19	23.75
24.	Teliya	78	17	21.79
	Total	**1770**	**672**	**37.9%**

Source: Field Work by the Scholar, 2012.

Next to Hadilpur, villages namely Lodhipur Harijan Tola (53.22), Karbandiya (51.89), Chakandara (51.35) and Bhikampur Harijan Tola (50.70), are greatly affected by air pollution. The number of affected inhabitants in these villages is 148 and their percentage share is 8.36 per cent to total. Majorly affected inhabitants suffer from ailments like Cough, Breathlessness and Chest Pain.

Table 8.6: Respiratory Diseases/Infections due to Air Pollution in the Study Area

Sl. No.	*Village/Quarrying Sites (Location)*	*Respiratory Diseases/Infections*		
		Cough/ Breathlessness/ Chest Pain	*Pneumoconios is*	*Asthama*
1.	Manpur & Gere	14	07	00
2.	Karjara	20	08	03
3.	Rajauli	12	06	04
4.	Karbandiya	21	13	07
5.	Pachna Baui	09	06	05
6.	Naugarhi	17	03	11
7.	Gere Harijan Tola	17	03	07
8.	Mirjapur Harijan Tola	22	04	06
9.	Lodhipur Harijan Tola	24	00	09
10.	Bhikampur Harijan Tola	28	02	06
11.	Lohjara Harijan Tola	18	03	05
12.	Belve	19	04	00
13.	Dhaurhi	16	02	03
14.	Majhla	19	03	08
15.	Hadiya	16	05	07
16.	Gopibigha	14	05	10
17.	Hadilpur	23	07	11
18.	Gayaghat	21	07	09
19.	Kare Paein	14	04	08
20.	Paigambarpur Hathiawa	16	00	06
21.	Chakandra	28	03	07
22.	Ramdiri	13	03	05
23.	Pattan	11	05	03
24.	Teliya	09	03	03
	Total/Percentage	**421/23.78%**	**106/0.33%**	**143/8.07%**

Source: Field Work by the Scholar, 2012.

The villages namely Gayaghat (49.33), Mirjapur Harijan Tola (46.37), Hadiya (42.42), Majhla (42.22) and Gere HarijanTola (41.53) have experienced the decreasing trend in the number of affected inhabitants. The number of affected inhabitants in these villages is 154 and their percentage share in total surveyed population is 8.70 per cent to total.

Further, the decreasing trend in affected inhabitants continues and villages namely Lohjara Harijan Tola (39.39), Naugarhi (38.75), Belve (37.09), Gopibigha (36.70), Kara Paein (34.21), Karjara (32.97) and Paigambarpur Hathiawa (30.55). The number of affected inhabitants in these villages is 188 and their percentage share is 10.62 per cent to total surveyed population.

The villages namely Dhaurhi (28.76), Ramdiri (28.76), Manpur and Gere (27.63), Rajauli (25.88), Pachna Baui (25.31), Pattan (23.75) and Teliya (21.79). The number of affected inhabitants in these villages is 141 and their percentage share is 7.96 per cent to the total. The decreasing trend in percentage of affected population shows the distance-decay trend. As the distance of the villages increases from the quarrying sites the percentage of affected population decreases.

It is evident from Table 8.5 that out of total surveyed population, 23.7 per cent are suffering from cough, breathlessness and chest pain, 0.33 per cent inhabitants are suffering from Pneumoconiosis and 8 per cent inhabitants are suffering from Asthama. The respiratory infections like cough, breathlessness and chest pain are common among the affected population because RSPM & SPM values are high during day time especially 14-22 hrs. and such high values of RSPM & SPM make the air unhealthy, unfit and unsuitable for breathing. But the affected population is composed of quarry workers, rickshaw pullers, fruit sellers, vegetable sellers, rag pickers, etc. and their nature of job compel them to breath in such an unhealthy, suffocating, low grade air and hence, resulting in cough, breathlessness and chest pain. The cases of Pneumoconiosis are more prevalent in people working as quarry workers for more than 25 years while asthama is prevalent among people working in the periphery of quarrying areas, but not near quarry sites. Out of 1770 surveyed inhabitants, 1077 are males and 693 are females. Out of 1077 males, 56 per cent males are affected while out of 693 females, 46.8 per cent females are affected by ailments caused due to air pollution.

Impact of Changing Levels of Noise and Vibrations

Sound is a normal feature of our life and a medium through which communication is possible. Noise pollution is an environmental problem that has only recently received much attention. The perception of noise as a problem is different for different people. Noise at certain level might be an aggravation or nuisance for some, while at higher levels, noise might become a more widespread or general aggravation. At still higher levels, noise might fall within discomfort range and at even higher levels, it may lead to physical and psychological damage. The effects of sound pollution in the study area are given in Table 8.7.

Table 8.7 shows the inhabitants affected by noise pollution caused due to quarrying related activities like drilling, digging, blasting, loading, unloading, crushing, cutting etc. About 74 per

Table 8.7: Population Affected by the Noise Pollution in the Study Area

Sl. No.	*Village/Quarrying Sites*	*Population Affected by Noise Pollution*	*Percentage of Population Affected by Noise Pollution*
1.	Manpur & Gere	63	82.89
2.	Karjara	52	55.31
3.	Rajauli	30	35.29
4.	Karbandiya	68	86.07
5.	Pachna Baui	56	70.88
6.	Naugarhi	64	80.00
7.	Gere Harijan Tola	51	78.46
8.	Mirjapur Harijan Tola	62	89.85
9.	Lodhipur Harijan Tola	42	67.74
10.	Bhikampur Harijan Tola	58	81.69
11.	Lohjara Harijan Tola	59	89.39
12.	Belve	60	96.77
13.	Dhaurhi	52	71.23
14.	Majhla	44	61.97
15.	Hadiya	62	93.93
16.	Gopibigha	67	84.81
17.	Hadilpur	42	64.61
18.	Gayaghat	40	53.33
19.	Kare Paein	59	77.63
20.	Paigambarpur Hathiawa	64	88.88
21.	Chakandra	43	58.10
22.	Ramdiri	45	61.64
23.	Pattan	68	85.00
24.	Teliya	63	80.76
	Total	**1314**	**74%**

cent inhabitants out of total surveyed population are affected by noise pollution. The number of inhabitants affected by noise pollution is surprisingly high in almost all villages except Rajauli due to its distance from the quarrying sites.

An examination of Table 8.8 reveals that 31.8 per cent of affected population is suffering from either hearing loss or deafness, 54.7 per cent from dizziness, headache, annoyance, speech interference, fatigue etc. and 12.6 per cent from psychosomatic disorders, tension, stress, mental illness and emotional distress.

Table 8.8: Direct, Behavioural and the Psychological Impacts Due to Noise Pollution

Sl. No.	*Village/Quarrying Sites (Location)*	*Direct Impact*	*Behavioral & Psychological Impacts*	
		Hearing Loss/ Deafness	*Dizziness/ Headache/ Annoyance/ Speech Interference/ Fatigue*	*Psychosomatic Disorders/Tension /Stress/Mental Illness/ Emotional Distress*
1.	Manpur & Gere	32	25	06
2.	Karjara	24	22	06
3.	Rajauli	00	26	04
4.	Karbandiya	33	27	08
5.	Pachna Baui	23	27	06
6.	Naugarhi	26	29	09
7.	Gere Harijan Tola	24	17	10
8.	Mirjapur Harijan Tola	23	30	09
9.	Lodhipur Harijan Tola	00	34	08
10.	Bhikampur Harijan Tola	22	26	10
11.	Lohjara Harijan Tola	22	29	08
12.	Belve	23	27	10
13.	Dhaurhi	22	21	09
14.	Majhla	00	39	05
15.	Hadiya	26	29	07
16.	Gopibigha	27	31	09
17.	Hadilpur	00	37	05
18.	Gayaghat	00	36	04
19.	Kare Paein	23	30	06
20.	Paigambarpur Hathiawa	27	32	05
21.	Chakandra	00	34	09
22.	Ramdiri	00	38	07
23.	Pattan	21	37	10
24.	Teliya	21	36	06
	Total	**419/31.8%**	**719/54.7%**	**166/12.6%**

Out of surveyed male population (1077), 57.7 per cent are affected and out of total female population (693), 53.6 per cent are affected by ailments caused due to noise pollution.

Key Findings

The key findings of my research study can be summed-up as under:

- On an average, the value of Respirable Suspended Particulate Matter (RSPM) is about 136.6 $\mu g/m^3$. This value of RSPM is much high as compared to the base value of 100.0 $\mu g/m^3$.
- On an average, the value of Suspended Particulate Material (SPM) is about 630 $\mu g/m^3$. This value of SPM is much higher as compared to the base value of 600 $\mu g/m^3$ (adopted by the Bihar State Pollution Control Board, Government of Bihar, Bihar).
- The levels of SO_2, NO_x, and Lead (Pb) are also in considerable volume, but their values need not to be matter of worry.
- The higher value of SPM in the air reduces environmental visibility to a considerable level and it is low during the period of 14-22, i.e. during the day. The environmental visibility is moderate during morning and evening hours.
- Out of total surveyed population of 1770, about 61.9 per cent inhabitants are suffering due to one or the other type of pollutions. Inhabitants affected by air pollution are about 37.9 per cent while those affected by noise pollution is about 37.8 per cent.
- Cough, breathlessness, chest pain are most prevalent in the study area as 23.7 per cent inhabitants are affected by these respiratory disorders while acute cases of Pneumoconiosis (0.93%) and Asthama (8%) is prevalent among the quarry workers.
- Out of the total surveyed population of 1770, 56 per cent affected males and 46.8 per cent affected females by the respiratory disorders have been recorded.
- Noise pollution is yet another aspect affecting Physical and Psychological health of inhabitants in the study area. Out of the surveyed population of 1770, 74 per cent

inhabitants are affected. Out of these 1314 affected inhabitants 31.8 per cent are cases of hearing loss or deafness, 54 per cent cases of Dizziness, Headache, Annoyance, Speech, Inference, Fatigue and 12.6 per cent cases of Psychosomatic disorders, Tensions, Stress, Mental illness, and Emotional distress.

- Out of the surveyed population of 1770, 35 per cent males and 21 per cent females are affected by one or more disorders related to noise pollution.

Recommendations and Suggestions

Therefore, a comprehensive, balanced and sustainable strategy is required to deal with challenges of stone quarrying. Such strategy may be broadly categorized into three parts:

- Firstly, mechanical measures which encompasses steps to minimize the adverse effects of quarrying at stone crusher units, stone crusher areas and overall mining areas.
- Secondly, Curative and Preventive measures to control the ill-effects of quarrying on health and general well-being of the inhabitants of the quarrying sites.
- Thirdly, Regulatory measures to minimize environmental impact of quarrying.

Acknowledgements

I would like to acknowledge, Prof. Manzoor Ahmad, Editor-in-Chief, *Jan Madhyam*, Lucknow, Uttar Pradesh for his guidance and comprehensive understanding related to various aspects of Quarrying related issues.

I would also like to acknowledge, Prof. Mohd. Ishtiaque, Honorable Vice-Chancellor, Magadh University, Bodh Gaya, Bihar, for his unending motivation and encouragement during the completion of this research article.

References

Argall, G.O. (1978). *Future of Small-Scale Mining—Important for the Future.* New York, USA.

Ashley, Steve, Kamal Kar, Abul Hossain and Shitabrata Nandi, (2000). *Bangladesh: The Chars Livelihood Assistance Scoping Study*. London

Bradshaw, A.D. (1983). *The Reconstruction of Ecosystems*. London.

Birabwa, E. (2006). *Small Scale Stone Quarrying: Its Contribution to People's Livelihoods*, A case study of Kasenge Parish, Nama Sub-County, Mukono District (Uganda). Norwegian University of Science and Technology,

Bodekar, R.N., Patel, J.N. and Hussain, A.N.M (1995). *Impact of Mining on Environment and The Measures to Control is Degradation—The Indian Scene*. Delhi.

Bebbington, A., (1999). *Capitals and Capabilities: A Framework for Analyzing Peasant Viability, Rural Livelihoods and Poverty*.

Blaikie, Piers, Terry, Cannon, Ian Davis, and Ben Wisner (1994). *At Risk: Natural Hazards, People's Vulnerability and Disasters*. London: Routledge.

Brock, K. (1999). *Implementing a Sustainable Livelihood Framework for Policy-directed Research: Reflections from Practice in Mali.*, Sussex, Brighton: Institute of Development Studies.

Brocklesby, Mary, Ann and Mary, Hobley (2003). The Practice of Design: Developing the Chars Livelihoods Programme in Bangladesh. *Journal of International Development*.

Carman, J.S. and Berger, A.R. (1990). *Small-Scale Mining: A General Review in Small Scale Mining: A Guide to Appropriate Equipment*. London: Intermediate Technology Publication.

Carmen, John (1985). *The Contribution of Small Scale Mining to World.* Mineral Production.

Carnegie, James. (2002). *Sustainable Livelihoods Approach and Artisanal and Small Scale Mining*. Seminar on Artisanal and Small-scale Mining in Africa, Identifying Best Practices and Building the Sustainable Livelihoods of Communities, Younde, Cameroon.

Carney, D., (1998). *Sustainable Rural Livelihoods: What Contribution Can We Make*? London.

Carswell, G., Haan, A.De, Dea, D., Konde, A., Seba, H., Shankland, A., Sinclair, A. (2000). *Sustainable Livelihoods in Southern Ethiopia*. Brighton.

Chakraborty, M.K. (2002). *Issues and Problems of Indian Small Scale Mines*. National Seminar on Policies, Statutes & Legislation, January, Dhanbad, India: CMRI.

Part II
Environmental Ethics and Sustainability

9

Cosmology and Environmental Ethics in Ancient Indian Geographical Thought

Rana P.B. Singh

The Perspective

Geography in ancient India refers to the metaphysical exposition of interconnectedness of man with nature aiming to understand humanity's residence on the earth. In geography, the "*geo-*" refers to the biological idea of mother Earth, Gaia, and "*-graphy*" to a cultural connotation referring to subjective meaning of place—with human interference and connectedness (e.g. love) space transfers to place. This was a kind of "deep" geography, where historical-cultural-ecological-landscape concerns altogether make a sense of meaning and understanding. In the present era of 'global understanding', the messages of geography in ancient India is being accepted as a light-tower for ecological awareness that commonly envisioned in the frame of 'sacred ecology'. Zukav (1979: 217) remarks that "Hindu mythology is virtually a large scientific discovery. Hindu deities such as Shiva and Vishnu continuously dance the creation and destruction of universe". The relevance for life is inherent in the Hindu religion with its pantheon of Gods; the Hindu view is God-filled space—of an animate universe. Initiated in the historical past, the Vedic, Puranic literature and treatises fully describe the sense of respect for nature and attempt to make awareness of the crisis calling for profound changes in the way human beings relate to the natural world (cf. Chaitanya, 1983). Some of these examples are illustrated here.

Attempts have also been made to elucidate the geography in

ancient India, however most of such works considered the notion and framework of concept of the universe and the earth, astronomical and climatic aspects, the places known and the settlement patterns. The description of regional identity and regional geography (natural and cultural landscapes) has further been taken into account with reference to the *Puranas* while emphasising some notions of cosmogony and cosmology (cf. Ali, 1983), however less emphasis is laid on the 'geographical thought' and metaphysical context, which may be compared with the scientific notion of modern geography. In fact, most of these studies deal with literary interpretation of the epics and ancient literature.

Primordial Frame of Evolution and Unity

The first reference of cosmic evolution is given in the *Purushasukta* of the *Rig Veda* (RgV) that explains that in the beginning came the golden germ (*hiraṇyagarbha*), i.e. the primal seed (RgV. 10.121.1). The other Vedic sources refer that the first seed was the sound, known as Oṁkāra—a combination of ***A, U, M***—the primeval sound from which the world and other planets came into existence (cf. Fig. 9.1). Thus, Oṁ (*praṇava* in Vedic terms) becomes the medium by which every eternal (inner) soul connects itself with the Creator of the cosmos (cf. Singh, 2009: 28).

The principal *Upanishads* set forth Oṁ as the object of profound religious meditation, the highest spiritual efficacy being attributed not only to the whole word, but also to the three sounds *A* (a-*kāra*), ***U*** (u-*kāra*), ***M*** (ma-*kāra*), of which it consists. A-*kāra* means form or shape like earth, trees, or any other object. U-*kāra* means formless or shapeless like water, air or fire (cf. Singh, 2009: 28-29). Ma-*kāra* means neither shape nor shapeless (but still exists) like the dark matter in the Universe. When we combine all three syllables we get *AUM* (Oṁ) which is a combination of A-*kāra*, U-*kāra*, and Ma-*kāra* (cf. Saraswati, 1976).

The three basic sound alphabets (*A, U, M*) represent the three Vedas—*Rig, Yajura,* and *Sāma*—symbolising the three states, i.e., waking, dream, and sleep. In the *Bhagavad Gita,* BgG (17.23) threefold symbol of the absolute reality is described as supremacy of Truth (*aum*), universality of Consciousness (*tat*) and reality of Bliss (*sat*). This mystical idea is similar to Big Bang theory, which deals with expanding universe and identifies the sound to be root cause of

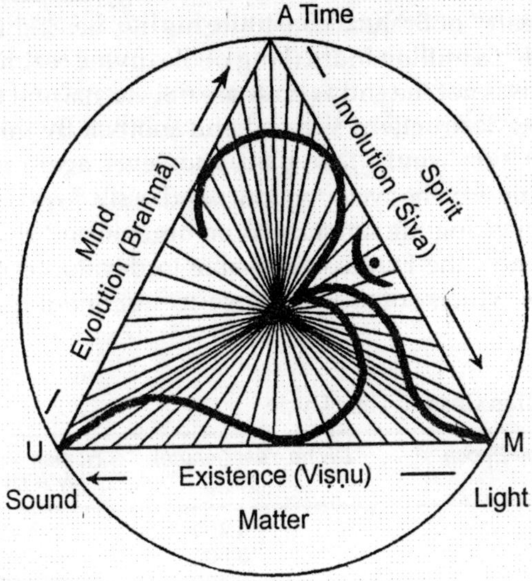

Fig. 9.1: The Triad of Oṁkara; after and © by Singh, Rana 2009: p. 28.

universal evolution (cf. Radhakrishna Rao, 1982: 79). Says *Chhandogya Upanishad* (2.23): "Prajapati brooded over the worlds. From the worlds issued forth the three-fold knowledge. Brooding on it arose the syllables: *bhur*, *bhuvah*, and *svar*. He brooded over them; there from arose the name Oṁ (*Oṁkāra*). As leaves are held together by the stalk, so all the words merge into *Oṁkāra*. The sound Oṁ is the whole universe." The *Mandukya Upanishad* begins by saying: "Hari is Oṁ. This syllable is this whole—the past, the present, the future—everything is just the phoneme Oṁ" (Kak, 1997-98: 118).

Following Edwin Hubble's law it is believed that the universe came into being about 10,000 million years ago (Capra, 1991: 197). According to Hindu cosmology this period comes to 8,640 million years, equal to Brahmā's one day (a *kalpa*) and one night (a *kalpa*). The *kalpa* is an unimaginable time span between the beginning and end of one creation. The Indian time is divided into four epochs (*yugas*), first defined as multiples of 4:3:3:1 of a *Kali Yuga* of 1,200 human years. Later they were explained by the device of replacing human years by divine years of 360 human years (Thompson, 2000: 228). One cycle of the four *yugas* is called as *Mahāyuga* (cf. Table 9.1). Thousand such *Mahāyugas* known as a *kalpa*, i.e. 4,320 million human years (cf. Eliade, 1991: 114). Mythology further says that a hundred "years" of Brahmā constitute his life, i.e. 3,11,040 billion years by which a million Indra (king of the divine realm) will pass away. But this is not the end as gods are not eternal and the cosmic creations and destructions succeed one another. By this period a great destruction would take place, however again re-creation starts. And this way the cycle continues endlessly. Says Capra (1991: 198), "Experiencing the universe as an organic and rhythmically moving cosmos, the Hindus were able to develop evolutionary cosmologies which come very close to our modern scientific models".

Table 9.1: Indian Cosmic Time Cycle

Yuga/Time Epoch	*Divine Year (length), DY*	*Human Year (HY), HY = DY X 360*
Satya/ Krita	4,800	1,728,000
Tretā	3,600	1,296,000
Dvāpara	2,400	864,000
Kali	1,200	432,000
Mahāyuga/ Divyayuga	12,000	4,320,000
Manvantara (71 *Mahāyuga*)	852,000	306,720,000
A day of Brahmā, a *Kalpa*	12,000,000	4,320,000,000
A day-night of Brahmā, 2 *Kalpa*	24,000,000	8,640,000,000

Source: *Mahābhārata*, 3.12.826; cf. Singh, 2009: 30.

The idea of endless cycles is described as *līlā*, the divine play of the Absolute Brahman: "the One becoming the many and the many returning into One". The Vedic cosmology describes the universe with respect to the three vertical levels: heaven, atmosphere, and earth. (RgV. 10.90.11-14). Having being associated to the top of the human body, the head, and earth is associated to its bottom, the feet (Lincoln, 1986: 5). The description goes on as to how from the Absolute Brahman, the transcendental 'primordial man' (*Purusha*), was created and in a process of self-transformation the various forms of micro-cosmic body and macro-scopic universe came into being (Lincoln, 1986: 32). However, on the other end the unified form of cosmos is also perceived. Says the *Bhagavad Gita*, BgG (10.8): "I am the origin of all; from Me the whole creation proceeds." And, again says the BgG (11.7): "Here today, behold the whole universe, moving and unmoving and whatever else thou desirest to see, all united in My body."

In Hindu tradition the basic thought is the awareness of unity and mutual interrelation of all things and events. The BgG (10.20) mentions: "The world is a living whole, a vast interconnectedness, a cosmic harmony inspired and sustained by the One Supreme". This is comparable to Bell's theorem demonstrating that the universe is fundamentally interconnected, interdependent, and inseparable (Capra, 1991: 313). The picture of an interconnected cosmic web is portrayed by modern atomic physics, however in ancient past Hindu mystics experienced the similar reality. Says the *Mundaka Upanishad* (2.2.5): "He on whom the sky, the earth, and the atmosphere are woven, and the wind, together with all life-breaths, Him alone know as the one Soul".

Organic Elements of Nature

According to Hindu cosmogony the Five Gross Elements (*Pañcha Mahābhutas*) are responsible for the life substance in the cosmic creation. These "elements create, nurture and sustain all forms of life, and after death or decay, they absorb what was created earlier; thus, they play an important role in preserving and sustaining the environment" (Dwivedi, 1997: 27). The Puranic theory of creation refers to Brahmā as *Svayambhu*, "one who is born at his will". He, being desirous of progeny, creates water first. He deposited in the water a seed out of which *Nara* was born and was thereafter called *Narayana*. Later from his navel a golden egg arose which gave birth to Brahmā, who divided the egg and made earth and heaven. From that movement the creation of all things began to take place (*Brahma Purana*: 137-140). A similar story in the *Bhagavata Purana* (1.3.2-5) also narrates that Primordial Man was lying down in the water of the universe.

The *Mahābhārata* (12. 182.14-19) states that the Supreme God created Primordial Man who first made sky; from sky water is made and from the seed of water, fire and air—these latter two together made the earth; hence in a metaphysical sense, these elements are not separated from each other. Altogether these five are considered as the five fundamental organic elements of nature (*Mahātattvas*). These elements are related to one another by means of their intrinsic nature leading to a bond among creatures (Singh, 1992: 143; cf. Singh, 2000).

Water

In Hindu mythology, water is considered as the first sacred fluid for purificatory ritual. The *Yajur Veda* (11.0.) states: "Human offerings in *yajñas* (sacrifices) pur'fy the water sucked by the sun in clouds with the air. Then that water rains and makes the medicines on earth sound." In the *Chandogya Upanishad* (7.10.1) water is described as an attribute linking subtler fire and grosser earth in different forms: "This earth, the air, the heavens, the mountains, gods and men, domestic animals and birds, vegetables and trees, wild creatures down to worms, flies and ants, are nothing but this water under solid conditions".

The environmental ethics and crisis of water pollution have been realized in Hindu thought in ancient period. One of the hymns of the *Rig Veda* (7.49.2) states, "The water in the sky, the waters of the rivers, and the waters in well whose source is ocean, may all these sacred waters protect me." To maintain the sacred power of water norms have also been suggested: "one should not cause urine, stool, cough in the water".

Air

In later Vedic mythologies *Praṇa* (breath of life) is identified as the superior vital force represented with the God of Wind (*Vayu*), who is responsible for the breath of universe and life, thus forming a cosmic integrity with nature. One of the texts says: "*Vayu* is our *Praṇa*" (*Vyasabhasyam* 3.4). It is said that the body of all organic beings can be sustained only as long as the *Praṇa* inhabits it: "All these creatures enter with the breath (into the body), and with the breath they again depart out" (*Chandogya Upanishad,* 1.11.5). This is comparable to a law of physics which states that "in the air, atoms collide millions of times every second and yet return to their original form after each collision" (Capra, 1991: 57).

Fire / Light (Agni / Tejah)

In Hindu mythology fire is conceived as divine body, *Agni* ("fire god") who stood as a powerful deity and a cosmic principal that pervades the creation, and accepted as the source of rain and also as a guest of all natural elements. The *Shatapatha Brahmana* (5.3, 5.17) says: "From *Agni* is born steam, from steam the cloud, and from the cloud rain." Wherever there is being, there too is Agni, the principle of life and growth. He is referred to as the ultimate being with various kinships *(Rig Veda,* 10.7.3). He is referred to as the ultimate being with various kinships (RgV. 10.7.3).

Earth

The earth is perceived as mother and an upholder of all *(Rig Veda,* 11.18; 1.155.2). The earth has been of immense symbolic significance in Hindu mythology, particularly with respect to identification, security, and maintenance of existence and continuity of human beings. The Vedic prayer to the Earth runs that, "The earth which possesses ocean, rivers and other bodies of water, and which gives us land to produce food grains and on which human beings depend for their survival, grant us all the eatable and drinkable objects like milk, fruit, water and cereals. .... On whom the trees, plants and herbs stand evermore immovable, we pay homage to that all-supporting motherland, whose independence we firmly protect" (*Atharva Veda,* 12.7).

The earth has also been described as possessing human qualities which pass from earth to man, and from one generation to another. Says the *Mbh* (12.84.7-29): "All human beings acquired from the Earth such characteristics as fluid (*rasa*), form (*rupa*), smell (*gandha*), touch (*sparsha*) and sound (*sabda*), hence our relationship to it is more eternal and maternal as one acquires many attributes from his mother". Since ancient times Hindus have been attached to agrarian life; the sense of attachment to earth had led to the idea of earth as goddess, mother, and overall the "generator of natural life." The *Prithvisukta* of the *Atharva Veda* (12.1.1-63), consisting 63 verses integrates most of the basic thoughts of Hindu sages concerning perceiving the nature, the human dependency on the Earth, and the resultant care and respect required; the hymn calls "the Earth as the mother and humanity as its children" (*mata bhumih putro aham prithivyah*).

Sky

Sky or space is referred to as synonymous with one another in the texts of the Vedic period. Sky is also conceived as dwelling place of the forces of Nature (air, water, fire, and so on), where the embryo of universe developed (AV, 1.11.2). This is fully elaborated in the *Chandogya Upanishad*, CU (3.9.2): "In the beginning this world was merely non-being. It was existent. It developed, it turned into an egg ... It was split asunder. One of the two egg-shells became one silver, and other gold. That which was silver is the earth. That which was gold is the sky".

Each of the above five elements according to Hindu mythologies is symbolised as some part of the body of primordial man, and the divine being is the inner soul of all. The *Vishnu Purana* (3.17.14) describes the cosmic form of Vishnu: "You are everything, earth, water, fire, air and space, the subtle world, the Nature-of-All (*pradhana*) and the Person *(purush)* who stands forever aloof."

According to mythology, there exist incarnations of Vishnu, of which the first five are considered fundamental, referring symbolically to the body and making for a symmetry of the origin of human being and his cosmic relationship (cf. Table 9.2).

The five incarnations of Vishnu symbolize the creation and evolution process that interconnects man and nature interconnectedness. According to the *Shatapatha Brahmana*, ShB (1.8.1.1-6), the first incarnation, *Fish*, symbolizes the origin of life in water; in this form He had saved organic life-seeds from the great cosmic flood. The second *Tortoise* form refers to the life form, which equally enjoys water and land. The third form of *Boar*, symbolising the life in forest and land, helped to save the Earth from the submergence in the cosmic flood. The *Man-Lion* refers to the phase of cooling earth, through whom human power was established over demons. The fifth form, *Dwarf*, a symbol of primitive man, attempted to control over the three realms of the world. According to geological time scale about 405 millions years ago when lands rose and small seas evolved and many kinds of fishes developed. This closely fits into the incarnation theory of creation. According to the Hindu time scale the *kalpa* (initial time) of life substance started around 432 million years ago and Vishnu took the form of a Fish. The latter five incarnations of Vishnu present the growth of vivid cognition of human psyche like victory over the world (*Parashurama*), ideal social rule (*Rama*), the model of *karma (Krishna)*, message of peace and synthesis (*Buddha*), and the era of falsehood *(Kalki*, yet to be born!; cf. Table 9.2).

Table 9.2: The Five Incarnations of Vishnu: Symbolism and meaning.

Incarnation (avatāra): VnP.4.2	*Element Symbol*		*Direction*	*Biological Symbol: AU. 2.5*	*Nature-Symbol*	*Body-Symbol*	*Textual Reference*
	Gross (Tattva)	*Subtle (Tanmatra)*					
1. *Matsya* (Fish)	Water	Taste	North	Semen	Origin of life in water	Blood	*SB* 1. 8. 1. 1-6
2. *Kurma* (Tortoise)	Air	Touch	East	Breath	Life in water and land	Breath	*SB* 7.5. 1.5
3. *Varaha* (Boar)	Earth	Smell	West	Body	Life in forest and land	Proper substance	*SB* 14. 1.2.11
4. *Narasimha* (Man-Lion)	Fire	Form	South	Speech	Phase of cooling earth	Warmth	*Mbh* 12. 339.77-102
5. *Vamana* (Dwarf)	Sky/Ether	Sound	Upward	Eye	Origin of primitive man	Mind	*SB* 1.2.5.1

Source: *VnP*, the *Vishnu Purana*, 4.2; *AU*, *Aitareya Upanishad*, 2.5; *SB*, the *Shatapatha Brahmana* 1.2.5.1; 1.8.1.1-6; 7.5.1.5; 14.1.2.11; *Mbh*, the *Mahābhārata*; S, *Shukla Paksha*, light-half, K, *Krishna Paksha*, dark-half both in the Hindu Lunar Calendar. See Singh, 1987: 308.

Sacrality and Natural Sites in the Hindu Tradition

In Hindu tradition, reverence for the *pavitrasthāna* or sacredscape or the inherent spirit at a natural site is as old as the foundations of *dharma* or religion. Several hymns in praise of the goddess *Prithvi* (mother Earth) are found in the *Rig Veda,* the oldest religious text of Hinduism (1.185, 6.70, and 5.84), dated *ca* 2000 BCE. She is perceived as a great and mighty goddess and also a living being, a cosmic organism. Reverence to *Prithvi* is continuously found in early medieval mythological literature were she is often mentioned as *Bhu Devi,* Earth Goddess. In these texts *Prithvi* is identified with the world-spirit and cosmic-force. According to another ancient book the *Devi Māhātmya* (11.5, now referred as DM), a *ca* seventh century CE text the world is filled *Prithvi* who constitutes every thing created (DM, 11.6).

The Indian subcontinent is projected as the sacred body of the goddess and the distinct sites are known as *pithas* (literally 'seats', symbolizing her body parts). The *tirthas,* holy centres/places, cover whole of the subcontinent to which the devotees undertake *tirthayātrā* or pilgrimage. Literally, pilgrimage is an act 'to cross', the profane to the sacred realm, from humanity to divinity, from this world to another world. Naturally, the purpose is to make contact with the divine and with these super objective human beings make arduous journey to remote places, usually a mountain, or hill top where the divinities supposedly live. Such geographical locales are considered to be the abode of divinities.

Connections between the place-geography and the spirit of place (*genus loci*) were formulated in ancient times. The geography provides a means to explain certain religious, philosophical and theological ideas. Classical and mythological texts have woven religious tales eulogizing the divinities and their place association. A map of India showing the places having divinity association, would hardly leave any space vacant. The history of India stands testimony to the fact that country had hardly any period when it was ruled by a single ruler. However, the sacred or holy places must be accredited importance for keeping, politically highly fragmented country historically and culturally united despite various diversities and dynamics at different levels.

With the belief that *devis* at all shrines (in Indian sub-continent) are manifestations of the goddess in different forms, the tradition of 51 *Shaktipithas* is supposed to have come into existence sometimes in the early medieval period, *ca* seventh century CE. This tradition is related to a mythology that clearly affirms the basic unity among all places sacred that embody the goddess who has the power to procreate, produce and protect (cf. Singh and Rana, 2016: 70).

All of the 51 *pithas* are closely associated with natural objects and indigenous local tales (Fig. 9.2). Most of the shrines occupy either hill/mountain tops or an elevated point. History suggests that, with the Aryan invasion around 2000 BCE, the aboriginal population moved east taking the goddess cult with them. Another interpretation, based on religious history, argues that with the

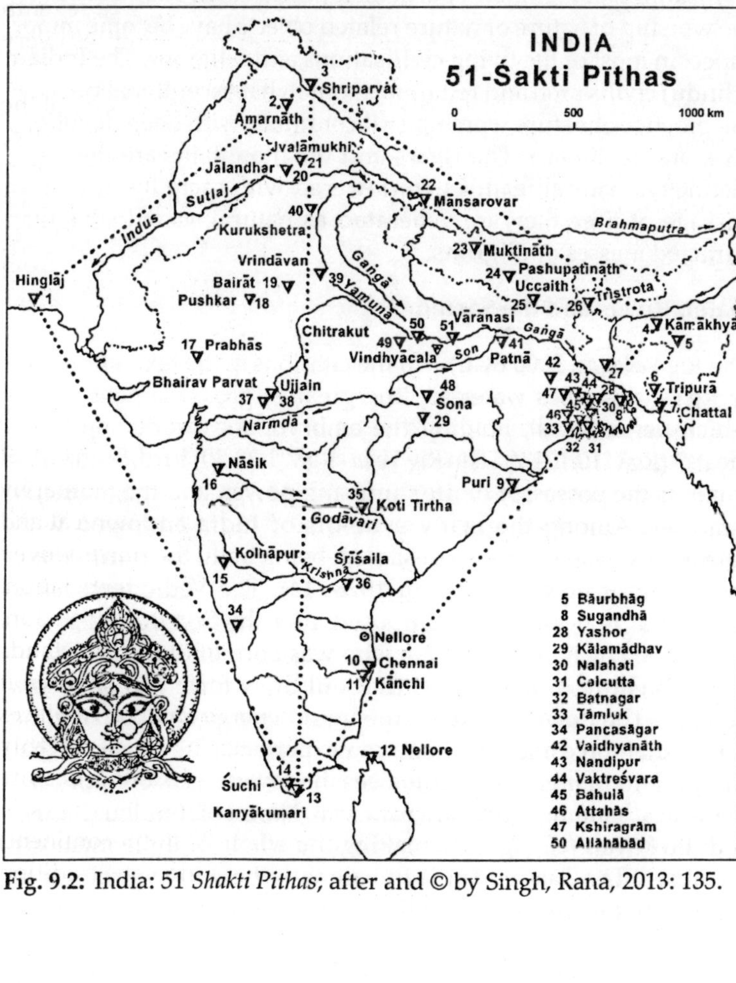

Fig. 9.2: India: 51 *Shakti Pithas*; after and © by Singh, Rana, 2013: 135.

growing rigidity and conservativeness in Hinduism, people started adhering to the cult of goddess instead. Possibly, due to the fear of losing a good number of adherents, this cult gradually was endorsed by the Brahmanical Hindu system. The scattered pattern of the 51 most important goddess shrines played their role in projecting the Greater India (*Mahā Bhārata*) as singular cultural entity (*see* Singh, 1997). They have held Indian people together, who otherwise belong to multiple and diverse ethnic-cultural groups with intra-social rampant divisions, since several hundred years (*cf*. Singh and Rana, 2016: 71).

The element of nature worship has been integral to all civilisations and religions, particularly the ancient ones. However, the worship of nature or nature related objects have become minor aspect in most of the living civilisations and religions. The Indian (Hindu) civilisation and religion is somewhat exceptional because the practice of nature worship still continues with deep devotion, awe, and reverence. The rivers and the mountains are the most distinctive natural features empowered with sacredness, and in passage of time they are venerated as natural sacred sites that attracted masses of pilgrims.

Water, Rivers and the Sacred

The *Rig Veda* (*ca*. 2000 BCE)—in the citations in the text referred to as RgV—describes water as "the greatest gross-element of life which pervades all, holding the embryo, and producing *agnih* (heat)" (RgV. 10.121.7). The *Rig Veda* (RgV. 1.23.20) further narrates water as the possessor of life's infusing power, and the motherly qualities. Among the many symbols of India endowed with spirituality, water is the most sacred, being both, the purifier and the origin of mystery (Darian 1978: 14). The Vedic text, *Katha Upanishad* (IV.6) arguably composed after the first Buddhist text around 500 BCE explains: "He who was born of old was born of water. Right from the waters, the soul drew forth and shaped a person". The flowing water is the liquid energy symbolizing the primordial force and ritual one can experience the power of that energy. Hindu mythology eulogises the seven rivers of India, viz. the Gaṅgā, Yamunā, Godāvari, Sarasvatī, Narmadā, Sindhu (Indus), and the Kāverī (cf. Fig. 9.3), making the whole of India intensely sacralised. The Gaṅgā in India functions as the archetype of sacred waters. By the process of spatial transposition of her identity in

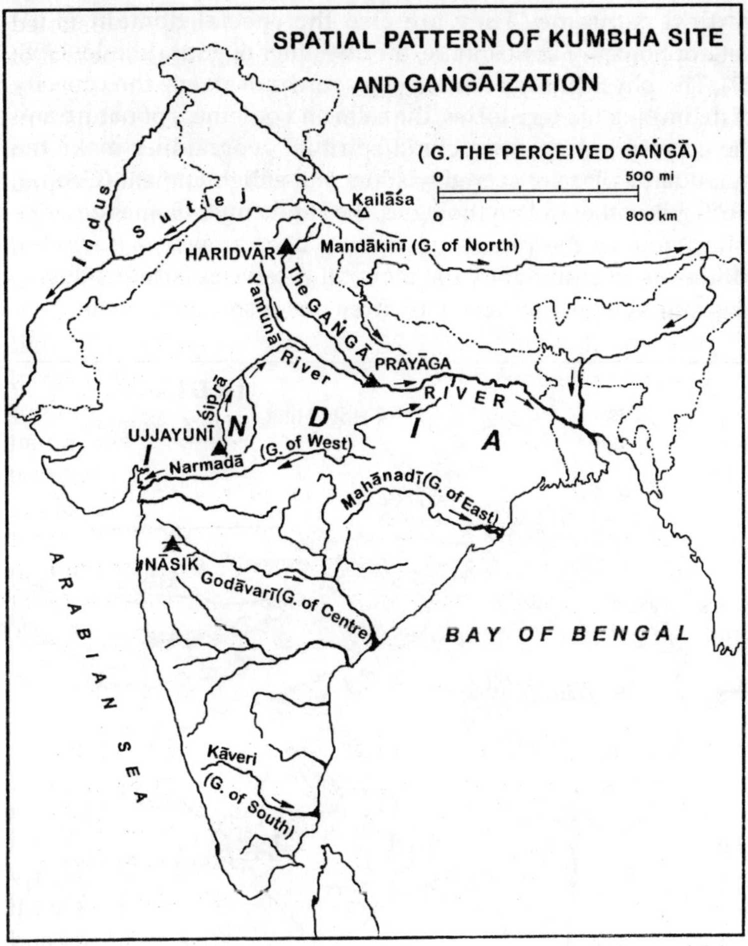

Fig. 9.3: The Gaṅgā River: Gaṅgāization and *Kumbha* sites; after and © by Singh, Rana 2013: 168.

different parts of India the major rivers of a given part represent her, e.g. the Gaṅgā of the east is the Godāvarī River, south: Kāverī, west: Narmadā, north: Mandākinī, and in the centre the Godāvarī River (Fig. 9.3).

Sacred Sites and Mountains

Mountains are the nearest natural attribute to the sky and they share the spatial symbolism of transcendence as they are high, vertical, supreme. They are also the special domain of all heterophonies of atmosphere, the dwellings of gods (Eliade, 1958: 99). The physical distinctness, the sources of rivers, the capacity of delimiting the territories, the calm and quietness of nature and the corresponding cosmic and spiritual geographies make the mountain a place of sacred wisdom and enlightenment (Cooper, 1997). Like other old mythologies, the Hindu mythologies describe mountains as the places possessing deep power of sacrality. Moreover, in cosmogony too mountains serve as cosmic pillar or axis mundi where one can pass from one cosmic zone to another.

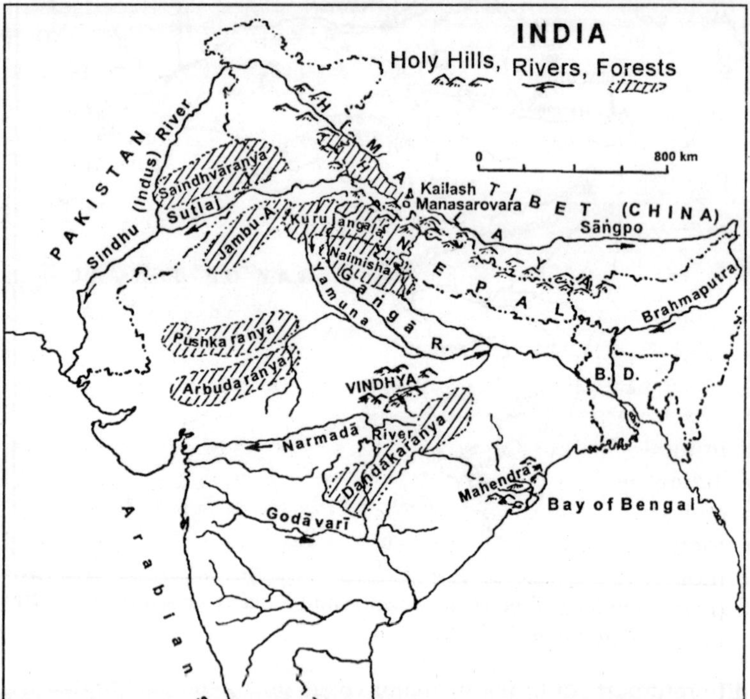

Fig. 9.4: India: The Holy Hills, Rivers and Forests; after and © Singh and Singh, 2010: 72.

In Hindu mythology Mount Meru stands in the middle of the world, and the polar star shines above it. Many temples located on a high hill are called as Meru or Sumeru temples. The Himalaya, especially the source-region of the Gaṅgā and the Yamunā Rivers, is full of sacred places and spots and their numerical archetype Mount Kailāsh (in Tibet, China) is equally venerated both by the Buddhists and the Hindus; it is the abode of Lord Shiva and his consort Pārvati. Additionally, seven sacred mountains described in the *Mārkandeya Purāna* (MkP. 5 7.10-11) are Mahendra (Odisha), Malaya (southern part of Western Ghats), Suktiman (the mountains in the eastern part), Riksha (Nilagiri and Deccan Plateau), Vindhya, and Panyātra (older part of Vindhya). The other attributes of nature received sacred and hierophantic connotations are 7 *Kshetras* (holy territories), 5 *Sarovaras* (sacred water pools) 9 *Āranyas*, sacred forest areas and Gaṅgāsāgar the sea island (cf. Fig. 9.4). Several other examples could also be cited to enlarge the list at the levels of pan-India, region, and locality.

Epilogue: Sensing Sustainability

The spirit of sustainability is also related to ecological identity referring to "all, the different ways people construe themselves in relationship to the earth as manifested in personality, values, actions and sense of self" (Thomashow, 1995: 3). Following the Vedic reflection, sustainability refers to the maintenance of a unified sensibility in search for wholeness and interrelationships among matter, life, and mind. This viewpoint is the essence of ethics behind the development and maintenance of Indian heritage, for which the Sanskrit/Hindu word, *dharohara,* is derived from "the mother earth" (*dharā*) and "endeavour of identity through time" (*ihara*), explained in terms of roots, and "our" deep glories of the past (Singh and Rana, 2016a: 66).

If geography is broadly defined as "the study of the Earth as home of humanity", then ethical values and sustainability can be accepted as the geographer's art. This helps in understanding and interpreting the sacred power inherent within a landscape. It offers "geography a coherent way of deepening its concern with a poetics of the World and with its understanding of humanity's residence on the Earth" (Bishop, 1994: 61). An awakened walk on the path of "Divine Nature", a major concern of the New Age movement, may lead to the deeper and sensible quest.

Without a way a pilgrim or traveller gets lost in the route. The way is a 'spirit'—spirit is an eternal sight for passing on the path in the right order. This 'spirit' is a blessing from the Mother Earth/ Mother Nature that blesses us to "Proceed from darkness to Light, from falseness to the Truth, and from death to Immortality" ("*Tamso mā jyotir gamaya, Asato mā sad gamaya, Mritur mā amritya gamaya*" ... *Brihadāranyaka Upanishad*, 1. 3. 27-28). Let us keep the spirit always awakened and pray the Mother to always direct us on the right path. Think *universally*, see *globally*, behave *regionally*, act *locally* but *insightfully*. This is an appeal for cosmic vision, global humanism, and Self-realization.

Bibiography

Primary Sources

AV, *Atharva Veda Samhita*, Commentary of Sayanacharya, 1895-1898 Pt. Shankar Panduranga Shastri (ed.). Bombay: Government Central Book Depot.

BgG, *Bhagavad Gita*. S. Radhakrishnan, 1956 (ed.). London: George Allen & Unwin.

Mbh, *Mahābhārata*. V.S. Sukthankar, *et al.*, (eds.), 1933-1959 19 Vols. Poona: Bhandarkar Oriental Research Institute.

RgV, *Rig Veda Samhita*, Commentary of Sayanacharya. F. Max Müller (ed.). 1966 Varanasi: Chowkhamba Sanskrit Series.

ShB, *Shatapatha Brahmana*. Albrecht Weber (ed.). 1964. Varanasi: Chowkhamba Sanskrit Series.

Upanishads: *Aitreya* (AU), *Chhandogya* (CU), and *Mundaka* (MU), see, Radhakrishnan, Sarvapalli (ed. & trans.) 1953. *The Principal Upanishads*. London: George Allen & Unwin.

VnP, *Vishnu Purana*. H.H. Wilson, (ed. and trans.), 1972. Calcutta: Punthi Pustak.

YV, *Yajur Veda Samhita*. Commentary of Sayanacharya, F. Max Müller (ed.). 1965. Varanasi: Chowkhamba Sanskrit Series.

References Books

Ali, S.M., 1983. *The Geography of the Puranas*: New Delhi, People's Publishing House, 3rd ed.

Bishop, Peter, 1994. Residence on Earth: Anima Mundi and a sense of geographical belonging. *Ecumene*, 1 (1): 51-64.

Capra, Fritjof, 1991. *The Tao of Physics*. Shambhala Pub., Boulder Co. 4th ed., 1999.

Chaitanya, Krishna, 1983. A profounder ecology—the Hindu view of man and nature. *The Ecologist*, 13 (4): 127-144.

Cooper, Adrian, 1997. *Sacred Mountains*. Ancient Wisdom and Modern Meanings. Edinburgh: Floris Book.

Darian, Steven G., 1978. *The Ganges in Myth and History*. Honolulu: University of Hawaii Press.

Dwevedi, O.P., 1997. Vedic heritage for environmental stewardship. *Worldviews: Environment and Religion*, 1 (1): 25-36.

Eliade, Mircea, 1958. *Patterns in Comparative Religion*. London: Sheed & Ward.

Eliade, Mircea, 1991. *The Myth of the Eternal Return*. Bollingen Series XLVI. Princeton: Princeton University Press.

Kak, Subhash, 1997-98. Vaishnava Metaphysics or a Science of Consciousness. *Prachya Pratibha*, 19: 113-141.

Lincoln, Bruce, 1986. *Myth, Cosmos, and Society*. Cambridge, MA: Harvard University Press.

Radhakrishna Rao, B., 1982. Concept of Ecology in Vedic Literature. *Mazingira*, 6 (4): 68-79.

Saraswati, Swami Dayanand, 1976. *Satyarth Prakash* ("Reflecting the radiant truth"). New Delhi: Arya Samaj Publications.

Singh, Rana P.B., 1987. Toward myth, cosmos, space and mandala in India. A search in the geography of belief systems. *National Geographical Journal of India*, 33: 305-326.

Singh, Rana P.B., 1992. Nature and cosmic integrity: A search in Hindu geographical thought. *GeoJournal* (Kluwer, Dordrecht), 25 (2): 139-147; and reprinted, Buttimer, Ann and Wallin, Luke (eds.) 1999, *Nature and Identity in Cross-Cultural Perspective*. *The GeoJournal Library* 48. Kluwer, Academic Publ., Dordrecht: 69-86.

Singh, Rana P.B., 1997. Sacredscape, cosmic territory, and faithscape: Goddess territory of Vindhyachal, India. *National Geographical Journal of India* (NGSI, Varanasi), vol. 43 (3): pp. 237-263.

Singh, Rana P.B., 2000. Ethical values and spirit of sustainability in Indian thought; in, Allen Noble, *et. al.* (eds.) *Geographic and Planning Research Themes for the New Millennium*. New Delhi: Vikas Publishing House, 445-458.

Singh, Rana P.B., 2009. Metaphysics and Sacred Ecology: Cosmos, Theos, Anthropos; in, his: *Geographical Thoughts in India: Snapshots and Vision for the 21st Century*. Planet Earth & Cultural Understanding Series, Pub. 2. Newcastle upon Tyne. U.K.: Cambridge Scholars Publishing, pp. 23-56.

Singh, Rana P.B., 2013. The 51 *Shaktipithas* (goddess sites) and sacred places; in, Singh, Rana P.B., (ed.), *Hindu Tradition of Pilgrimage: Sacred Space and System*. New Delhi: Dev Publishers & Distributors, 112-158.

Singh, Rana P.B. and Rana, Pravin, S., 2016. Indian Sacred Natural Sites: Ancient traditions of reverence and conservation explained from a

Hindu perspective; in, Verschuuren, Bas and Furuta, Naoya (ed.): *Asian Sacred Natural Sites: Ancient Philosophy and Practice in Conservation and Protected Areas*. London and New York: Routledge, Taylor and Francis, 69-80.

Singh, Rana P.B. and Rana, Pravin, S., 2016a. Heritagescapes of India: Contemporary Scenario and Programmes for Conservation; in, Enstedt, Daniel; Larsson, Göran, and Sardella, Ferdinando (eds.) *Religionens varp och Trasor/ Warp and Rags of Religion: Festschrift to Prof. Åke Sander*. Institutionen för Litterature Gothenburg. LIR, Skrifter. Varia, Gothenburg (Sweden): 65-77.

Singh, Rana P.B. and Singh, Ravi S., 2010. Sacred Places of Goddesses in India: Spatiality and Symbolism; in Singh, Rana P.B. (ed.), *Sacred Geography of Goddesses in South Asia: Essays in memory of David Kinsley*. Planet Earth & Cultural Understanding Series, no. 5. Newcastle upon Tyne, U.K.: Cambridge Scholars Publishing, pp. 45-78.

Thomashow, Mitchell, 1995. *Ecological Identity*. Cambridge: MIT Press.

Thompson, Richard L., 2000. *Mysteries of the Sacred Universe. The Cosmology of the Bhagavata Purana*. Govardhan Hill Publ., Alachua FL.

Zukav, G. 1979. *The Dancing Wu Li Masters*. Bantam, New York.

10

Environmental Ethics and Resource Depletion

Haseena Hashia

Introduction

Humans modify their natural environment according to their interests and this human modified world is characterized by the rapid growth of population, high rate of consumerism, unequal distribution of wealth, exclusion of aboriginal people and fear of global warming. Still the lives of human beings are lived in a natural ecology where resources—soil, air, water, photosynthesis, climate—are matters of survival. In this way, culture and nature share a reciprocal relationship and are interwoven in similar way as minds are inseparable from bodies. Now, environmental quality is necessary for quality of human life and in order to maintain environmental quality, there is urgent need of ethics to be applied to the environment.

Till the early 1970's, environmental ethics was not known to people and it was only after the social movements of the 1960's that people started questioning about humans' moral relationship with the rest of the natural world. Initially, thinkers and researchers were not able to give adequate account of environmental ethics, but later on they published dozens of anthologies and systematic works in this field, and courses were taught in several universities and colleges in many countries. There are four professional journals. The International Society for Environmental Ethics (ISEE) which has 400 members in 20 countries. The World Congress of Philosophy (1998) devoted four sections to environmental philosophy, with dozens of the related papers. The website bibliography of the Society for Environmental Ethics (SEE) contains 8000 articles and books not only by philosophers, ethicists and theologians, but also by policy-makers, lawyers, environmental professionals, foresters, conservation and wildlife biologists, ecologists, economists, sociologists, historians, developers and business persons—all with an ethical concern about human uses of the natural environment.

Environmental ethics is theory and practice about appropriate concern for, values in and duties regarding the natural world. Environmental ethics shows the ethical relationship of human beings with the natural environment. Further, environmental ethics outline our 'Moral Obligations' towards the environment. In simple words, environmental ethics list out the Do's and Don'ts while interacting with environment. Environmental ethics applies ethics to the environment, analogously ethics applied to business, Medicine, Engineering, Law and Technology.

Contemporary ethics has been concerned to be inclusive: the poor as well as the rich, women as well as men, future generations as well as the present generations. Environmental ethics is even more inclusive. Whales slaughtered, wolves extirpated, whooping cranes and their habitats disrupted, ancient forests cut, Earth threatened by global warming—these are ethical questions intrinsically, owing to values destroyed in nature, as well as also instrumentally, owing to human resources jeopardized. Humans need to include nature in their ethics; humans need to include themselves in nature.

Somewhat ironically, just when humans, with their increasing industry and technology, seemed further and further from nature, having more knowledge about natural processes and more power to manage them, the natural world has emerged as a focus of ethical concern. Human power to affect nature has dramatically escalated, as with species loss or global warming. Exploding populations raise concerns that humans are not in a sustainable relationship with their environment nor have they distributed the benefits derived from natural resources equitably. Nor have they been sensitive enough to the welfare of the myriads of other species.

Major Ethical Perspective

Anthropocentrism

This viewpoint advocates that human have no direct moral obligations to the natural world and says that "human beings and/ or their interests matter morally in their own right while everything else matters morally only insofar as it affects human beings and/ or their interests". This viewpoint fails to capture the reciprocal relationship between the human beings and the natural world. An anthropocentric ethics claims that people are both the subject and the object of ethics. Humans can have no duties to rocks, rivers nor to wildflowers or ecosystems, and almost none to birds or bears. Humans have serious duties only to each other. Anthropocentrists may wish to serve these things for the believe that nature is for human beings but human beings are not for nature.

Humans deliberately and extensively rebuild the spontaneous natural environment and make the rural and urban environments in which they reside. We care about the quality of life in these hybrids of nature and culture. Ethics arises to protect various goods within our culture, and hence, ethics is a feature of the human "Social Contract". People arrange a society where they and the others with whom they live do not lie, steal, kill. This is right, and one reason it is right is that people must co-operate to survive; and the more they reliably co-operate the more they flourish. In other words, individual enters into contract, figuring out what is best for a person on average, oblivious to the specific circumstances of one's time and place.

Biocentrism

Biocentrism is an ethical point of view that extends inherent value to all living things and emphasize on appropriate respect toward all living things, not only the wildlife and farm animals, but now the butterflies and the sequoia trees. It is an understanding of how earth works, particularly as it relates to biodiversity. It stands in contrast to anthropocentrism. Biocentrism does not imply the idea of equality among the animal kingdom, for no such notion can be observed in nature. Biometric thought is nature based, not human based. Advocates of biocentrism often promote the preservation of biodiversity, animal rights and environmental protection.

The following example of plant makes it easier to understand this point of view. A plant is a spontaneous life system, self-maintaining with a controlling genetic programme (though with no controlling centre, no brain). A plant is not a subject, but neither is it an inanimate object, like a stone. Plants, quite alive, are unified entities of the botanical although not of the zoological kind; that is, they are not unitary organisms highly integrated with centred neural control, but they are not unitary organisms, with a meristem that can repeatedly and indefinitely produce new vegetative modules, additional stem nodes and leaves when there is available space and resources, as well as new reproductive modules, fruits and seeds.

Ecocentrism

Ecocentrism is a term used to denote a nature-centred, as opposed to human-centred system of values. The justification for ecocentrism usually consists in antological claim and subsequent ethical claim. The ontological belief denies that there are any existential divisions between human and non-human nature sufficient to claim that humans are either the sole bearers of intrinsic value or possess greater intrinsic value than non-human nature. Thus, the subsequent ethical claim is for an equality of intrinsic values across human and non-human nature.

The ecocentric ethics was conceived by Aldo Leopold and he recognizes humans, as the product of a long evolutionary process and are inter-related in their life processes. In the words of Aldo Leopold "A thing is right when it tends to preserve the integrity, stability, and beauty of the biotic community. It is wrong when it tends otherwise." "That land is a community is the basic concept of ecology, but that land is to be loved and respected is an extension of ethics" (Leopold, 1969: 224-25, vii-ix). In holistic ethic, this ecosystem level in which all organisms are embedded also counts morally—in some respects more than any of the component organisms, because the systemic processes have generated, continue to support, and integrate tens of thousands of member organisms. The appropriate unit for moral concern is the fundamental unit of development and survival but a species is what it is, where it is, encircled by the ecology. These are the reasons because of which Aldo Leopold is popularly known as father of environmental ethics.

The human environment encompasses three main territories: the urban, the rural and the wild—all the three are necessary if we are to be three dimensional persons. Nature is much present in the hybrid habitats of rural landscapes put to multiple use; and so we need ethics of wildlife management. We need ethics for forests and farmlands and for the countryside. Nature is present in, and a support of, our cities as well.

Resources and Resource Depletion

According to Organization for Economic Co-operation and Development (OECD), "Resource is anything directly used by human beings" and hence, it is obvious that resources cover a broad field. Now, these resources can be classified differently on the basis of differences in point of views. The Objective Study divides resources into Environmental Resources, Material Resources and the Energy Resources. The objective study do not include Human Resources and the Non-Exhaustible Resources.

Secondly, resources on the basis of Regeneration Rate can be

Table 10.1: Classification of Resources

	Time for Regeneration	*Environmental Resources*	*Energy Resources*	*Material Resources*
Renewable Resources	< 1 Year, Controllable by Humans	Agricultural Products, (Non-Permanent) Pollution of Water and Air	Solar Energy, Water, Ethanol	Salt
Semi-Renewable Resources	1-200 Years, No Human Influence	Fish, Forests, Ground Water, (Permanent) Pollution of Water and Air	Geothermal Energy, Water, Firewood	
Non-Renewable Resources	No Economic Relevance	Ozone, Endangered Fauna and Flora	Oil, Gas, Coal, Uranium	Minerals and Soil

Source: Wacker, Blank (1999).

classified into Renewable Resources, Semi-Renewable Resources and Non-Renewable Resources. Renewable Resources includes food, water, forests, and wildlife and the consumption rate of these resources should be maintained within the capacity of the natural systems to regenerate in a human relevant period; Semi-Renewable Resources are in an intermediate stage of their possibility to renew or to deplete and Non-Renewable Resources includes oil, Gas, minerals and wildlife and their use as material and energy resources leads to depletion of the earth's reserves and are characterized that they do not renew in human relevant periods.

Thirdly, resources on the basis of ownership regimes can be classified as Open Access Ownership Regimes in which nobody is excluded from resources exploitation; Private Ownership Regimes in which right for exploitation are well defined and lastly, Common Ownership Regimes which have an intermediate stage including the types with restricted access and public ownership.

Resource depletion is most commonly used in reference to rapidly increasing population and overall increase in standards of living and concurrent expansion in spheres of agriculture, fishing, mining, ground water consumption, consumption of fossil fuels, deforestation, industrialization, urbanization etc. On Earth, the developed nations hold about one-fifth of the world's 5 billion persons, and they produce and consume about four-fifths of all goods and services. The underdeveloped nations, with four-fifths world's people, produce and consume one-fifth. Of the 90 million new people on Earth each year, 85 million appear in the Third World, the countries least able to support them, and the result is poverty and environmental degradation in a feedback loop. Meanwhile, the 5 million new people in industrial countries will put as much strain on the environment as the 85 million new poor people.

The over-consumption problem in the developed nations is linked with the under-consumption problem in the developing nations, and this result in increasing environmental degradation in both sets of nations. Sustainable development must close the gap between the rich and the poor, and also within nations. Even if there were an equitable distribution of wealth, human population cannot go on escalating without people becoming more and more poor, because the pie has to be constantly divided into smaller pieces. Even if there were no future population growth, consumption patterns cannot go on escalating on a finite Earth. There are three problems: Over-Population, Over-Consumption and Under-Distribution.

Sustainable Development

The fast pace of resource exploitation is posing threat of exhaustibility and the injustice to the intergenerational equity. At this vary point comes the concept of sustainable development and according to this concept, "Sustainable Development meets the needs of the present without compromising the needs of future generations." This concept is based on the following two ideas, these are:

- The idea of needs, in particular the essential needs of the world's poor, to which over-riding priority should be given.
- The idea of limitations imposed by the state of technology and social organization on the environment's liability to meet present and future needs.

The concept of sustainable development gives recognition to the globally relevant survival unit: Earth and its Biosphere. The bottom line, trans-cultural and non-negotiable, is a sustainable biosphere, i.e. the full Earth. The us and our sustainable resources view is not a systemic analysis of what is taking place. The planet is a self-organizing biosphere, which has produced and continues to support all the Earthbound values. Earth is the source of values and so is value-able, able to produce value itself.

References

Botzler, R.G. and Armstrong, S.J. (1998): *Environmental Ethics: Divergence and Convergence*, New York: McGraw Hill.

Collins, M. (1980): *Our Universe*, Washington, D.C.: National Geographic Society.

Des Jardins, J.R. (1997): *Environmental Ethics: An Introduction to Environmental Philosophy*, Belmont, CA: Wordsworth.

Johnson, L.E. (1991): *A Morally Deep World: An Essay on Moral Significance and Environmental Ethics*, Cambridge: Cambridge University Press.

Leopold, A. (1969): *A Sand County Alamanac,* New York: Oxford University Press.

Norton, B.G. (1991): *Toward Unity among Environmentalists,* New York: Oxford University Press.

Pojman, L.P. (2001): *Environmental Ethics: Readings in Theory and Application,* Belmont, CA: Wordsworth.

Sale, K. (1985): *Dwellers in the Land: The Bioregional Vision.* San Fransisco: Siera Club.

Serres, M. (1995): *The Natural Contract. Ann Arbor*: University of Michigan Press.

11

Environmental Morality, and Sustainable Development (Permanent Solution)

Anula Maurya

1. In this age of development, the natural resources are diminishing at a rapid pace owing to uncontrolled utilisation and improper planning. Presently, mankind is bent upon inviting self-obliteration in the name of development as a sequel not only the humans, but other beings such as animals, birds, plants, forests etc. are on the verge of extinction. It means we are moving towards the jaws of self-annihilation and posterity will never forgive as for this negligence.

2. Everybody knows that with increase in comforts, mind goes on becoming more and more conservative and self comes on the top of the priority. Naturally, a side effect is neglected and problem starts from this points.

According to Sanskrit texts, the meaning of the word 'BHAGAVAN' is the entire environment.

BH = *Bhumi* (Earth)
G = *Gagan* (Sky)
V = *Vayu* (Air)
N = *Neer* (Water)

Hence, the reason of worshiping Bhagavan (God) is clear from above explanation. Since, Bhagavan is visible in the form of nature, we worship and respect nature to please the Almighty. Probably our ancestors were great scientist to discover this core aspect of our existence.

3. In our reversed *Vedas*, Fire, Air, Water, Earth, River, Mountain etc. have been designated as Gods.

In view of *"Sarva aasha mum mitram bhavantu"* feeling of friendship (maitre bhavna) has been explored. In the *"Atharva veda"* the earth appears for the mother and self for son— *"Mata bhumi putrodhan prithivya"*.

Sant Tulsidas describes the Socio-economic conditions of the *Ramayana* period as—

> *"Daihik, Daivik, Bhautik, Tapa.*
> *Ram Rajya hi kab nahi Byapa."*

That means, during *Ram Rajya*, everyone was enjoying happiness of all kind and nobody confronted any type of problem.

Indian philosophy also endorses the same thoughts.

In *Sankhya Darshan* the great sage Kapil Muni declass three types of sorrows—

1. *Adhyatmik* (Spiritual)
2. *Adhibhautik* (Physical)
3. *Aadhidaivik* (Supernatural)

Everyone living on this planet wants happiness but sorrows appear in the way two disturb the same. So, efforts should be made to overcome these various forms of sorrows to gain happiness in life.

It is this needless to say that the environmental pollution invites all types of calamities and perturbations on this earth on regular intervals.

4. One of the great poets of Sanskrit, Kalidas is considered as a poet of nature. His creations such as — *"Meghduta"*, *Ritu Samhara*, *"Abhigyan Shakuntalam"* etc. has been written under the shadow of nature. In *"Abhigyan Shakuntalam"*, Shakuntala love for plants, animals and birds has been tangibly depicted. All these writings are worth reading and emulating.

The most important teaching of Mahatma "Buddha" and Mahavir is *"Ahimsa"* (non-violence) which is intrinsically attached to nature.

5. In *"Padma Purana"* efforts has been made to show the

importance of forests and their growth and presentation. It says the—

> *"Daskupa Samvapi Dasrapi Samhupadah.*
> *Dashud Samputro Dasputrasamo Dharmah."*

That means planting a single tree is equal to giving birth to tens sons on this earth. This perception was envisaged to encourage people to understand the need of forest augmentation and proper preservation.

6. If we watch closely our classical music, we find that all the *ragas* have been named keeping in view the importance of environment.

They are—

Kumud Prava, Rag pushpa, Hemant, Vasant, Jaldhar, Kedar, Sawani Kalyan, Champak, Champakali, Govardhan, Kalhans, rag prabhar etc.

Luckily, I happen to teach *"Bharatiya Sanskrit Nidhi"* to girl student of B.A. 2nd year, wherein there are forecasts of climate conditions through scientific means. This invention has helped every sector to decide their course of action during the assessed period.

The writer of *"Brihat Samhita"* Varahmihir has mentioned as many as 107 subjects like — *Vriksha Aayurveda, Sadyaovarshan* etc. his writings emerge from nature and are centred around the welfare of all beings.

In *"Yajurveda"* we come across prayers for tranquillity in nature and its perpetual growth. The famous *mantra* for *"Santi Path"* is—well being of all living or non-living.

Mantra:

> *"Ghovath shantih, Vishvadevo Shantih, Brahma Shantih, Sarva Shantih, Santi Revashantih, Sa Ma Shanti redhi."*

7. In ancient times, there were a number of *"Ashrama"* and *"Tapovans"* on our pious land. In thousands *"Yagyans"* were organised with great fanfare, people led simple and obstinate life—not slave of lusts and craze. Their living style never interfered the nature. So, there were nc environmental related problems. People were happy limited means of comforts.

However, with the invent of science and multiple discoveries, our desire has become more dominant on living style. Availability of all means of comforts, because of globalisations has accelerated our needs. We have forgotten the nature and its vital role in our existence. The result is not adorable even most deadly diseases are spreading in all parts of the world because of water, air and sound pollution caused by various reasons.

In one of the poems written by world famous poets Ravindra Nath Tagore, there is an urge and wish to clean the inner and outer environment of human mind and make it healthy for better. This poem is relevant even in today's context.

It begins—

Desh ki maati, Desh ka jal
Hawa Desh ki, Desh ka phal,
Saras bane, Prabhu saras bane.....
Desh ka ghar, Desh ke ghat
Desh ka van, Desh ke bat
Saral bane, Prabhu saral bane....
Desh ke tan aur, Desh ke mann
Desh ke sare bhai bahan
Vimal bane, Prabhu vimal bane.....

8. The definition of real development is to decide the steps by which the present generation meets its needs without harming the interests and requirements of prosperity.

9. Presently the need of the hour is to change our mind set and think about the mounting problem of environmental pollution. This is not at all the work of a single individual. This requires participation of one and all living on this planet earth.

It is admirable that this topic being discussed by reading leaders of the world and remedial measure are being explored. We are now serious after losing the race. Anyway, the situation will change automatically once. We start moving in right direction.

In the word of Rashtra Kavi, Maithili Sharan Gupta—

"Hum kaun the, kya ho gaye hain, aur kya honge abhi,
Aao vichare aaj milkar, ye samasyayen sabhi".

12

Environment and Community Resilience

Pankaj Kumar and *Rashmi*

Introduction

The term 'environment' etymologically means surroundings. Everything that surrounds and affects living organism is environment. The word 'Environment' is derived from the French word "Environ" which means "surrounding". Thus, environment is a complex of many variables which surrounds man as well as all living organism. Any external force, substance or condition, which surround and affects the life of the organism in any way becomes a factor of its environment. The natural environment consist of four interlinking systems namely, the atmosphere, the hydrosphere, the lithosphere and the biosphere. These four systems are in constant change and such changes are affected by human activities and *vice-versa*.

Ecological Issues of Environment

An environmental exertion arises when on earth there is a change in the quality or quantity of any environmental factor which directly or indirectly affects the health and well-being of man in an adverse manner. As we look around our surrounding in which we live, we found that our surroundings were originally a natural landscape such as a forest, a river, a mountain, a desert, or a combination of these elements. These landscapes is heavily changed by human beings and those who live in cities get our food supply from surrounding villages and these in turn are dependent on natural landscapes for agriculture, fuel wood, fodder, and fish. Thus our diurnal lives are linked with our encircle and necessarily affects them. The anthropogenic impact on natural environment is one of the most burning issues of the present times and a subject of discussion in geographical literature.

Environmental problems can be studied from two different viewpoints. One is simply to look for adverse effects without regard to their origin in order to detect trends that call for further investigation; the other is to try to understand the cause and effect relationships, which make better prediction and proper management possible. Most of the environmental problems which are critical at the present time are fairly widely known because of the growing awareness of all levels of society, including governments, general public and the scientific community.

Ozone Depletion

When an ozone layer is depleted, adverse ultra violet rays reach the earth's surface, causing health hazards such as skin cancer or cataracts. Ozone layer is depleting globally except over tropical areas and the rate of depletion is higher in the highest latitude regions. In Japan, a statistically revealing trend has been verified in Sapporo, and in South Pole, the largest ozone hole in history was observed in 2000. The ozone layers are in a fragile condition due to the emission of anthropogenic chemicals.

Acid Rain

Acid rain is a rain that shows strong acidity for dissolved sulphur oxides and nitrogen oxides that are generated from combustion of fossil fuels and so on. The degree of acidity is measured in terms of pH value of rainwater. The pH of rainwater as measured in the laboratory is 5.65 owing to the dissolution of atmospheric CO_2 in it. Rain, having a pH value of less than 5.65, the value resulting from the equilibrium between atmospheric CO_2 and pure distilled rain water at 25°C, can be termed acid rain. The impact of acid rain over a wide range Pisces for the acidification of inland water was such as lakes, swamps, and rivers, and forests by acidification of soils, and acceleration of deterioration or collapse of trees and cultural heritage buildings by acid deposition. Many forests in Europe and North America now receive as much as 30 times more acidity than they would if rain and snow fell without pollutants

Global Warming

With the current spreading out of human activities, a large amount of greenhouse gases (GHG) such as carbon dioxide and methane gas is emitted in the air, enhancing greenhouse effects and increasing the prospects of global warming. The report of the Intergovernmental Panel on Climate Change (IPCC, 2001) indicates a rise of the average global surface temperature by 0.6±0.2°C since 1861 and forecasts a further rise by 1.4°C to 5.8°C until 2100 and a increase of the sea level of between 9 cm and 88 cm. The observation by Japan Meteorological Agency indicates that a rise of the average annual temperature by about 1.0°C over the last 100 years and the influence of global warming on the natural environment is already detected such as reduction of the sea ice area of Sea of Okhotsk and a shift of natural habitat areas of animals and plants. The atmospheric concentration greenhouse gases has relatively increased while the beginning of the industrial era. These has emerged as a growing consensus in the scientific community that the anthropogenic greenhouse gases emissions of carbon dioxide, nitrous oxide, CFCs, methane and low level ozone threatens to dislocate human societies and natural ecosystems.

Water Pollution

Water pollution refers to contamination of water due to any external material, or in other words, introduction of something to natural water which makes it incompatible for human consumption. WHO has defined water pollution as "any foreign material either from natural or other sources that may contaminate the water supply and makes it harmful to life, cause of their toxicity, leads to reduction of normal oxygen level of water, causes aesthetically unpalatable effects and spread of epidemic diseases". Water pollution is caused by several sources, which are not independent in nature, but interact with one another. The water pollution sources mainly are of two types—natural sources and anthropogenic sources. The major sources of pollution includes domestic effluents, sewage, industrial effluents, agricultural effluents, radioactive wastes, thermal pollution and oil pollution.

Community Resilience

The meaning of resilience differ by corrective perspective. In simple words, resilience (with its roots in the Latin word *resilio*) means to adapt and "bounce back" from a event. Similarly, resilience also refers to the ability of a system to absorb, change, and still carry on. Community resilience has become a key policy issue, especially in recent years. Resilience is the ability of a system to suck disturbance and still retain basic functions and structure. Building resilience means deliberately guiding the complex process of adaptation in an attempt to preserve some qualities and allow others to fade away, all while retaining the essence—or "identity"—of the system. In a human community identity is determined by what people value about where they live. However, what a community of people collectively values is open to interpretation and subject to disagreement. This suggest that people and the ways they come to rough consensus are necessarily at the centre of community resilience building.

The Six Foundations

Although many resilience configuration and tools for building community resilience are now available, no single approach will likely work for all communities and their heterogeneous social and economic contexture. Therefore, we have distinguish six, foundations for community resilience. The foundations support building community resilience, rather than achieving resilience as a fixed goal, so as to emphasize resilience building as an ongoing process.

The six foundations are:

1. ***People***: The power to imagine the future of the community and build its resilience resides with community members.
2. ***Systems thinking***: Systems thinking is integral for understanding the complex, interrelated crises now unfolding and what they mean for our similarly complex communities.
3. ***Adaptability***: A community that accommodate to change is resilient. But because communities and the challenges we face are dynamic, adaptation is an ongoing process.

4. ***Transformability***: Some challenges are so big that it's not possible for the community to simply adapt; fundamental, transformative changes may be necessary.
5. ***Sustainability***: Community resilience is not sustainable if it serves only us, and only now; it needs to work for other communities, future generations, and the ecosystems on which we all depend.
6. ***Courage***: As individuals and as a community, we need courage to face formidable issues and take responsibility for our collective future.

Governments, non-governmental organizations, community people in many countries trying in coping mechanism with all ecological problems. In highly developed societies, this task is often compounded by associated problems such as aged, overburdened, and complex critical infrastructure systems; the catastrophic potential of chemical, biological, radiological, nuclear, and explosive (CBRNE) threats; and the increasing interconnectivity of many global systems of transportation and communication. The idea of building resilience to natural and man-made problems is now a dominant strategic theme of every nation.

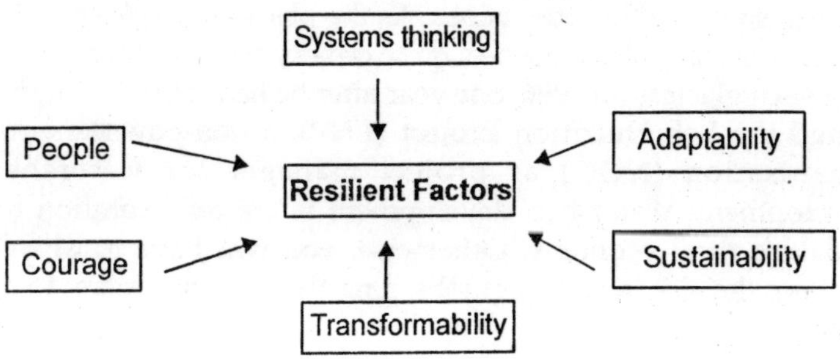

Fig. 12.1: Flow diagram of Resilient factors

Community Resilience from Local People

Chewang Norphel

Ladakh is a cold, mountainous desert, falling in the rain-shadow area of the Himalayas. During winters, temperature drops below –30°C mark and annual average rainfall of 50 mm. Dearth of water is the most important problem in the Ladakh region and the only source of water is glacier water from the mountains. They melt in summer, releasing the little water that the people of Ladakh gets. This water is however managed by the people with the utmost care. It is stored for use throughout the year. Norphel realised the importance of water and has made several *zings* (tanks) and artificial glaciers in Ladakh region for the daily requirement of the native people.

Norphel Comes from a middle class family of Leh. He realised that all the problems in the region were mostly related to water and in most of the areas, it was scarce. He realised that the best way to deal with this is the construction of clean, efficient channels. The channels he makes brings water from distant areas with minimal losses. While working on the *zings* and channels that he evolved the idea of making an artificial glacier. His method involves channelling glacier water to the shadow area of a mountain, covered from the sunlight. He puts in half-inch-wide iron pipes perpendicular to the edge of the depression where the water collects. After seeping into the pipe the water freezes. As more water seeps in, it pushes out the frozen block. This also freezes, continuing the cycle. On the other side emerges a neat, artificial glacier.

He noticed in Leh that water did not freeze in the channels but did so in the thin iron pipes. As the pipes are made of metal and are very thin, they lose heat quite rapidly. He has already made four such glaciers. In 1996, one year after he had retired, Norphel joined the Leh Nutrition Project (LNP), a non-governmental organisation (NGO) as project manager for watershed development. Watershed development is the only solution for Ladakh's rural economy. Otherwise, you will have rural folk flocking the city in search of jobs. And there are not many to go around.

Balbir Singh Seechewal or Eco Baba

Balbir Singh Seechewal, one of the most renowned environmentalists from Punjab who is also known as Eco Baba. In the 2000, Balbir Singh decided that something had to be done about the domestic and industrial waste that was killing the Kali Bein river—160 km long tributary of Beas in Doaba region of Punjab. The river, which is considered sacred by many in the state, had reduced to nothing but a drain because of all the waste that was being discarded in it. Some portions of the river had even dried-up, resulting in immense water problems in the neighbouring farms.

His efforts have made the sacred Kale Bein river lively again. However, the Eco Baba saw the problem and took the initiative of teaching the people about the importance and benefits of protecting and cleaning the river water. He knew that he cannot clean the entire river all alone so he gathered people from 24 villages. He bought the equipment to clean the river with the help of financial contributions made by the villagers. It took more than a decade for the Eco Baba along with his followers to clean the river, restore water and fill the dried patches. He took help from the Punjab Government to build a low-cost underground sewerage system model that collects sewage water from ponds and treats it in a natural way so it can be used for agriculture and irrigation purposes. In addition, he has put efforts in making the river banks a beauty site by planting trees, bathing ghats, roads and drawing several artworks. Eco Baba also started a public awareness campaign, urging villagers to dispose sewage somewhere else and not in the river. With a clean riverbed, natural springs were restored and the river started to fill-up once again.

He has also developed an underground sewerage system model with the help of the Punjab Government. It is a low cost model that collects sewage water from ponds and treats it in a natural way so it can be used for agriculture and irrigation purposes. With restoration of its water flow, thousands of hectares of land have been reclaimed from water-logging in Tehsil Dasuya of Hoshiarpur District, from desertification in Kapurthala district, and from floods in the sand area of confluence of Beas and Satluj rivers. His work throughout the years has been praised by many in the country and abroad. Other than working towards the conservation of environment, Balbir Singh has also established schools and colleges at different places. In February this year, he came up with a solution to treat solid waste with a machine developed in the Sant Avtar Singh Yadgari Technical Research Centre under his guidance. The machine can help separate heavy particles like polythene, glass, and iron from the garbage. It can be cheaply manufactured and is being tested for further improvements. His reputable work has received appreciation not only from India, but foreign countries as well.

Jaya Devi

Jaya Devi was just 12 when she got married. After this, she not only went on to change her life, but also led to the development of her entire village. From fighting with Naxalites to planting trees and doing rain water harvesting, Jaya Devi is truly the "Green Lady" of Bihar. She was forced to discontinue her studies due to Naxalites threats and faced many other struggles while growing up. But Jaya was not a regular girl. She was determined to change the situation of her life and the village she lived in.

One day, during a regular medical check-up, she shared her desire to bring a change with the nurse. The lady advised her to form a group as fighting alone in Bihar was not an easy task. She then set-up a Self-Help Group in 1997 in Saradhi village of Bihar to help marginalised communities, especially women, avoid money lenders and become financially independent. She started bringing women together and helping them save money. A large part of her work revolved around freeing her villagers from the grip of moneylenders. She enabled women to educate themselves, send their children to school and take advantage of already existing schemes of the government. She met a social worker from a nearby village, Kishore Jaiswal, who introduced her to the various methods of rain water conservation. Jaya brought the villagers together and constructed a tank to catch the rain water. She also managed to get people to give voluntary labour and construct the tank all by themselves.

Her efforts started to gradually show results. The well irrigated fields gave bumper crops in the next season, which raised the confidence of the farmers and encouraged them to submit a proposal to NABARD. Inspired by their efforts, NABARD came forward to support them and helped in the construction of six more tanks in the village. For every Rs.100 worth of work, the villagers contributed Rs.16 as 'shramdaan' and the rest of the cost was borne by NABARD. Not only this, to take their efforts to a new level, the villagers laid an 800-feet pipeline to bring water from the Kareli hills to the ground. This project was a huge success and gave a good boost to agricultural growth in that low rainfall area. Her love for nature enabled her to spread awareness about tree plantation, and she, along with the help of the villagers, planted over 1 lakh trees in her village and nearby areas.

With the success of their initiatives, the face of the village changed. People, especially women, became self-dependent, confident and empowered. The farmers got together to fight for their rights and got liberated from the money-lenders. Children started going to school and women too learnt to write their names. With their constant efforts, the soil became more fertile and gave a better harvest too.

C.K. Ganguly and Mary Vattamattam

In 1989, the area near Chennakothapalli village of Anantapur (the second driest area in India) in Andhra Pradesh was a wasteland. Till C.K. Ganguly and Mary Vattamattam chanced upon it in 1991 and saw its immense potential to blossom into a green paradise. The couple, along with friend John D'Souza, then bought 32 acres of this barren land. Inspired by Japanese author Masanobu Fufuoka's seminal book on natural farming, they began to plant trees regularly and help the land regenerate itself. Along with this their friends began to nurture a dream of transforming it into a green agro-forest. The couple named the land Timbaktu. In Telugu it means Sarihaddu Rekha—the last horizon where the earth meets the sky.

Soon they formed the Timbaktu Collective, an NGO, to empower villagers in the area. The scanty rainfall set their agenda for restoration or creation of new rainwater-harvesting structures. They tried to solve the issue through watershed development work in 14 villages and by constructing and repairing 260 water bodies through governmental scheme Food for Work. They began their work by constructing small earthen bunds and small rock-filled check dams. Water-harvesting trenches were dug in the revenue wastelands belonging to Kogira, Kambalapalli and Shyapuram villages of Roddam Mandal and Mushtikovela, Subbarayunipalli and Guvvalagovindampalli villages of Chennakothapalli mandal. This was taken-up in the Kalpavalli area. The idea was to plug the gullies so as to reduce the run-off and get as much water as possible to stay on the land and percolate into the soil. Later, bigger check-dams and rock-filled dams were built to save as much rainwater as possible. Today, the main check dam of Timbaktu holds water almost 3-5 months after the monsoon.

What initially started with 32 acres of barren land has now

spread to over 2,800 hectares (covering seven villages) of wasteland that has been regenerated into a forest. Timbaktu is also famous for its use of clean energy and organic farming. Currently, around 1,190 families grow organic food on 3,570 acres of land. The farmers had adopted dry land techniques for cultivation of millets. Slowly, they realized they were taking loans for pesticides and fertilisers. After they showed them the potential of organic farming, they have started growing millets, castor, corn, red gram, green gram, pulses and groundnut with organic inputs produced locally. The area relies completely on solar power supplemented by a generator for emergencies.

Conclusion

Everything that surrounds and affects living organism is environment. Thus, environment is a complex of many variables which surrounds man as well as all living organism. An environmental exertion arises when on earth there is a change in the quality or quantity of any environmental factor which directly or indirectly affects the health and well-being of man in an adverse manner. The important environmental issues which affect human health is are ozone depletion, acid rain, global warming, water pollution etc. These problems are solved by community resilience. Community resilience is the ability of a system to suck disturbance and still retain basic functions and structure. Building resilience means deliberately guiding the complex process of adaptation in an attempt to preserve some qualities and allow others to fade away. Therefore, we have distinguish six foundations for community resilience. The foundations support building community resilience, rather than achieving resilience as a fixed goal, so as to emphasize resilience building as an ongoing process. The local people like: Chewing Norphel, Balbir Singh Seechewal, Jaya Devi, C.K. Ganguly and Marry Vattamattam have took the initiative and started cleaning and protecting the environment in their own manner. The local native community people have started the initiative to conserve environment in a small step which will become a major weapon in future in conserving environment.

References

Danar, O.R., Pushpalal, D. (2014). Building Community Resilience Conceptual Framwork and its application in Post-Tsunami Resettlement. 4th International Conference on Building Resilience 8-10 September, Salfard Quays, U.K. *Proceeding Economicy and Finance,* 18 (2014) 489-496.

Daniel (2015). *6 Foundations for Building Community Resilience.* Post Carbon Institute.

Kaushik, A. and Kaushik, C.P. (2014). *Perspectives in Environmental Studies,* New Age International Publishers, New Delhi.

Longstaff, P.H., Armstrong, N.J., Perrin, K. and May, W. (2010). Building Resilient Community: A Preliminary Framework for Assessment, *Homeland Security Affairs,* Vol. 5 (3).

Morrow, B.H. (2008). *Community Resilience—A Social Justice Perspective,* CARRI research report 4.

Saxena, H.M. (2004). *Environmental Geography,* Rawat Publications, Jaipur and New Delhi.

Tarhan, Adydin, C., and Tecim, V. (2015). How can be disaster resilience built with using sustainable development? Urban Planning and Architecture Design for Sustainable Development, 14-16 October, 2015. *Proceeding Social and Behaviour Sciences,* 216 (2016), 452-459.

13
Impact of Environmental Regulations on Climate Change

Indu Chaudhary and *Mansi Sachdeva*

Introduction

The resolve of countries around the world is getting stronger as the impending dangers of climate change begin to demonstrate themselves in terms of growing desertification, melting of snow-capped mountains and glaciers, rising sea-levels, catastrophic cyclones and tsunamis with adverse effect on the ecosystem. It is therefore important to understand the mechanics of climate change and global efforts to encounter this formidable problem.

One of the prime drivers of climate change (or global warming) is the excess emission of gases such as Carbon dioxide (CO_2), Methane (CH_4), Nitrous oxide (N_2O), Hydrofluorocarbons (HFCs), Perfluorocarbons (PFCs) and Sulphur hexafluoride (SF_6) that aggravate the greenhouse effect. The greenhouse effect is a natural process that warms the Earth's surface. The process involves absorption of solar radiations reflected by earth's surface by greenhouse gases (GHGs) like water vapor, carbon dioxide, methane, nitrous oxide and ozone. This process helps in maintaining the temperature of the Earth around 33 degrees Celsius which ensures sustainability of life on Earth.[1] The problem that we are facing today is that due to human interference particularly through burning of fossil fuels (coal, oil and gas), deforestation, agriculture and industrialization, there is enhanced greenhouse effect leading to an increase in global temperatures causing global warming.

The need for regulating greenhouse gas emissions arises because of the externality inherent in various agricultural and industrial processes. The bulk of the climate change is caused by carbon dioxide released from combustion of fossil fuels during industrial processes, followed by release of methane and nitrous oxide by livestock in agriculture. In addition, clearing of forests for agriculture or industrial use cause discharge of carbon dioxide trapped in trees particularly when the trees are burned. According to FAO estimates, between 1990 and 2005, deforestation has occurred over 13 million hectares of land per year.

Global Efforts for Climate Change

The first effort towards discussion of problems associated with climate change dates back to 1979 with the conduct of the World Climate Conference in Geneva, Switzerland. Over the years concerted efforts have been undertaken to find solution to the problem of climate change. We discuss the chronology of the events below:

- 1979—World Climate Conference (WCC) held.
- 1988—Intergovernmental Panel on Climate Change (IPCC) was set-up.
- 1990—WCC and IPCC call for a global treaty on climate.
- 1992—Adoption of United Nations Framework Convention on Climate Change (UNFCCC) text at the Rio Earth Summit.
- 1994—UNFCCC comes into force.
- 1995—First meeting of Conference of Parties (CoP), the major decision-making body, in Berlin.
- 1997—Kyoto Protocol formally adopted at CoP 3.
- 2001—Marrakesh Accord adopted at CoP 7 which laid down in detail the rules for implementation of the Kyoto Protocol.
- 2005—Kyoto Protocol comes into force. First Conference of the Parties serving as Meeting of the Parties to the Kyoto Protocol (CMP) is held in Montreal. An *Ad-hoc* Working Group on Further Commitment for Annex 1 parties under Kyoto Protocol (AWG-KP) is formed that launches the negotiation for the next phase.

- 2007—Bali Action Plan charted the way for post 2012 outcomes by forming another *Ad-hoc* Working Group on Long-term Cooperative Action.
- 2009—Under Copenhagen Accord, parties submitted pledges for mitigation or limitation of GHG emissions that were non-binding.
- 2010—Cancun Agreements which displayed the first largest collective effort to reduce emissions through National Plans and their timely reviews to ensure that average global temperatures increase below 2°C. Besides, it contained the most comprehensive package ever agreed to help developing countries deal with climate change through financial, technological and capacity-building support.
- 2011—Durban Plan for Enhanced Action wherein Governments recognized need to create a blueprint for a fresh universal, legal agreement to deal with climate change beyond 2020. The four main pillars of the Durban Plan were: (i) the second commitment period of the Kyoto Protocol; (ii) delivery of a new universal legal protocol for period beyond 2020 with legal force by 2015; (iii) conclusion of existing broad based stream of negotiations in 2012; and (iv) conduct of a fresh global review of the climate change challenge based on science and data and take collective action to meet it.
- 2012—Doha Amendment was adopted at CMP 8 in Doha, Qatar. An amendment to Kyoto Protocol, it establishes the beginning of second commitment period from 1st January 2013—31st December 2020. It requires submission of Instrument of Acceptance (IoA) by at least 144 countries for the amendment to come into force. As on 11th February, 2016, only 60 parties had deposited their IoA.
- 2013—Warsaw Outcomes at CoP 19 included four key decisions: (i) parties furthering advancement of the Durban Platform by agreeing to submit their Intended nationally Determined Contribution (INDC) well before the Paris Conference in 2015; (ii) Setting-up of a Green Climate Fund to help reduce or limit emissions in developing countries and to help adapt vulnerable societies to the unavoidable impacts of climate change; (iii) Warsaw Framework for Reducing Emissions from

Deforestation and Forest Degradation (REDD); and (iv) Warsaw International Mechanism For Loss and Damage.

- 2014—Lima Call for Action at CoP 20 elaborated key elements of forthcoming Paris Agreement 2015.
- 2015—Paris Agreement was adopted. The major decisions included: (i) agreement to set a goal for limiting global warming to less than 2 degrees Celsius relative to pre-industrial level; (ii) parties will also pursue efforts to limit the increases in temperature to 1.5 degree Celsius; and (iii) call for zero anthropogenic GHG emission during second half of the century. The Paris Agreement will become binding on its members only when at least 55 parties producing over 55 per cent of world's GHG emissions ratify it.

The Kyoto Protocol

Till date, Kyoto protocol is the most effective climate change agreement that has laid binding requirements on the developed countries of the world. The protocol acknowledges that the responsibility for present day GHG emission scenario rests on the developed nations who in their process of industrialization have caused large scale emission of GHGs. Thus, for the purpose of imposing these binding emission reduction targets, countries have been classified as Annex 1 and Non-Annex countries. Annex 1 countries comprise the industrialized countries of Europe including Economies in Transition (EIT) after the disintegration of the erstwhile USSR, the United States of America, Canada, Australia, New Zealand and Japan. Non-Annex 1 countries are primarily developing countries. Forty nine parties classified as the least developed countries are given special consideration under the UNFCCC because of their limited capacity to respond to adverse impacts of global warming.

Annex A of the Kyoto Protocol mentions the GHGs whose emissions have to be controlled. These are Carbon dioxide (CO_2), Methane (CH_4), Nitrous oxide (N_2O), Hydrofluorocarbons (HFCs), Perfluorocarbons (PFCs) and Sulphur hexafluoride (SF_6). The individual target of each Annex 1 country for the first commitment period is listed in Annex B of the protocol. These countries are required to reduce emissions of GHGs to a certain percentage of their 1990 emission level calculated over the period 2008-12. The targets for Annex 1 countries are listed below:

Table 13.1: List of Annex 1 Countries

Country	*Target (1990** — 2008/2012)*
EU-15*, Bulgaria (1988), Czech Republic, Estonia, Latvia, Liechtenstein, Lithuania, Monaco, Romania (1989), Slovakia, Slovenia (1986), Switzerland	–8%
USA	–7%
Canada, Hungary (average of 1985-87), Japan, Poland (1988)	–6%
Croatia	–5%
New Zealand, Russian Federation, Ukraine	0
Norway	+1%
Australia	+8%
Iceland	+10%

Note: * The 15 States who were EU members in 1997 when the Kyoto Protocol was adopted, took on that 8 per cent target that was to be redistributed among themselves.

** Some EITs had a baseline other than 1990 mentioned in parenthesis. *Source*: http://unfccc.int/kyoto_protocol/items/3145.php

It must be noted that the United States of America which among the largest emitters of GHGs has not ratified the Kyoto Protocol. Besides, Canada also withdrew from the protocol in 2011.

The Kyoto Protocol provides certain flexibility mechanisms which may be used by the Annex 1 parties to reduce emissions to meet their respective targets. These are: (i) International Emission Trading (IET), (ii) Clean Development Mechanism (CDM), and (iii) Joint Implementation.

International Emission Trading (IET)

Under IET, the targets for limiting emissions are expressed as levels of emissions allowed over the 2008-12 commitment period. These are divided into Assigned Amount Units (AAU). Countries that achieve emission levels below their targeted amount can sell the spare emission units to countries that overshoot their emission targets. This trading of emission units gives rise to the emission trading market, more popularly known as the carbon market.

Certain other types of units, each unit equal to 1 ton of CO_2, can be transferred under IET. These are:

- RMU—Removal Units based on the land-use, land-use changes and forestry activities such as reforestation.
- ERU—Emission Reduction Units generated under the Joint Implementation projects.
- CER—Certified Reduction Units generated from a Clean Development Mechanism Project.

Fearing the possibility of overselling of units during the commitment period and subsequently being unable to meet ones emission targets, the Kyoto Protocol mandates countries to maintain a reserve of AAUs, RMUs, ERUs and/or CERs in their national registry such that the commitment period reserve of units does not fall below 90 per cent of their assigned emission amount or 100 per cent of five times of the country's most recently reviewed inventory, whichever is the lowest.[2]

Clean Development Mechanism (CDM)

The Clean Development Mechanism allows Annex 1 countries to implement emission reduction projects in developing countries. Each certified reduction unit generated from a Clean Development Mechanism Project equals 1 ton of CO_2, which is counted towards meeting emission targets of the Annex 1 country. The advantage of this mechanism is that in addition to providing flexibility to the Annex 1 countries, it enables sustainable development and emission reduction in developing countries. The range of CDM projects is varied, encompassing agriculture, biomass/wind/solar/tidal/geo-thermal energy, fossil fuel switching, energy efficiency in households/industry/utilities, coal mines methane leakages, carbon capture and usage, reforestation and afforestation, landfill gas and waste handling etc.

Recent trends reveal that 75.2 per cent of CDM projects are energy-based (renewable and non-renewable), 10.8 per cent relate to waste handling and disposal, 4.3 per cent are in the manufacturing and 2.4 per cent in agriculture. An analysis of the regional distribution reveals that around 83.9 per cent CDM projects are based in the Asia and Pacific Region, followed by Latin

America and Caribbean. There are only a few projects in Africa and economies in transition. China alone accounts for roughly 50 per cent of these projects.

Joint Implementation

Joint Implementation (JI) allows Annex 1 countries to earn emission reduction units for meeting their targets from projects in other Annex 1 countries. Apart from providing flexibility, JI benefits the host country through technology transfers and foreign investment. Some important JI projects:

- Nitrous oxide emission reduction plant set-up in Czech Republic with the help of Denmark. It aims to achieve about 1 billion ton of carbon dioxide equivalent emission reduction.
- Handing of landfill gas in Poland by Denmark. The targeted reduction is 618 million ton of CO_2.
- Sawdust Project in Romania by Denmark, aiming at emission reduction equal to 500 million tons of CO_2.
- Wind Power Project in Lithuania for Netherlands aiming for 231 million of CO_2 emission reduction.
- Biomass Fuel plant in France for Germany targets at 384 million tons of CO_2 reduction.

Trends in Climate Change

As pointed out above, the first commitment period of the Kyoto Protocol was from 2008 till 2012. It involved reduction of GHG emissions by Annex 1 countries by a certain per centage relative to the 1990 level. We examine below the performance of Annex 1 countries over the 1990-2012 period.

Over 1990-2012, we observe an average 10.6 per cent reduction in GHG emissions. This is largely attributable to the transition of certain Annex 1 countries to market economy with a resultant drop in Gross Domestic Product (GDP) and demand for energy. Besides, adoption of more efficient technologies is also responsible for this significant reduction in the level of GHGs.

While over the period 1990-2000, the reductions were driven by economies in transition (EIT); between 2000 and 2007, a modest reduction of just 3.4 per cent was on account of slowing down of the non-EIT parties and an increase in emissions as a result of strong economic growth in the EITs. In addition, during early 2000 we find increased implementation of mitigation policies and measures.

The 7.3 per cent reduction observed over the period 2008-12 was caused by the following four factors: fall in energy demand due to global financial crisis, implementation of new and stringer policies and measures, autonomous technological improvements and behavioral changes towards global warming.

Overall, there was a 15.2 per cent reduction in emissions per capita and a drop of 35.5 per cent in the intensity of emissions. In 1990, the use of energy by EITs was 16.6 per cent higher than the non-EITs. This became almost equal by 2012. In fact, the total primary energy supply (TPES) per unit of GDP fell as much as 28 per cent for all Annex 1 countries over the above mentioned period.

Many non-EIT countries such as UK, Denmark, Germany, Sweden, Finland, France etc. have achieved reductions in GHG emission despite strong economic growth owing to greater energy efficiency, larger use of renewable sources of energy and fuel switching.

We find that the emissions of all GHGs, namely, Carbon dioxide (CO_2), Methane (CH_4), Nitrous oxide (N_2O) fell except Hydrofluorocarbons which show a rise of about 176 per cent. This increase in the use of HFCs occurred because these were used to substitute for ozone-depleting substance controlled under the Montreal Protocol.

While there was an overall reduction in all GHGs except HFCs, slight changes in relative shares of individual gases were witnessed over the period 1990-2012. The share of CO_2 rose to over 81 per cent indicating that CO_2 formed the bulk of the GHGs responsible for global warming. The second most important gas is Methane whose share fell by about two per centage points to 10.9 per cent. Further, although share of nitrous oxide fell by 1 percentage points to account for 6 per cent of the share, the combined share of HFCs, PFCs and SF_6 rose from 0.2 to 0.7 per cent. It must be noted that whereas CO_2 forms the bulk of GHGs, other gases are more harmful in terms of impact.

Total emissions measured in terms of 1000 kilotons of CO_2 equivalent was 19041 in 1990 which dropped to about 17024 by

2012. Sector-wise GHG emissions were highest in the energy sector (82%), followed by agriculture (8.5%), industry (6.6%) and waste (2.7%). The reductions during 1990-2012 period were maximum by agriculture sector (18%) and minimum for energy sector (9%).

Within the energy sector, all sub-sectors show a decline in emissions except transportation which depicts a rise of 10.4 per cent over the above period. Although, there is a steady rise in emissions from transportation till 2007, in the subsequent period the emissions from the sector illustrate a declining trend. Most decrease is in manufacturing and construction (22.5%), followed by residential and industrial (21%), fugitive emissions from fuels (17%) and electricity and heat production (3%).

There is a lot of variation with regard to controlling GHG emission by different Annex 1 countries. Around a third of the Annex 1 countries showed an increase in GHG emissions over 1990 levels. More significant among these are Turkey (163%), New Zealand (111%), Malta (58%), Canada (42%), Japan (8.6%), US (2.7%), Australia (2.4%).[3] The sharpest declines in emissions are for Latvia (121%), Lithuania, Romania, Ukraine, Bulgaria, Russia (50%), Czech, Norway, Sweden, UK (26%), EU (21%) etc.

The projections derived by the UNFCCC based on the National Communications from various Annex 1 countries points towards a 9.7 per cent fall in emissions by 2020 relative to 1990 level. Compared to 2010, emissions are expected to rise slightly for the EITs given their process of economic growth while emissions will remain stable for the non-EIT Annex 1 countries. It remains to be seen though if efforts such as the recent Paris Agreement with nations resolving to restrict the increase in global temperature below 2 degrees Celsius of the pre-industrial level will lead to a more significant reduction in GHG emissions.

Environmental Regulation

As countries make efforts to achieve emission reduction to prevent destructive impact of climate change, it is important to analyze the various policy measures or forms of environmental regulation available at their disposal. We have highlighted in the beginning of this paper that the need to regulate the control of GHG emissions arises because pollution is an externality. The utility functions of people or profit-maximizing functions of units producing pollution do not in normal course consider pollution as an argument in their optimization problem. As a result, they over-consume or over-produce without taking into account the damage that their economic activities cause to the society at large. It is therefore important that polluters are made to pay for the damages they cause and also devise ways to restrict the amount of externality generated.

There are two main types of environmental regulations: (i) Command and Control regulation and (ii) Economic Incentives. Under the command and control regulation, emission limits and compliance methods are prescribed by the regulator for each facility or source. Though this approach is useful in restricting the amount of emissions generated, the information demands for following such a regulation are enormous as the regulator is required to possess all relevant information for every single facility or source. In the absence of full knowledge about each firm's control costs, this method of regulating emissions turns out to be inefficient as the equi-marginal principle of equating marginal cost of emission across firms generating the same level of emissions no longer holds. This implies that the cost of emission reduction tends to be unnecessarily high.

In contrast to command and control regulation, economic incentives provide incentives to the polluters to internalize the externality and provide a solution that is in the best interest socially. Taxes and permits are two most important types of economic incentives. Theoretically, both of these incentives result in the same efficient outcome.

Taxes are a form of a price regulation with the tax being levied at the socially optimal level of emissions. The socially optimum level of emissions is reached at the point where the marginal cost of emission reduction equals the marginal damage from emission generation. When the polluter is made to pay a tax on each unit of emission that he/she generates, it becomes in the polluter's interest to reduce the level of emissions.

On the other hand, in case of permits, the regulation is in the nature of a quantity regulation wherein the total amount of emissions that are generated is directly linked to the number of permits issued. The initial permits could be allocated by the regulator for free (also known as grandfathering) or through auctions. Each permit issued allows the firm to emit a specific amount of pollution.

The polluters can indulge in trading of these permits. This means that they can buy and sell the right to pollute. Trading of permits induces a price on the permits or the permission to pollute. When producing emissions becomes expensive for the polluter, he/she has a natural incentive to reduce it. In other words, the system of permit trading creates an opportunity cost of emitting since the firm that emits less has more permits to sell.

Though with taxes we know what exactly would be the marginal cost of emission reduction, with permits it is difficult to decipher. The volatility in the permit price may arise due to fluctuating demand and supply of permits with changing economic conditions. The experience of EU's emission trading scheme (ETS) shows that there was an over-supply of permits leading to an extremely low price for carbon permits.

However, this is not to suggest that there is no uncertainty with regard to taxes. In case of a tax, the cost of abatement is known but not the quantity that would eventually result. Nonetheless, it is interesting to note that both permits and taxes satisfy the equi-marginal principle of emission control and are thus efficient.

In the context of climate change, it has been observed that there is not one policy that every Annex 1 country follows to meet its emission target. The current status of various Annex 1 countries is as follows:

- *Emission tax (carbon tax)*: Australia and Belgium.
- *Emission trading*: Austria, Bulgaria, Croatia, Czech Republic, Italy, Japan, Lithuania, New Zealand, Romania, Spain, USA, Ukraine and Slovakia.
- *Both emission tax and emission trading* : Canada, Denmark, Estonia, Finland, France, Germany, Greece, Hungary, Iceland, Ireland, Latvia, Liechtenstein, Luxembourg, Netherlands, Norway, Poland, Portugal, Slovenia, Sweden, Switzerland, and United Kingdom.

Econometric Application and Discussion

Simple Ordinary Least Square regression has been done to capture the impact of different emission regulations of Annex 1 countries on climate change. Data on carbon emission for year 2011 and type of regulations imposed have been collected from World Bank and

In-Depth Review reports respectively. On an average, 39 countries emitted 346295.8 metric tons of carbon dioxide.[4] Log of carbon dioxide emission in thousand metric tons is taken as dependent variable. Type of regulation is taken as an independent variable. 13 and 2 countries out of 39 have implemented emission trading scheme and tax mechanism respectively.

Twenty one countries have used both taxes and emission trading scheme to control emissions of carbon. Countries not only have used carbon taxation, but have also imposed taxes on fuel, vehicles etc. to control the level of pollution. Following table shows the results of ordinary least square:

Table 13.2: Regression Results

	*ln (Carbon Emissions 2011)**		
	Model 1	*Model 2*	*Model 3*
ETS	0.744	–	–
	(0.678)	–	–
Carbon Tax	–	0.966	–
	–	(1.465)	–
Both Tax & ETS	–	–	–1.311**
	–	–	(0.602)
Constant	10.99***	11.19***	11.94***
	(0.392)	(0.332)	(0.378)
Observations	39	39	39
R-squared	0.031	0.012	0.109

Carbon emissions per 1000 metric tons for year 2011

*** p<0.01, ** p<0.05, * p<0.1

Standard errors in parentheses.

Results from model 1 and model 2 highlight that the mere imposition of individual type of regulation will not help countries in controlling the carbon dioxide emissions. It is quite evident from the table that the collective usage of quantitative and pricing mechanism helps in controlling the carbon emissions level significantly.

The collective mechanism have 131.11 per cent higher tendency to control the pollution being caused by carbon dioxide than the other individual regulations.

Conclusions

It is not the single system which can alone reduce the level of carbon emissions. Both pricing and quantitative mechanism together can control the level of pollution. Countries like Norway, Poland, Sweden, Switzerland etc. have less carbon emissions as compared to the countries which have used single mechanism. The chapter has further scope of study but the paucity of data could not allow to do the same.

Notes

1. https://www.environment.gov.au/climate-change/climate-science/greenhouse-effect
2. The Kyoto Protocol requires maintenance of a Registry System to track and record transactions by parties under the flexibility mechanism. An International Transactions Log is also maintained by the UN Climate Secretariat which verifies that the transactions are consistent with the rules of the protocol.
3. These figures are inclusive of LULUCF estimates.
4. Reports are available online at http://unfccc.int/national_reports/annex_i_natcom/idr_reports/items/4056.php

References

In-Depth Review Report, Annex 1 Countries.

http://unfccc.int/national_reports/annex_i_natcom/idr_reports/items/4056.php

Kolstad, Charles, D. (2000), *Environmental Economics*, Oxford University Press.

14

Dimensions of Sustainable Development

Preeti Tewari

Introduction

In their quest for higher and better standards of living, human beings have begun to consume more and more renewable and non-renewable resources. Improved technology has extended their reach further, higher and deeper into the Earth and its life-sustaining systems. Consequently, human activities have affected the environment in a manner so profound that its aesthetic and productive values have declined substantially. Millions of people suffer from severe poverty and humankind is more vulnerable to disasters on account of environmental degradation. As the consequences of human activities became more and more apparent, the concept of sustainable development gained currency in the last three decades of the preceding century. It is now almost universally accepted that if humankind wants to improve and maintain its standards of living, indeed, if it wants to ensure its existence on this planet, it must adopt a blueprint for sustainable development.

A widely accepted definition of sustainable development is the very familiar one that was first used by the Brundtland Commission Report in 1987. "Our Common Future" defined sustainable development as "development that meets the needs of the present generation without compromising the ability of future generations to meet their own needs". While this definition focuses adequately on sustainability, it fails to spell out the kind of development that is considered desirable. Other views on sustainable development, especially those offered by geographers, either tend to be similarly focused on the sustainability aspect, or tend to elaborate on sustainable development in the context of environmental and resource conservation. However, development is a holistic concept and it is necessary to focus adequately on other dimensions of development in order to ensure its sustainability. It is very important to adopt the right model of development, because that will determine whether development will be sustainable or not.

Various scholars have offered a number of views on what constitutes sustainable development. However, most views agree on certain points. As mentioned above, development is a holistic concept. It may be viewed as a process that results in increased human well-being and happiness. The process involves various systems, both natural as well as human-made. Natural systems include the atmospheric, lithospheric, hydrologic and biospheric systems. The human-made systems include the economic, social and political systems. All these systems are closely and intricately interlinked, and the health of one impacts the others. Current models of development disrupt the functioning of the natural systems, and the consequent degradation of the environment results in poverty and migration, thus affecting the economic and social systems. The ecological aspects of sustainability have received adequate attention. The subsequent sections of this chapter deal with certain aspects of the human-made systems that make development unsustainable.

The Economic Dimension

The economic system focuses on what is produced and how it is produced. We produce goods and services using natural and human resources. Unfortunately, the producers of these goods and services do not take into account the needs of the people. Instead, production takes place in response to demands, ignoring needs that are not backed by purchasing power. So, the system produces villas and luxury apartments for the rich while the housing needs of the poorer sections of society go unmet, forcing them to live in slums. Again, we produce healthcare services. However, the best of these services cater to the needs of not just rich Indians but also medical tourists from other parts of the world, while poor Indian citizens are deprived of even the very basic health care. In short, the economic system fails to ensure that the basic needs of all sections of society are fulfilled, choosing instead to use precious resources to produce luxuries for the rich.

Precious resources are also devoted to the production of good that we later advise people not to use. For example, fertile land, irrigation water, fertilisers and labour are used to grow tobacco. Tobacco is then processed and transported to factories where it is converted into beedis, cigarettes and other products using factory space, energy and labour. Once again, the finished products from these factories are transported to the market and sold to the final consumers, with the warning that tobacco consumption (in any form) is detrimental to their health and can even be the cause of their death! Aerated beverages, junk food, and plastic bags are other examples of goods that are produced with the help of precious resources, but whose use is subsequently discouraged on account of their harmful effects on human and environmental health.

Ironically, the production of all these harmful products is considered as contribution to the GNP. On the other hand, the work that women do in their homes and in family enterprises is not acknowledged as economically productive work, even though it enhances the productivity of labour and looks after the physical, mental, psychological, and emotional health of the country's citizens. Instead women who are not engaged in the formal wage-labour relationship are categorised as non-workers and clubbed together with prisoners and beggars, among others, by the Census of India.

A discussion on the economic system must also consider the distribution of goods and services. One may look at the distribution of productive assets such as land and capital, and also at the distribution of what is produced. Even a cursory look at the distribution of both shows a high level of inequity. Access to, and right over, resources have been among the most contested issues in recent years. The poor and marginalised sections, like small farmers and tribals, have had to wage prolonged, and sometimes violent battles against the state to protect their rights over farmland and forest land. In their desire for rapid economic growth, states have joined hands with multinational corporations and indigenous big business houses to deprive poor farmers and tribals of their lands and livelihoods. The Indian Rural Development Report of 1992 reveals that nearly half of India's rural population either owns no land or is nearly landless. The Scheduled Caste and Scheduled Tribe population of India is increasingly becoming landless. Data collected by the NSSO in 2003-04 shows that just over 31.12 per cent of households are landless and roughly another 30 per cent own less than 0.4 hectares. More than 60 per cent of households owned 5.11 per cent of land while less than 1 per cent of the households owned more than 11 per cent of the land (Draft National Land Reforms Policy 2013). The inequalities in our economic system become starkly apparent when one reads regular news items about farmers in different parts of the country committing suicide while rich industrialists owing thousands of crores of rupees to banks continue to evade action.

It is also necessary to examine how our economic system produces goods and services. While the Indian economy was growing at a relatively fast pace as compared to other countries in the world, it was observed that "growth in job creation has not kept pace with overall economic growth, as the corporate sector, particularly manufacturing, is not producing more." (Jha, 2015). The failure of the economy to create jobs leads to desperate and violent attempts by various powerful caste groups (like the Patidars in Gujarat, the Kapus in Andhra Pradesh and the Jats in Haryana) to be included in the list of Backward Classes. It also leads to corruption practices in recruitment for government jobs (manifested in the Vyapam scam in Madhya Pradesh).

Production of goods and services must also be evaluated in terms of the amount of energy used and the source of this energy. Per capita energy consumption in India is low, but will increase as the economy grows. Coal is the major source of energy, meeting about 47 per cent of our primary energy needs. Fossil fuels together account for 82 per cent of our primary energy, with nuclear energy, renewable resources and hydroelectricity accounting for a mere 3 per cent. Coal is expected to remain the major source of primary energy in 2047 (Report of NITI Aayog, 2015). Per capita emission of greenhouse gases is expected to rise from 1.7 tons in 2012 to 5.8 tons in 2047. While per capita emissions may be low, total emissions will be substantial. While the government plans to greatly increase energy efficiency in transportation, industry and buildings, enforcing and monitoring remain major challenges (Bhaskar Sarma, 2014).

In addition to goods and services, the economic system also

produces 'bads'. The bads can be seen as the emissions, effluents, solid waste, toxic chemicals and harmful radiation generated during various stages in the production and distribution processes. These bads are released into the environment to pollute and degrade the land, air and surface and ground water. These in turn affect the productivity of natural and human-made ecosystems as well as the health and productivity of human beings. Unlike the distribution of goods, the distribution of bads is such that the poor and disadvantaged get a disproportionately larger share. Consequently, their health and productivity are compromised, making it difficult for them to lift themselves above the poverty line.

A sustainable economic system should be geared towards the reduction and elimination of poverty. Special attention should be paid to the working poor to help them increase their incomes to a level that enables them not just to remain alive but also to rise out of absolute poverty. Creation of jobs should be an essential part of the model for economic growth. More of these jobs need to be created in smaller towns and villages in order to check the migration into larger cities that are already bursting at the scams. An enabling environment must be created so that disadvantaged sections like women and the disabled are able to acquire skills and find jobs in order to be economically independent. Their economic empowerment is a necessary step towards their overall empowerment. Safety issues in public places and at workplaces also need to be addressed so that women are not limited in their choice of employment.

The manufacturing, agricultural and transportation sectors must adopt green technology in order to reduce their environmental impact. Formulation of policies and a legal framework for pollution control and disposal of solid and toxic waste is necessary. Equally important is the stringent implementation of these laws. Finally, it is time to initiate a campaign to put a stop to mindless and endless consumption. Sustainable consumption is an integral part of sustainable development. Following Mahatma Gandhi, we should focus on fulfilling the needs of people, and not on catering to their greed.

The Social Dimension

The term social system is used very broadly here to include

demographic characteristics of the population and the relationship between different sections of society. India is the second most populous country in the world. 17.5 per cent of the world's population lives in India on 2.4 per cent of the world's land area. Between 2001 and 2011, India's population grew at an annual rate of 1.76 per cent. While this growth rate is lower than it has been for several decades it is considerably higher than China's growth rate of 0.53 per cent in the corresponding period. Consequently, India is poised to displace China from the position of the world's most populous country by the year 2030. The implications of this population growth are many. Rapid population growth is at the root of most environmental problems as the ecosystem of a given area can sustainably support only a certain number of people. Once population exceeds the carrying capacity, the ecosystem may be irreparably damaged. Pressure is also exerted on the physical and social infrastructure as more people need more food, shelter, education and healthcare. Ranked a lowly 135th according to the Human Development Index, India is already struggling to meet these needs of its existing population, and to create additional facilities will pose a serious challenge. A well-nourished, educated, skilled and healthy population can be a vast human resource, but in the absence of these attributes the population would be a liability. Another challenge would be to find jobs for this demographic dividend. A million young people would join the work force every month for many years to come. Without sustainable employment opportunities they would join the army of self-employed who barely manage to keep body and soul together. On the other hand, increased life expectancy means that there will be a large number of senior citizens. The social system will have to devise a mechanism to meet the special requirements of this group, which includes emotional and financial support, security and geriatric health care.

Another enormous social problem confronting the Indian society is the issue of 'missing women', a phrase coined by Amartya Sen to describe the horribly skewed sex ratio in India (and some other Asian countries). There were 940 females per thousand males in India in 2011. And if this was not bad enough, the child sex-ratio was 919 girls per thousand boys. The situation was even more dismal in some states of India, reflecting abject neglect of women in them. The already poor status of women becomes worse as the sex-ratio becomes more unfavourable. There is a corresponding increase in crimes against women and trafficking and sale of women. It also gives rise to undesirable social practices like sharing of wives among brothers.

The other demographic indicators that are a cause for concern are the low level of urbanisation and low literacy rates. With just over 30 per cent of its population residing in urban areas, the percentage of urbanisation in India is low by world standards. Despite their many problems, the higher density of population in urban areas makes it cheaper to provide basic infrastructural facilities. However, planned urbanisation is desirable in comparison to the haphazard growth that we are experiencing at present. India's failure to achieve 100 per cent literacy nearly seven decades after Independence is a matter of shame. The literacy rate in 2011 was only 74 per cent. Even more shameful is the huge gender gap of 17 per cent in literacy levels. Equally a matter of concern is the poor quality of education being imparted in our schools. The current system has failed to equip students with either knowledge, analytical skills, life skills or professional skills to face the challenges of adult life.

Indian society also faces several other challenges. Discrimination based on caste, religion, gender, race and sexual orientation remains deeply entrenched. Constitutional provisions notwithstanding, oppression of Dalits continues both overtly and covertly. The status of women continues to be poor and Indian society has a long way to go before women can claim economic, political and social equality with men. Issues of women's safety within and outside their homes have still not been resolved. Moral policing of women, both by their families and by society at large, is carried out with impunity and it is not uncommon to have strictures passed on what women should wear, how they should behave in public places and whom they should marry. Honour killings enjoy sanction among certain sections of society. Racial discrimination is experienced by persons from the north-eastern states of India. It may be in the form of verbal abuse, difficulty in renting accommodation and in more extreme cases, violent and sometimes fatal attacks. Similar intolerance is experienced by the LGBT community as people with different sexual orientation are not generally accepted by society. Society is also divided on the lines of religion so much so that an ordinary incident easily assumes communal overtones. Indian society also remains insensitive to the needs of those with physical and mental disabilities. Few efforts have been made to make public spaces and transportation accessible to them.

A social system that suffers from so many ills cannot be sustainable. It is important to take steps to achieve a stable population. Urgent steps are also required to correct the sex-ratio as a skewed sex-ratio has terrible social implications. Planned urban growth, with cities that provide economic opportunities, is the need of the hour. Planning is also necessary to improve the education system and to cater to the needs of the growing geriatric population. A society that discriminates against its own on grounds of gender, religion, race, disability and sexual orientation cannot be stable. We must work towards creating a society that accepts all its members in an environment of tolerance.

The Political Dimension

The political system is taken here to include the state (which encompasses the government, bureaucracy and other institutions), political parties, the citizens and the media (which has an important role as a watchdog). The state is responsible for policy making, legislating, implementing and monitoring. Government policy should work towards removal of poverty, creating jobs, providing universal education and health care, removal of discrimination, protecting the environment and so on. So, if seven decades after independence, high levels of poverty, unemployment, illiteracy, malnutrition and ill health, various forms of discrimination and environmental pollution still persist, it represents a failure of successive governments in either formulating right policies or in their effective implementation. This may be the result of general ineptitude, lack of will, corruption, (or more likely a combination of all these) on the part of the government and the bureaucracy. The overburdened judiciary has been effective in certain areas but not so effective in others. The implementing and monitoring agencies have been generally ineffective in upholding the rule of law, their autonomy having been compromised by government interference.

Political parties have a vital role in a democracy. Unfortunately, Indian political parties have often let the nation down. They have invested in vote bank politics and never desisted from dividing society on the lines of caste, community, religion or region whenever it suited their interests. None of the political parties have genuinely supported progressive measures to empower women or reduce corruption, conspiring together to either block the bills or diluting them to such an extent that they become ineffective. None of the parties have ever given prominence to environmental issues in their manifestos. The Parliament and assemblies seldom witness debates on serious issues, with parties preferring to stage protests rather than hold discussions. The media too does not always do justice to its role as a watchdog. It reveals a strong urban bias in its coverage, and prefers scandalous and sensational issues to serious ones. It also loses interest in one issue as soon as another one crops up.

The citizens of India have also been a weak link in the political system so far. They are guilty of voting on the lines of caste and religion rather than ideology, issues and individual merit of candidates. Political parties have exploited the ignorance, indifference and helplessness of citizens. People fail to see themselves as empowered citizens who form the government that should be accountable to them. Instead, the old notion of the government as the ruler and the people as subjects continues to persist in their minds.

It is this same citizen who also holds a ray of hope. Aware, involved and empowered citizens can become the force that can change the system. They can demand effective policies and laws that can ensure that our economic, social and political systems become sustainable and protective of the natural systems.

References

Census of India, 2011. Various Publications.

Government of India, Ministry of Rural Development 2013. *Draft National Land Reforms Policy*.

Jha, S., 2015. Manufacturing job growth remains under stress. *Business Standard*, New Delhi.

NITI Aayog, 2015. *A Report On Energy Efficiency And Energy Mix in the Indian Energy System (2030)*.

Sarma, B., 2014. *Energy Efficiency in India: Challenges and Lessons*.

15

Environmental Education: A Way for Knowledge of Nature

Pravendra Singh Birla and *Priyanka Mittal*

Introduction

Environmental Education (EE) refers to organized efforts to teach how natural environments function, and particularly, how human beings can manage behaviour and ecosystems to live sustainably. It is a multi-disciplinary field integrating disciplines such as biology, chemistry, physics, ecology, earth science, atmospheric science, mathematics, and geography. The term often implies education within the school system, from primary to post-secondary. However, it sometimes includes all efforts to educate the public and other audiences, including print materials, websites, media campaigns, etc.

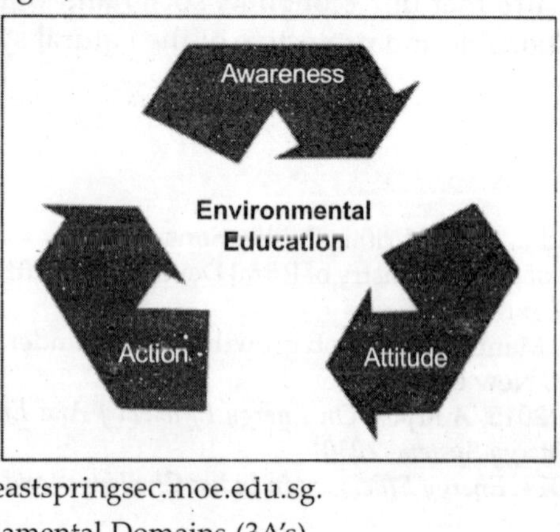

Source: www.eastspringsec.moe.edu.sg.

Fig.15.1: Fundamental Domains (3A's)

Environmental Education (EE) is the teaching of individuals, and communities, in transitioning to a society that is knowledgeable of the environment and its associated problems, aware of the solutions to these problems, and motivated to solve them. The United Nations Educational, Scientific and Cultural Organisation (UNESCO) states that EE is vital in imparting an inherent respect for nature amongst society and in enhancing public environmental awareness. UNESCO emphasises the role of EE in safeguarding future global developments of societal quality of life (QOL), through the protection of the environment, eradication of poverty, minimization of inequalities and insurance of sustainable development (UNESCO, 2014). Environmental Education may best be defined as *a process directed at creating awareness and understanding about environmental issues that leads to responsible individual and group actions.* Successful environmental education focuses *on processes that promote critical thinking, problem solving, and effective decision-making skills.* Environmental Education utilizes processes that involve students in observing, measuring, classifying, experimenting, and other data gathering techniques. These processes assist students in discussing, inferring, predicting, and interpreting data about environmental issues.

Environmental Education is not environmental information: Environmental information is providing facts about specific environmental issues or problems. This may be accomplished through news releases, informational brochures, bulletins, videos, or other media techniques. It is often geared toward the general public instead of targeting a specific group or audience. Information can be very useful to the highly motivated individual who is concerned about a specific topic or issue and can be a critical element of environmental education.

Environmental Education is not environmental advocacy: Quality environmental education concentrates on the educational process. It is non-biased and science-based. Environmental educators may consider themselves environmental advocates in their personal lives. However, in their role as environmental educator they must remain neutral; there is no room for personal beliefs to take centre stage. It is important for environmental educators to remember which role they are in when working with an audience.

Environmental problems and issues are complex and there

are not simple answers. Often there are many possible solutions or no obvious solution at all. It is through the processes of quality environmental education that students can sort through the frequently biased, emotional, and propagandized elements of environmental issues, weighing various sides of an issue in order to make informed, balanced, and responsible decisions.

Objectives of Environmental Education

Of course, one major reason is that it is critical to maintaining our quality of life. Whether we are talking about destruction of the tropical forest, global warming, toxic waste disposal, the ocean crisis or air quality—environmental education is essential if we participate fully in solving environmental problems facing us today and on into the future. There are also many positive educational outcomes.

The following are the objectives of Environmental Education:

1. *Awareness:* To help the social groups and individuals to acquire knowledge of pollution and environmental degradation.
2. *Knowledge:* To help social groups and individuals to acquire knowledge of the environment beyond the immediate environment including distant environment.
3. *Attitudes:* To help social groups and individuals to acquire a set of values for environmental protection.
4. *Skills and Capacity* Building: To help social groups and individuals to develop skills required for making discriminations in form, shape, sound, touch, habits and habitats. Further, to develop ability to draw unbiased inferences and conclusions.
5. *Participation:* To provide social groups and individuals with an opportunity to be actively involved at all levels in environmental decision-making.

There are four areas of decision-making:

- The types of environmental issues on which decisions might be made;
- The physical setting of the prospective environmental decision, including its spatial scale;

- The types of social groups and individuals who might interact in a process leading up to an environmental decision; and
- The time frame within which the decision must be made.

Areas of Environmental Education

Environmental studies discipline has multiple and multilevel scopes. This study is important and necessary not only for children, but also for everyone. The scopes are summarized as follows:

1. The study creates awareness among the people to know about various renewable and non-renewable resources of the region. The endowment or potential, patterns of utilization and the balance of various resources available for future use in the state of a country are analysed in the study.
2. It provides the knowledge about ecological systems and cause and effect relationships.
3. It provides necessary information about biodiversity richness and the potential dangers to the species of plants, animals and micro-organisms in the environment.
4. The study enables one to understand the causes and consequences due to natural and main induced disasters (flood, earthquake, landslide, cyclones etc.) and pollutions and measures to minimize the effects.
5. It enables one to evaluate alternative responses to environmental issues before deciding an alternative course of action.
6. The study enables environmentally literate citizens (by knowing the environmental acts, rights, rules, legislations, etc.) to make appropriate judgements and decisions for the protection and improvement of the earth.
7. The study exposes the problems of over population, health, hygiene, etc. and the role of arts, science and technology in eliminating/minimizing the evils from the society.
8. The study tries to identify and develop appropriate and indigenous eco-friendly skills and technologies to various environmental issues.

9. It teaches the citizens the need for sustainable utilization of resources as these resources are inherited from our ancestors to the younger generating without deteriorating their quality.
10. The study enables theoretical knowledge into practice and the multiple uses of environment.

Relevance of Environmental Study

Environmental study is based upon a comprehensive view of various environmental systems. It aims to make the citizens competent to do scientific work and to find out practical solutions to current environmental problems. The citizens acquire the ability to analyze the environmental parametres like the aquatic, terrestrial and atmospheric systems and their interactions with the biosphere and astrosphere. The importance of Environment study can be envisaged through the following points:

- World population is increasing at an alarming rate especially in developing countries.
- The natural resources endowment in the earth is limited.
- The methods and techniques of exploiting natural resources are advanced.
- The resources are over-exploited and there is no foresight of leaving the resources to the future generations.
- The unplanned exploitation of natural resources lead to pollution of all types and at all levels.
- The pollution and degraded environment seriously affect the health of all living things on earth, including man.
- The people should take a combined responsibility for the deteriorating environment and begin to take appropriate actions to space the earth.
- Education and training are needed to save the biodiversity and species extinction.
- The urban area, coupled with industries, is major sources of pollution.
- The number and area extinct under protected area should be increased so that the wild life is protected at least in these sites.
- The study enables the people to understand the

complexities of the environment and need for the people to adapt appropriate activities and pursue sustainable development, which are harmonious with the environment.

- The study motivates students to get involved in community action, and to participate in various environmental and management projects.
- It is a high time to reorient educational systems and curricula towards these needs.
- Environmental studies take a multidisciplinary approach to the study of human interactions with the natural environment. It integrates different approaches of the humanities, social sciences, biological sciences and physical sciences and applies these approaches to investigate environmental concerns.
- Environmental study is a key instrument for bringing about the changes in the knowledge, values, behaviours and lifestyles required to achieve sustainability and stability within and among countries.

Environmental studies deals with every issue that affects an organism. It is essentially a multidisciplinary approach that brings about an appreciation of our natural world and human impacts on its integrity. It is an applied science as it seeks practical answers to making human civilization sustainable on the earth's finite resources. Its components include: Biology, Geology, Chemistry, Physics, Engineering, Sociology, Health, Anthropology, Economics, Statistics, Philosophy, and Education.

Diversity in Environmental Education

Now-a-days, environmental education is sometimes integrated into school curricula as an interdisciplinary goal of formal education. It is also part of informal education, and a part of daily life during leisure time activities, as well as a substitute for or extension to the formal education sector.

Environmental education is about experiencing, sharing, creativity, pleasure and sensitivity: environmental education activities can be informing the population, discovery activities (guided visits, games, outings), but can also consists of the active participation of the public (workshops, volunteering, excursions, role play, field trips or holidays). The public sector, as well as NGOs, provides materials, education and guidelines on environmental education. Protected Areas also play a vital role in environmental education in regions, having the scientific and protection issues at hand and being able to transfer the knowledge using participation opportunities to a broad public.

Education for sustainable development became more and more important at the beginning of the twenty first century and can be viewed as a broadening and strengthening of environmental education. It takes into account not only the education about ecology and how to protect naturally functioning environments, but also the social, democratic, cultural and economic well-being of humans in these environments. It aims at enabling people to enforce and support sustainable development in their regions and globally.

In 2002, the United Nations decided to organize the Decade of Education for Sustainable Development (DESD) from 2005 to 2014, in order to promote the value of respect to others and to nature as a basis of sustainable development. UNESCO states the following on their website regarding Education for Sustainable Development (ESD): "The founding value of ESD is respect: respect for others and respect for the planet and what it provides us with (resources, fauna and flora). ESD wants to challenge us all to adopt new behaviours and practices to secure our future."

The Role of Environmental Education in the Indian Context

Thus, there are many challenges for environmental educators in India. Apart from the obvious ones of helping strengthen environmental management and conservation, one of the important ones is to bring about awareness of the need that the country develops in less wasteful ways than is the current paradigm. EE is one of the tools that can help India achieve this goal. There are considerable initiatives in EE in India today. There are also several challenges. Some of these are:

- The challenge, in a large and diverse country, to find the right blend between centralized and de-centralized efforts and approaches.

- The challenge of reaching out to large numbers cost-effectively.
- The challenge of making environmental considerations relevant and meaningful to various groups.
- The challenge of putting EE on the agenda of educational decision makers.
- The challenge of putting sustainable development concerns high on the agenda of policy makers, and
- Finding and developing human and financial resources for EE.

Barriers and Constraints in Indian Environmental Education

The widespread practices of Environmental Education in India have been unsuccessful through the years in many ways. Unfortunately, to-date the subject of Environmental Education is linked with the subject of Environment studies, which focuses on providing children with scientific facts and figures on global environmental problems. It addresses environmental issues from a viewer's point of view by identifying the primary sources and proposing corrective measures needed to redress the symptoms, for example, ozone depletion and global warming. Therefore, students end-up knowing what is wrong with the planet but do prevent such damage, neither can they see how to become responsible for the environmental problems and hence, understand how they need to help solve issues by changing their own styles.

The main problems that India seems to be facing regarding Environmental Education can be summarized as follows:

1. *Lack of Environmental Awareness and Lack of Organizational Support:* There is also need of better communication and collaboration with developed countries. There is need of extensive teachers training and their participation in workshops and conferences to expose them with new environmental education materials, techniques and information.
2. *Role of Media in Promoting Environmental Education:* No one can deny the proactive role of Media in promoting and acting as a catalyst in initiating change in the society. However, with reference to Environmental Education,

whether Print media, electronic media or social media has not done justice and we rarely see any structured approach when dealing with environmental issues.

3. *Lack of Attitude towards Environmental Management and Resistance to Change:* Lack of Environmental Education is a major factor that has an important bearing on environmental attitude/behaviour.
4. *Lack of Environmental Training Modules:* The status of Environmental Training programmes and its contents is not satisfactory.
5. *Lack of Preparedness of teachers:* Another barrier to environmental education activities is the reluctance of support and lack of preparedness on part of the teachers.
6. *Inadequate School Curriculum:* No one can deny that the current curriculum is focused on age old teaching practices prevailing over decades, and is responsible for development of stress among students and thereby affecting their normal developments. We need to develop curriculum which will develop skills and attitudes in the students.
7. *Ineffective Environmental Educational Programmes and Policies:* Without a doubt the present EE Programmes and policies are not sufficient to drive students for opting Environment as a career option. Few steps are taken by Ministry of Environment and Forest (MoEF), India. However, the implementation of these steps and policies is a major challenge.

Evolving an Effective Government Strategy to Promote EE in India

1. *Roles of MOEF, MHRD and other Ministries:* While the principal responsibility for Environmental Education through the formal educational system is with the Ministry of Human Resource Development, the parallel responsibility of EE through non-formal efforts lies with the Ministry of Environment and Ministry of Environmental Forestry (MoEF). But these efforts are by no means exclusive. There is a large amount of co-operation between the Ministries and with the

institutions associated with them.

2. *Environmental Education in the Curriculum:* The national system of education, as defined in the National Policy on Education, 1986, visualizes a national curricular framework which contains a common core including several elements having a direct bearing on the natural and social environment of the pupils. The National Policy on Education, 1986 (NPE) states that the "protection of the environment" is a value which along with certain other values, must from an integral part of the curriculum at all stages of education. The policy states: "There is a paramount need to create a consciousness of the environment. It must permeate all ages and all sections of society, beginning with the child. Environmental consciousness should inform teaching in schools and colleges. This aspect will be integrated in the entire educational process."

   There has been special emphasis on the need to give importance to environmental education, and this has been kept in view while designing curricula, framing the syllabi and developing text books. The philosophy behind the curricula is that environmental education could be infused into the curricula especially at the primary level.

   The National Council of Educational Training and Research (NCERT), the apex body in the area of developing curriculum for the formal education system. Currently, there is a national debate going on about how to make EE not only widespread, but also effective at all levels of education. The strategy under discussion envisages a four pronged approach. The four elements of the strategy are:

   - Strengthening Infusion of EE.
   - Teacher Training for effective EE.
   - Introduction of Environment as a separate subject.
   - Use of non-formal methods of EE through the involvement of NGOs.

The success of the above strategy will depend upon the close synergy and partnership between the MHRD and the MOEF, their key institutions, State Governments, NGOs as well as educational institutions throughout the country. In addition, the four components are closely linked and one cannot be viewed in isolation from the other. The operationalization would need to keep this in view.

Centre for Environmental Education (CEE) is closely involved in this process, part of which is being supported by the World Bank. The first step which is ongoing is the analysis of curricula across India to review the degree and quality of infusion of EE. The exercise is being undertaken by a partner organization Bharati Vidyapeeth Institute of Environment Education and Research (BVIEER).

3. *Environmental Orientation to School Education (EOSE):* EOSE, most EE programmes are designed and implemented with National and State level perspectives, hence, the full intent to environmental education will not be achieved because environmental concerns and problems may be locale specific and, therefore do not include consideration of global solutions. Therefore, the Ministry of Human Resource Development (MHRD) supports a centrally sponsored scheme under its financial assistance is provided to government and voluntary organizations and other institutions working in the field of environmental education to develop locale specific programmes and materials. Under this scheme, CEE is one of the designated nodal agencies. To date approximately projects to support development of locale specific programmes and materials by NGOs have been facilitated.
4. *Centres of Excellence:* One of the strategies of the Department was to establish "Centres of Excellence" for research, training and education which would play a pivotal role in strengthening the country's infrastructure and thereby its ability to deal with these issues. The Centre for Environment Education was set-up in 1984 at Ahmedabad under this programme. A second Centre, the C.P. Ramaswamy Environmental Education Centre at Chennai was set-up in 1988 under the same scheme. The main activities of both the Centres are the development of environmental resource materials, organization of training programmes and creation of environmental awareness among teachers, students and the general community.

5. *National Environmental Awareness Programme (NEAC):* The Ministry of Environment and Forests (MOEF), Government of India started National Environment Awareness Campaign (NEAC) in 1986 with the aim of creating environmental awareness at all levels of society. Under NEAC, the Ministry provides financial assistance to selected non-governmental organizations (NGOs), education and training institutes, community organizations, etc. to create massive awareness among citizens of India. Diverse target groups ranging from students/youth/teachers to rural and tribal population, women, professionals and the general public are covered under this campaign. The Campaign programmes are basically composed of a spectrum of short duration programmes.
6. *Environmental Information System (ENVIS):* The Ministry of Environment and Forests has set-up ENVIS for different aspects of environment. The objective of this system are to provide national environmental information service to the users of originators, processors and disseminators; to build-up storage, retrieval and dissemination capabilities; to promote support and assist education and personnel training programmes designed to enhance environmental information processing and utilizing capabilities; to promote exchange of information amongst developing countries. CEE has been designated as the National ENVIS Centre for Environmental Education.
7. *Museums of Natural History:* Setting-up of Natural History of Museums as unique facilities to promote non-formal environmental education and to create environmental awareness among people is a strategy of the Ministry of Environment and Forests. The National Museum of Natural History is located at Delhi. Regional Museums are also being established at Mysore, Bhopal and Bhubaneshwar.
8. *Promoting Mass Media:* The Ministry provide financial assistance for the production of films, video-spots and other audio-visuals on important environmental issues for creation of mass awareness. These are normally telecasted by our National Television (Door Darshan) Channels. There are slots in our National TV Channel especially for

environment.

Conclusion

Teachers need to be prepared to become EE facilitators, who will proactively adopt the activity oriented approach to teaching and learning through, about for the environment. This will require in addition to teacher training, ongoing support that will reach into schools/colleges and influence the EE programme. This support could be perhaps from an external resource agency that closely interacts with the educational system on an ongoing basis.

From the above discussion the following suggestions emerge:

- The problem of environment abuse is a serious one and needs to be addressed at the local, national and international levels. To achieve a good quality of life on earth for all living beings, it is essential to spread awareness about and educate human kind in sustainable development and environmental problems.
- It is agreed, that teachers are potential change agents and are capable of generating a workforce of enlightened, skilled and motivated learners. They can empower the citizens with the ability attitude and values to protect the environment using formal and non-formal channels of education. It is essential that teachers themselves need to be trained and equipped with the requisite knowledge skills and values to effect such a change.
- Universities and schools have to play an important role to translate the objectives and recommendations of the various commissions and committees into practice for achieving environmental literacy and awareness among learners.
- Technological interventions and mass media should be employed to create environmental awareness among the teaching community. A convergence of the conventional and open and distance learning systems should be employed to meet this challenge.
- There is a need to train teachers in additional competencies regarding environment education (UNESCO-1985). The teacher training curricula should integrate environment

education with the methodology component of all disciplines, since environment is a part of all areas of study. Non-formal channels of education like T.V., radio, press and satellite technology can be effectively utilized for capacity building of environment educators.

- Online courses on environment education with a thrust on the practical, skill and value development aspect could be developed for the teachers, educators' administrators, development workers or any person interested to become knowledgeable and aware of environmental issues, on the lines of Green Teacher Programme of the Centre for Environment Education, Ahmadabad, India.
- User friendly, multi-media courseware on environment problems and awareness can be prepared, particularly for the rural-agro-based communities in India.
- Collaborative ventures could be created between the teachers and community through the agencies of schools, colleges, universities and other institutions. Such collaborations could include campaigns on environment awareness, tree plantations, and waste management or also in developing instructional materials.
- Electronic and computer networks could be employed to connect globally and acquire information and expertise on latest developments in the area of environment education and training. Hence, technology mediated learning can play a major role in dissemination of knowledge, skills and values regarding environment, among teachers and through them to our future generations.

References

Agarwal, A., Shankar, R. and Tiwari, M.K., (2006). Modelling agility of supply chain, *Industrial Marketing Management*, 3(6): 443-457.

Cranton, P. (2006). *Understanding and Promoting Transformative Learning: A guide for educators of adults*. San Francisco, CA: Jossey-Bass.

Hutchison, D. (2004). *A Natural History of Place in Education*. New York: Teachers College Press.

Irwin, A. (1995). *Citizen Science: A Study of People, Expertise, and Sustainable Development*. London: Routledge Publications.

Jickling, B., & Wals, A.E.J. (2008). Globalization and environmental education: Looking beyond sustainable development. *Journal of Curriculum Studies*, 40(1): 1–21.

Kagawa, F., & Selby, D. (Eds.). (2010). *Education and Climate Change: Living and Learning in interesting Times*. London: Routledge Publications.

López, R., & Toman, M.A. (2006). *Economic Development and Environmental Sustainability: New Policy*. Oxford, UK: Oxford University Press.

Raj, T. and Attri, R., (2011). Identification and modelling of barriers in the implementation of TQM, *International Journal of Productivity and Quality Management*, 28(2): 153-179.

Ravi, V. and Shankar, R., (2005). Analysis of interactions among the barriers of reverse logistics, *Technological Forecasting and Social Change*, 7(2): 1011-1029.

16

Environmental Issues in Development

Case Studies from Himachal Himalayas

Ankur Srivastava and *Poonam Sharma*

Introduction

Environment and development have been in conflicting scenario whenever put together. There are many cases around the world which reveals the ongoing development paradigm and the environmental issues evolved thereof. As considered development always show the positive trend for a change but there are other faces too. When it comes to developing nations the environmental cost is heavier as compared to developed nation. Most of the mountain areas of the world are facing a situation of change in form of their utilization.

The arrival of tourists in the Kullu valley is mainly credited to the facility of road transport as pre-motor days were almost devoid of tourism in the valley. The opening of the Mandi-Larji gorge in 1930 made the Kullu valley accessible to the outside world and this laid the foundation of tourism industry (Sharma, 1989). In 1964-65 the tourists coming into the valley were around 10,000 this rose to nearly 70,000 in the 80s (Singh, 1989). However, up to this period tourism was in juvenile stage of its growth and no adverse impacts arising out of accommodating these numbers in the concern area were noticeable. The interrelationships among host-tourist-nature at that time could be said to be holistic and eco-friendly. However, in the late 1980s and 1990s traffic of tourists rose exponentially. The tourists were as high as 11 lakh in Manali and 3 lakh in Kullu (Anonymous, 1994a; Ram and Kuniyal, 1994).

Although this rapid growth in the number of tourists was a golden period for hoteliers and travel agents but it proved costly for the environment. Construction of hotels began in full swing and environmentalists began to perceive the danger signs not only to environment but also to the tourist industry.

The adverse environmental impact of tourism and hydroelectric projects in Kullu and Kinnaur districts in the north-western Himalayas has reached to an alarming situation.

Study area

Kullu district situated in the lesser Himalayas between 31°20′–32°26′ north latitudes and 76°59′–77°50′ east longitudes. The district is bounded by Pir-Panjal range in the north; Bara Bhangal in the north-west; the Greater Himalayas in the eastern boundary and Dhauladhar range in the south-west while River Satluj marks the southern boundary of the district. It enjoys pleasant climate with average annual rainfall varying between 100 cm and 137 cm. The minimum temperature drops as low as –2°C during winter as recorded at upstream Manali, while the maximum temperature rises to 30°C during summer as observed at downstream Bhuntar.

Kinnaur, located on the Indo-Tibetan border, is very scenic and is surrounded by the Tibet on the east, Garhwal Himalaya on south, Spiti Valley on the north and Kullu on the west. Kinnaur is extended between 77° 45′ and 79° 00′ 35″ longitude, 31° 05′ 50″ and 32° 05′ 15″ latitude. Kinnaur is about 235 kilometres from Shimla. The district is divided into three administrative areas—Pooh, Kalpa, and Nichar and have five tehsils (counties) with administrative headquarter at Reckong Peo. The annual rainfall varies from 45.4 mm at Pooh to 380 mm at Nichar. The minimum temperature ranges from –6.9 to 14.6°C and maximum from 7.5 to 23.1°C. The wide range of environmental gradients, topography, climate and geographical conditions have endowed the landscape with a rich floral diversity dominated by conifers in the temperate zone, and medicinal and aromatic herbs in the alpine meadows.

Methodology

This chapter includes primary as well as secondary data sources. People perception has been also taken into consideration for

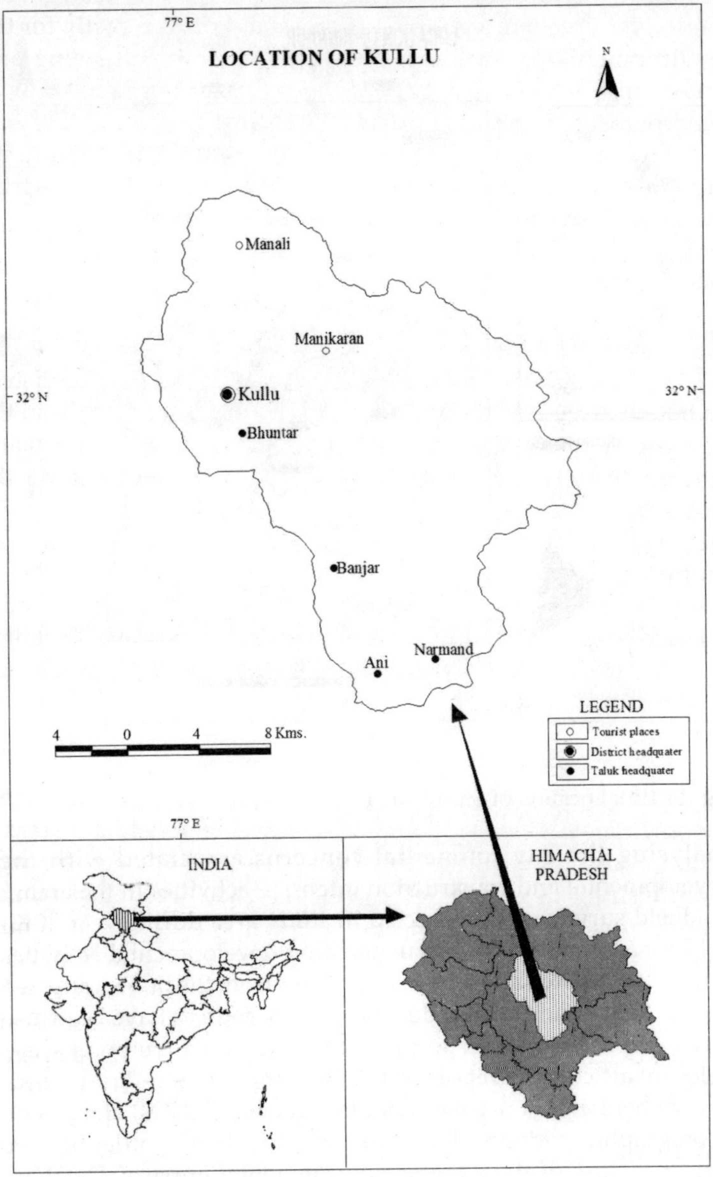

Fig. 1 (a): Location of Study Area

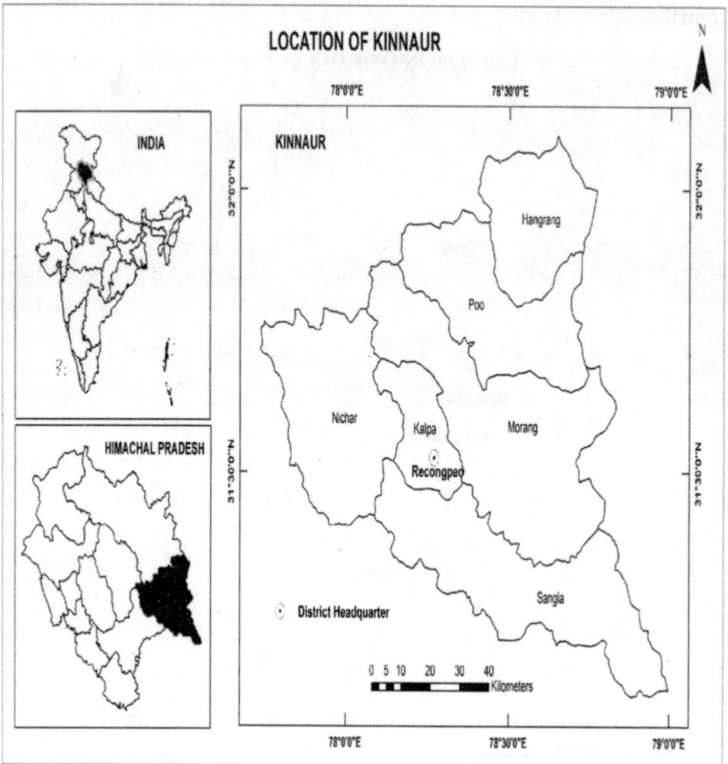

Fig. 16.1(b): Location of Study Area

analysing the environmental concerns associated with the developmental and construction intensive activities in the area.

Field survey was conducted in study area during year 2012-2015 for assessment of various ongoing developmental activities in the concern area along with interviews from the project affected people (PAP) and stakeholders Secondary sources have been also given emphasis in order to relate the study on a temporal scale. Relevant articles and reports published from time-to-time by both government and non-governmental agencies (NGOs) along with photographic evidences have been incorporated in order to have a clear picture of the adverse environmental impacts. Database regarding status of ongoing hydro power projects have been assessed from MOP (Ministry of Power) and NHPC (National hydro power corporation).

Results and Discussion

Development and Mountains

Development in the mountains, need to have an entirely different approach given the fragility and vulnerability of the ecosystems. Development interventions in such sensitive ecosystem may result in accelerated environmental degradation, which may further hamper the downstream attributes. In many cases the physical settings of mountain ecosystem does not allow any outside intervention. The negative impacts of unplanned development, insensitive to mountain specificities, are already becoming common, and the most frequent being the regular incidences of landslides, river obstructions and flash floods in the mountain and recurrent floods in the plains. Mt. ecosystems are more vulnerable to large scale activities such as construction of roads, hydro projects, and massive dams. The impact of these activities is accentuated in mt. areas due to steep surface topography, problem in site selection and other zone of influence in vicinity. The State of Himachal Pradesh may have immense hydropower potential, but the environmental cost that it has to bear for such projects is something not many have looked at. Authorities have been working to use all four major Rivers of the State, Ravi, Satluj, Chenab and Beas, to generate electricity. This is certainly going to leave riverbeds parched and cause damage to flora and fauna.

Impact of Hydro Projects

Installation of small and large hydro power projects along with reservoirs are the recent development trend in Himachal Himalayas. There are two types of beliefs about the environment friendly profile of run of river hydro projects; both are widely prevalent:

(a) That hydro power is all 'green' it has no adverse environmental impact at all.
(b) That hydro power does have some negative impacts but the impacts are too small to be of any concern.

Deforestation

Besides enhancing the scenic beauty, forests also plays vital role in regulating temperature and rainfall, and minimising adverse impacts arising due to over interference on the part of human beings. Forests also determine economic activities, development and livelihood of the people. They control the climate and regulate the hydrological cycle, protect soil erosion and stabilise carbon, nitrogen and oxygen contents in the atmosphere. Initially, the valley was rich in forest cover, fauna and water resources (Singh, 1989). These species were covering the high altitude areas of Rohtang Pass with dense coverage (Harcourt, 1871). Now-a-days, this tree line is receding and exists only between Marhi-Kothi and Manali.

Construction activity in the alpine areas and high forested slopes require large scale deforestation. The further implication of these activities could be disastrous as most of them goes in unplanned manner. The larger and the long term impact of commercial activity on the slopes would be on the entire ecosystem affecting the flow of natural resource like fodder, fuelwood, grass and medicinal herbs to the villages which are located lower down along the slopes. Soil erosion is considered as the very first outcome of degradation activities operational in hilly and mountainous areas. These activities further accentuate problems like flooding, landslides, loss of flora and siltation directly affecting the habitats nearby. Road, tunnel and hydro power stations along with increasing tourism pressure in Kullu district have resulted in deforestation on a large scale. Other than deforestation due to development aspect, the demand for timber and firewood across the country has had an impact on the forests of the Himalaya and deforestation in the Himalaya affects the flood situation in the Gangetic Plains.

More than 10,000 green trees have been felled down during the past two years and about 30,000 are awaiting the axe of development in this district. The Rs. 2,000 crore project of the Rohtang tunnel would require felling of 684 fully grown and 350 small trees, just to make an approach road to the south portal of the tunnel, besides 20,000 trees would be cut to complete the 2051-MW Parbati hydroelectric project in the Manikaran and Sainj valleys of the district. Table 16.1 accounts the environmental cost of hydro power development in eco-sensitive zones of Kinnaur district.

Table 16.1: Hydro projects in Kinnaur

Hydro Power Project	*Status*	*Capacity (MW)*	*Trees Felled/Damaged*	*Forest/Agricultural Area Diverted (Hectares)*
Nathpa-Jhakri	C	1500	10759	147.50
Karcham-Wangtoo	C	1000	11277	496.71
Baspa-2	C	300	5471	44.179
Bhabha	C	120	76	0.98
Sorang	UC	100	206	19.17
Tidong-1	UC	60	6780	39.04
Kashang-1	UC	66	591	34
Yangthang	P	NA	NA	NA
Poo Spiloo	P	NA	NA	NA
Tidong II	P	NA	NA	NA

Source: Compiled by author, 2013.

Slope Destabilization and Landslides

Developmental and various construction intensive activities have also increased the rate of landslides in the study area. The Himachal section being a prominent part of young and still rising Himalayas is experiencing frequent landslides incidences. Road construction over unstable slope is the major reason behind trigger of such phenomenon. There are many sites in Kullu and Kinnaur district which experience frequent land sliding. The steep and fragile slope in Kinnaur accelerates this phenomenon and often triggered by incessant heavy rains and snow. Such an event occurred in June 2013 and Kinnaur was cut off from the state from Tapri onwards as most of the approach roads and Hindustan-Tibet national highway was blocked at several places due to landslides and about 1700 persons were stranded.

Kinnaur is a mountainous district having rugged topography and deep and narrow valleys and steep slopes. The main cause of slope failure/landslide etc. is steep and fragile slopes, loose soil, fissured/fractured rock strata, some tectonic activity, heavy rainfall, toe erosion by running water and human intervention like various unplanned construction activity, deforestation, faulty land-use planning, use of explosives in construction, practicing unscientific mining, quarrying, tunneling methods, unscientific dumping on the valleys etc. The shooting stone, which is very common in many parts of Kinnaur is caused, among others, by the animal movements and winds. The landslides have caused loss of life and infrastructure in the past. The major effect is observed mainly near the villages and along National Highway-22 (Now NH 5), old Hindustan-Tibet Road and other link roads connecting the villages of the district. The important landslides of the district are Malling landslide, Dubling landslide, Spillow landslide, Khadra Dhaank landslide, Lippa landslide, Pangi Nala landslide, Powari landslide, Sapni landslide, Brua landslide, Kuppa landslide, Urni landslides, Sholding landslide, Nathpa landslide etc. The main road leading to Kinnaur has many flashpoints which if triggered by natural events block the connectivity to the district. Such susceptibility is very for other internal roads of the districts.

Impact on Water Resources

Construction of proposed project may lead to two types of impact on the hydrology of the area, i.e. surface water and ground water hydrology. The water during construction and operational phase is drawn from local water resources, putting pressure on them. The diversion also includes channel engineering which is often executed trough help of blasting process, this not only destabilizes the slope regime, but also have negative impacts on the local water resources. Protesters have been especially agitated over assessments of the minimum distance between projects, and the minimum volume of flow in the channel during the dry season.

Diversion of Rivers and Streams

In Kullu district concerns are over Kothi Beas and Harnola Nalas as the upcoming hydro installation will tap raw water at 1440 kilo litre per day. These nallas or streams are the main source of drinking and irrigation water in the villages downstream. There are also concerns from the villager's side that the construction activities will pollute the water sources rendering them unpotable. There are clearly visible evidences which show the pathetic condition of rivers affected by large hydro power

Fig. 16.2: Status at Kharcham Wantoo Project
Source: South Asia Network on Dams River and People, 2010.

construction. The impact is much more prominent in the downstream region. The minimum environmental flow criteria which should be 15 per cent as decided by the state are often violated by the developers resulting in conflict between local community and the developer. The local people have concerns regarding water sharing as the apple orchards and crop field uses lift irrigation for which water has be driven from near by water source.

Muck Disposal

Muck disposal has always been an issue with construction activities in eco-sensitive zones. The excavation and blasting process produces significant amount of waste which is often dumped along the river course side. This practice has direct adverse impacts on the local environment which can be easily seen while travelling along major river channels. The unscientific and haphazard muck disposal results in increased turbidity having direct adverse impacts on the river ecology. Although the detail project reports (DPRs) and EIA reports suggests scientific waste disposal mechanism at specific points but practically the environmental norms are being violated in many cases. The muck generated by the power projects and excavation activities is being dumped along the main river course. The Project Colonies such as the one constructed at Tapri which has historically faced many devastation is virtually on the river course. The repeat of 60 feet high floods in the year on the pattern of 2000 would cause huge devastation both to the power project, residential locations and road network.

Table 16.2: Level of Noise Pollution at Hydro Power Construction Site

Sl. No.	*Machine*	*Noise Level (dB)*
1.	Compacter	80-85
2.	DG set	80-110
3.	Dozer	80-85
4.	Drilling Machine	120-130
5.	Dump Truck	80-90
6.	Face Shovel	80-90
7.	Granting Machine	100-120
8.	Motor Scrapper	85-90
9.	Pumps	80-100

Source: Detailed Project Report (DPR, 2012)

Impact on Flora and Fauna

The effect of more than one plant over a river is much greater than that of a single plant due to the cumulative impacts resulting from consecutive construction (Odom, 2010). Leucauge decorate (*Araneae:Tetragnathidae*), an orb-weaving spider, that basically breed near watery and moist sources. This species is an excellent indicator of water-rich environment where there is thick presence of insect-prey. The results of baseline survey on the flora carried out during the study in the project and its adjoining area revealed that some of the species viz.; *Hyoscyamus niger, Ephedra gerardiana, Ferula jaeschkeana, Heracleum candicans, Betula utilis, Juniperus macropoda, Dactylorhiza hatagirea, Datisca cannabina, Rheum webbianum, Dioscorea deltoidea, Rheum austral* recorded from the region fall under category of threat status (Rare/Endangered/Vulnerable) as per the Red Data Book. These threatened plant and animal species may have an adverse impact with the project activities.

A study conducted by Dr. Jagdish C. Kuniyal, Mr. Arun P. Jain and Mr. Ardhendu S. Shannigrahi of the GB Pant Institute of Himalayan Environment and Development, Himachal unit at Mohal, 4 km from here, reflected that the environmental situation arising at Kullu and Manali due to increasing pressure of tourism and deforestation has registered dangerous proportions of polluted air, water and an increase in suspended particulate matter (SPM).

An in-depth study over a period of four years (1996-1999) showed that the SPM has gone up to 112 μg/m^3 at Manali during summers beyond permissible level (100 μg/m^3) and in Kullu 118.8 μg/m^3. The total waste generated was nearly 63 per cent in Kullu and 72 per cent in Manali which is higher than that of the non-biodegradable level. The study further reveals that the indiscriminate throwing of municipal solid waste into rivers is a common practice in this the area which results in polluting of the river water.

Table 16.3: Heavy Construction and Related Adverse Impacts

Forms of Activity	*Pressure on*	*Adverse Impacts*
Over construction	Land	Increase in disasters (deforestation, floods, cloud bursts and landslides, etc.)
Increase in roads	Forests	Soil erosion, landslides, floods
Fuelwood		Air pollution and shrinkage in forests
Timber extraction		Air pollution and loss of forests cover
Forest fires		Drying up of springs
Trekking	Fauna	Disturb wildlife habitat reduction in wildlife Hunting & poaching
Increase in road traffic	Air	Increase in air and/or noise pollution and Respiratory problems begin
Waste dumping Sewage disposal	Water	Water borne disease/ contamination of water sources, fading scenic beauty

Source: Kuniyal *et al.*, 1999.

Impact on River Ecology

Hydro electric projects and water reservoir schemes in mt. areas not only effects the ecology of the water system, but also alter the local climate to some extent. There is also impact on the inter relationship between aquatic and terrestrial systems. One of the main environmental challenges of hydropower development is related to fish passage both upstream and downstream. These migrations are ecological imperatives for populations of anadromous fish. Entire populations of these migratory species can be eliminated if either up or downstream migrations are blocked. The consequences can sometimes be very negative since some species are disappearing and others are arriving due to the morphological change of the river basin and/or the characteristics of the water composition due to the thermal pollution, the increased turbidity or the likely alteration of nutrients. For example, in some cases strong variation of the flow can destroy fish eggs.

Impact of Unplanned Tourism

Today, more than 70 lakh tourists flock to the state and a bulk of these are domestic tourists. Within the state it has been the Kullu and Shimla districts, which are comparatively easily accessible, with substantial and growing transport and communication infrastructure which receives the majority of the tourist traffic of the two districts, it is the Kullu valley which is home to the river Beas that is more popular, with Manali, which receives snow in the winter, being the point of attraction. The number of visitors to the Kullu-Manali circuit grew from 38,000 in 1975 to 1,30,000 in 1985 and visitations were projected to be 250,000 by 1990. This figure has been between 30 to 50 lakhs in 2007. Kinnaur being tribal belt of the state is now emerging as a adventure tourism destination. The difficult terrain of the district is adding new dimensions to the tourism industry. Nature camps at Nako and LToday, tourism contributes more than 5 billion rupees to the state revenue, forming 2 per cent of the State Domestic Product. But while this might be the bright side of the story, there is more to consider. There have been various studies and assessments of the adverse impacts that tourism has had on the environment of mountain states like Himachal in general and the Kullu Valley in particular. "Manali in Himachal Pradesh was a small hill resort catering to the needs of people who loved nature. Now, it is an overcrowded city with ugly multi-storied buildings."

Researchers have discovered that the ecological footprint of Manali is now 25 times greater than its size (Cole and Sinclair 2002). "The chaotic, sudden nature of Manali's development has caused the town to now face serious environmental problems. The town should be focusing on waste management, decreasing *fossil fuel* dependency, forest protection, economy minded tourism, and informing both tourists and residents to be environmentally aware to prevent further environmental problems in the future. In addition to this, in 2007 the central Ministry of Tourism provided in-principle approvals to projects worth almost Rs. 29 crore for tourism related activities in Himachal. The Asian Development Bank (ADB) has also asked the State Government to submit proposals for developing theme-based tourism circuits so that it can release funds for building the necessary infrastructure for these projects. The ADB is showing a special interest in eco-tourism projects. The stage has been set for massive private and foreign investment in the tourism sector and the environmental along with socio-cultural implications that have played out till now are about to increase manifold.

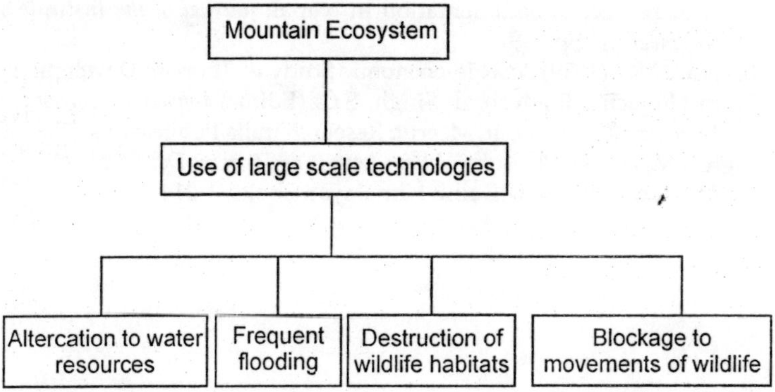

Fig. 16.3: Mountain Ecosystem and Impact of Large Scale Technologies

Conclusion

The environmental issues in development need a timely review as further delay may worsen the whole scenario. Environmental policies need a more liberal perspective towards the indigenous population who deserve the first right over the local resources. Environment and development have always been challenging phenomena occurring together. Thus, the upcoming altercations between them should be taken care of. As the water towers i.e, mountains, of worlds are feeling immense pressure from the consumption side and further stress is obvious, there is a need for concrete solution in order to minimize the impact intensity. Development paradigm has also given access to basic amenities to people living in isolated and difficult terrain. Health facilities are now within reach due to improvement in communication links. The adjectives such as Ecotourism, sustainable development need a practical implementation.

References

Harcourt, A.F.P., (1871) *The Himalayan Districts of Kooloo, Lahoul and Spiti*. Reprinted in 1982, New Delhi: Vivek Publishing Co., 1-119.

Kuniyal, J.C., Vishvakarma, S.C.R., Badola, H.K. and Jain, A.P., (1999) Tourism in Kullu Valley: An Environmental Assessment: A report (unpublished), Kosi-Katarmal (Almora): GBPIHED, 1-206.

Ram, S.C. and Kuniyal, J.C., (1994) *Potentials of Tourism in Kullu, Himachal Himalaya* (unpublished report), Kullu (India)-Shamshi: GBPIHED, Himachal Unit, 1-133.

Sangroula, D.P. (2009) Hydropower Development and its Sustainability with respect to Sedimentation in Nepal. *Journal of the Institute of Engineering*, pp. 1-9.

Sharma, N.K., (1989) A Socio-economic Study of Tourism Development in Himachal Pradesh, in Singh, S.C. (Editor) *Impact of Tourism on Mountain Environment*, Meerut: Research India Publications, 230-236.

Singh, T.V., (1989) *The Kullu Valley: Impact of Tourism Development in the Mountain area*, New Delhi: Himalayan Books, 1-214.

17

Women as Environmental Managers for Sustainability

Monica Ahlawat

"...... the future of this planet depends on women."

—**Kofi Annan**

Introduction

The term 'environment' is much used in current times. Its content is defined as variously or as broadly as its user determines. Environment denotes all these resources, which make-up the totality of the productive base of a region, which is inhabited by people. These resources include land, forests, water, livestock and people. The real meaning is in the interaction between people who are the users of the environment. While all human beings interact with the environment, the people who are closest to it, both as users and as nurturers are women (Mitra, 1988). UNICEF drew attention to the depletion of natural resources and the consequent hardships to women. The important role of women in economic and social development in both their communities and their countries is increasingly being recognized. Numerous formal "events" have helped to enhance recognition of this role. For example, the United Nations Decade for Women from 1975 to 1985 drew global attention to women, especially the trying conditions under which many of the poorest live. The United Nations Conference on Environment and Development (UNCED) in Rio de Janeiro during 1992 presented a global action plan to institutionalize the role of women in environment and development. The United Nations Fourth World Conference on Women, held in Beijing, China, during September 1995, further highlighted important issues if the gap between men and women is to be narrowed. This conference followed earlier major meetings in Mexico City (1975), Copenhagen (1980) and Nairobi (1985). Representatives attended the Beijing Conference from 189 countries, and involved an official conference held in Beijing as well as a parallel conference for non-governmental organizations (NGOs) in nearby Huariou. Together the two conferences attracted some 50,000 people. The *Constitution of India* ensures equal status for both men and women.

> *"You can tell the condition of a nation by looking at the status of its women."*
> —***Jawaharlal Nehru***

The history of the relationship of rural women to nature's resources has been marked by a struggle to provide subsistence for the family in the face of growing alienation from, and increasing erosion of the means. Since, the early 1970s there has been considerable interest in the relationship between women, particularly low-income rural women in developing countries, and the environment. The poor rural women, the main users of household biomass and providers of subsistence needs, were seen as the main victims of the deepening environmental crisis. But gradually, there has been a shift in that perception. Women are no longer viewed as mere victims; it is increasingly recognized that they could have a key role to play in natural resource management as they have the knowledge and experience gained from working closely with their environment. They are seen as the solution to the developing environment crises, as major assets to be harnessed initiatives to conserve resources and fix ecological problems. Rural women constitute an important component of rural development. Economic self-sufficiency of rural women can greatly contribute to the eradication of poverty in rural areas. Economic upliftment of rural women will bring about the desired social change in them. It will provide them social status, a rightful share in the national wealth, a sense of participation in national affairs and will thus bring them in the main-stream of national development. In order to understand the problems of the rural women, it is essential to have a clear idea of its infrastructure with regards to its natural resources, the potentialities of the region and the prospects of the economic upliftment of the rural women. They deserve to be given top priority, if the rural poverty is to be eradicated and the rural households are to be made not only economically viable, but also self-generating economic units. Rural communities will continue to depend heavily on agriculture and natural resources for their livelihood. Environmental degradation will only deepen their poverty, so environmental conservation and poverty alleviation are parallel objectives. In most situations where they enjoy secure tenure, the poor will invest to protect their land and their environment.

Why Gender? Women compose one-half of the world's population and perform 2/3rd of the world's work hours, yet are any where poorer in resources and poorly represented in positions of decision-making power. Women are traditionally associated with child bearing, child rearing, emotional care taking and responsibility for the physical maintenance of the household. In many societies, women's position in the family and in the community is determined by traditional practices and customs of overall constraints of a patriarchal system. Women perform multiple roles such as productive, reproductive, social and community etc. (Figure 17.1).

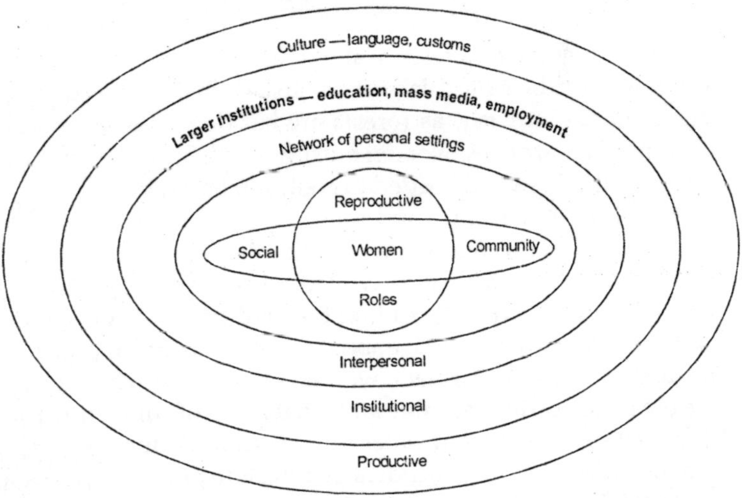

Fig. 17.1: Woman and their Social Relationships
Source: Millican and Smithells, 1992.

The basic purpose of this study will be to highlight the role that women play in the environmental management and development in rural Delhi. It is because women have more close relationship with their surroundings, are more sensitive and more willing to care for it. Most men who migrated to cities did not make enough money to be the breadwinners for women and children left behind in rural areas, which had to try to survive through marginalised subsistence farming. Often this situation led to men's abandonment of their families, producing a significant rise in the number of poor female-headed households. All human beings have an impact on the natural environment and all are affected by the degradation of the environment by "man-made" pollution.

Denying women any appreciable role in decision-making about use of the environment has led directly to food-fuel-water crises in the rural areas of the Third World. Such crisis results from resource depletion that threatens the survival of people in subsistence economies, but also deforestation and desertification. Women are the main food producers and processors in most of the rural areas of the Third World, and they must have access to clean water and firewood for fuel. As their land is lost of corporate farms and water resources are polluted by agricultural run-off from fertilizers and pesticides, rural women are forced to travel farther-and-farther in search of clean water. Because the amount they carry is limited, they have to fetch water several times a day, adding more hours to their hard labour to sustain the meager diets of their families. Similarly, as forests are cut down for large-scale agricultural enterprises, women must go further to field in order to look for the firewood needed to cook and boil water, making it safe to drink. When water and fuel sources are being depleted, not only does food become scarce, but also the basis for ecologically sound agricultural practices is eroded. Most women agricultural workers work closely with and on the land and have developed significant informal knowledge about eco-systems and appropriate land-use patterns. As farmers, women often know which plants have the most nutritional value and what farms of cultivation lead to the least soil erosion and water consumption. As fuel gatherers, women known they are dependent on forests to provide renewable sources of firewood.

"Major social transformation major social transformations are impossible without ferment among the women." —**Karl Max**

It is important to study women's work because:

1. Substantial part of women's time and energy is spent in working.
2. Women's work is most of the time invisible and unrecognized, primarily because in the accepted capitalist paradigm any 'economic' activity is synonymous with 'market' activity and much of women's work is done outside the realm of the market. It is also usually undervalued since the unpaid element is not taken into consideration while computing national income.
3. A number of issues confronting the women's movement today, particularly in developing countries such as in India, are related to different aspect of women's work.
4. In the contest of globalization women's work is probably one of the most important areas that are being affected by the changing situation.

The significance of the present study lies in the fact that it is one of the few empirical attempts to study the actual conditions of women in nature. It brings into focus the systematic pattern of discrimination against women at every level. It also emphasizes the decisive role played by traditional cultural norms in determining the position of women in agrarian society.

Environmental Degradation Affecting Women

Women have the responsibility for managing household resources, but they typically do not have managerial control. Given the variety of women's daily interactions with the environment, they are the most keenly affected by its degradation. For example:

- Deforestation or contamination increases the time women must spend seeking fuel wood or safe, clean water, and increase women's risk of water-borne disease. In the State of Gujarat, India, women now spend four or five hours a day collecting fuel wood, where previously they would have done so once every four to five days.

- Soil erosion, water shortage and crop failures reduce harvest yields; soil exhausted from over-use reduces the productivity of household gardens.
- Toxic chemicals and pesticides in air, water and land are responsible for a variety of women's health risks. They enter body tissues and breast milk, through which they are passed on to infants. In a village in China's Gansu province, discharges from a state-run fertilizer factory have been linked to a high number of stillbirths and miscarriages. Water pollution in three Russian Rivers is a factor in the doubling of bladder and kidney disorders in pregnant women, and in Sudan a link has been established between exposure to pesticides and prenatal mortality with the risk higher among women farmers.
- In urban settings in particular, air and water pollution can be extreme, and sanitation and waste treatment poor or non-existent, presenting new threats to health, particularly for women, who have the highest levels of exposure. In the Indian cities of Delhi and Agra, for example, drinking water comes from rivers heavily polluted by DDT and other pesticides.

Degraded environments mean that women must spend more time and effort to find fuel or produce food, but their other responsibilities, for meeting household needs and ensuring family health, do not diminish. Gendered divisions of labour have so far resisted real change. In many countries, women already work 12 hours or more a day in and out of the home; in Africa and Asia, women work an average of 13 hours more each week than do men (Mitchell, 1997).

> *Women have a vital role in environmental management and development. Their full participation is therefore essential to achieve sustainable development.*
>
> —**Rio Declaration Principle 20**

Rural Women and Environment Management

Poor women in rural areas have become increasingly marginalized

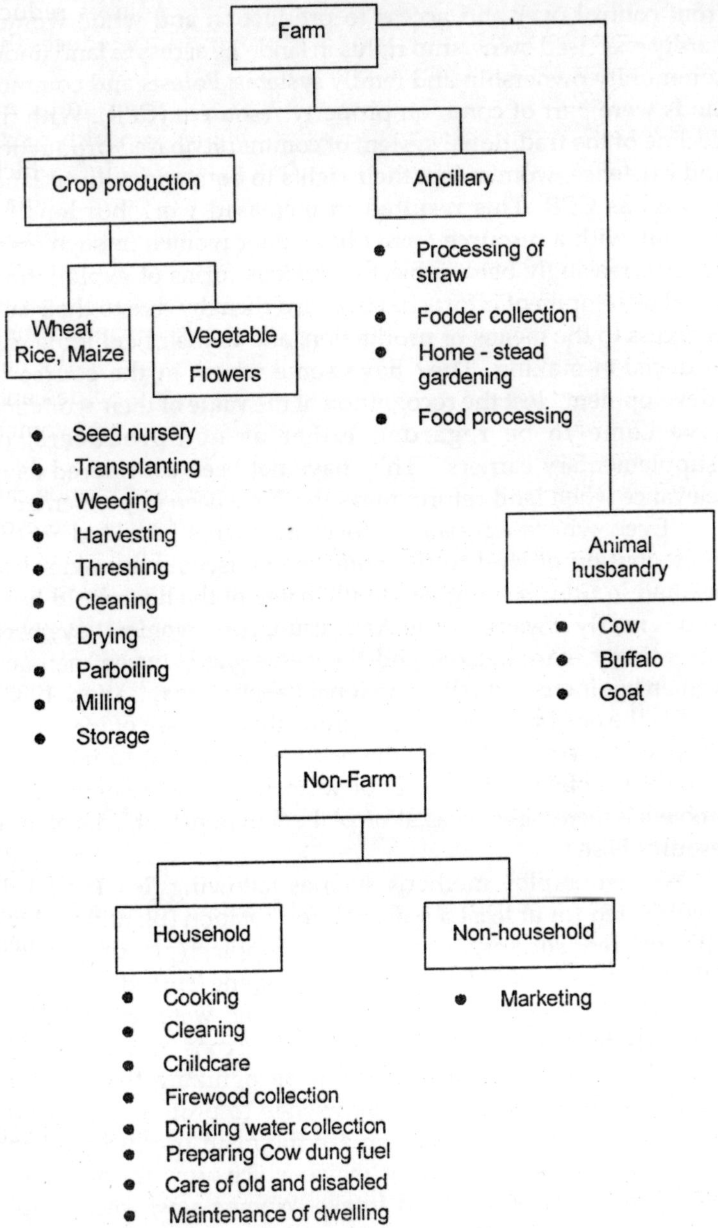

Fig. 17.2: Facets of Farm Women's Work
Source: Mitra, 1990.

from control over and access to production and while women hardly exercised ownership rights in land, the access to land under community ownership and family systems. Forests and common lands were part of common property resources (CPR). With the decline of the traditional system of community based production and existence, women lost their rights to both agricultural land, as well as CPR. This resulted in increased work burdens for women, with a resource / asset base. Poor women in such areas have increasingly been subject to various forms of exploitation. Rural development efforts have passed them by due to their lack of access to the means of production, and to their negligible role in decision-making. They have some where in the course of "development" lost the recognition of the value of their work and have come to be regarded either as non-producers, or "supplementary earners". They have not been considered as of relevance when land reform measures have been implemented.

"Even where agrarian reform measures have led to the redistribution of land to the poor, the household approach has resulted in titles being given in the name of the household head who is nearly always a man. As a result, rural women have been increasingly marginalized and the status gap between men and women has increased" (International Labour Organisation, 1988).

On the one hand there is therefore, this problem of increasing poverty in terms of loss of the asset base leading to increased survival problems for rural poor women. On the other side, the problem is increasing devastation of the "environment", the natural resource base.

Women employ methods such as fallowing (leaving fields uncultivated for at least a season), crop rotation (planting a field with different successive crops), intercropping (planting several different crops in a field at one time), mulching (spreading organic material on the soil around plants to avoid water evaporation) and a variety of techniques that promote soil conservation, fertility and enrichment. Planners are now recognizing the value of learning from women's local knowledge to protect and sustain the environment. Rural women are the main producers of the world's staple crops-rice, wheat, maize-which provide up to 90 per cent of the rural poor's food intake. Women sow, weed, apply fertilizer and pesticides, harvest and thresh the crops. Their contribution to secondary crop production, such as legumes and vegetables, is even greater.

Grown mainly in home gardens, these crops provide essential nutrients and are often the only food available during the lean seasons or if the main harvest fails. Women's specialized knowledge about genetic resources for food and agriculture makes them essential custodians of agro-biodiversity. In the livestock sector, women feed and milk the larger animals, while raising poultry and small animals such as sheep, goats, rabbits and guinea pigs. Also, once the harvest is in, rural women provide most of the labour for post-harvest activities, taking responsibility for storage, handling, stocking, processing and marketing.

Women and Environmental Governance

Environmental governance refers to the rules, processes and behaviour that affects the way power is exercised at all levels in the field of environmental policy. It also includes other areas that have an impact on the environment, and concepts such as openness participation, accountability, effectiveness and coherence. Women do not exist in environmental governance. Women are unreasonably positioned in environmental governance. Women are less involved in environmental decision-making. Women have less capacity in participating environmental decision-making. The disparity between men and women are hardly addressed in environmental decision-making. The impacts of environmental decision-making to women are barely assessed (Figure 17.3).

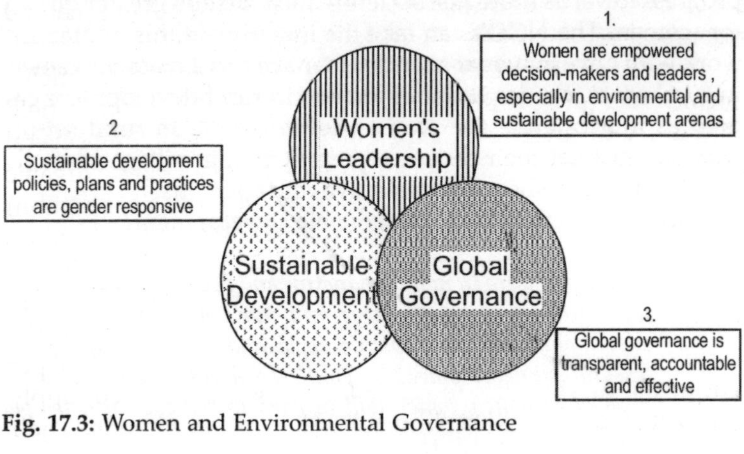

Fig. 17.3: Women and Environmental Governance

Half of the world's population-women has no say in environment and development policies which affect them and their family lives. There is a need to recognize the traditional role of women as natural resource managers and in improvement of environmental conditions. There has been gradual awakening among some planners, officials and experts to the fact that women in rural areas of developing countries like India are often important even key actors in the development process. Enlightened well meant plans for overall increase in production and rural development, for providing primary health care to all people, for expanding domestic food production, for controlling population growth and many more targets, seem unattainable without the cooperation of rural women. But even where its importance is recognised, programmes for their betterment are not easily designed and implemented. The mechanics of cooperation have not evolved very far. And there remain many influential people particularly among planners and policy-makers-who are unaware or unconvinced of the need to deal specifically with the roles of women. Successful development can not be pursued without rural womens participation, condemning them to low productivity menial jobs under utilises human resources and thus retards the process of growth. Concern for human rights and the dignity of individual's demands great improvements in their conditions of work, their access to productive resources and their participation in decision-making at all levels. In other words, to achieve substantial growth in production depends partly on women and progress towards more just societies must include greater quality for women. The NGO's can take the initiative in this matter and work with governmental agencies to make this a mass movement in rural areas. Participation of women in rural development can help us to accelerate the pace of development. In rural set-up, women must get their proper representation in village councils, panchayats and other administrative organisations.

Are Women the Key to Sustainable Development?

> *"If women were in more productive and decision-making roles, we could be moving faster and more assuredly towards sustainability in the economic, social and environmental sense. Sustainable development is a political concept because it is about good governance, which will be hard to achieve until we get closer to gender parity."*
>
> **—2012, UN Conference on Sustainability Development.**

References

Agarwal, B., 1992, Gender and Environment Debate, Lessons from India, *Feminist Studies*, Vol. 18, No. 1.

Aggarwal, Bina, 1994, *A Field of One's Own: Gender and Land Rights in South Asia*, Cambridge: Cambridge University Press.

Merchant, Carolyn, 1995, *Earth care: Women and the Environment*, New York: Routledge Press.

Mies, Maria, 1986, *Indian Women in Subsistence and Agricultural Labour*, Geneva: International Labour Office.

Mitra, Manoshi, 1988, *Environmental Degradation and Regeneration: Alternative Strategies for Development*, 4th National Conference on Women's Studies, Andhra University, 28-31 December, 1988.

Mitchell, B., 1997, *Resource and Environmental Management*, Geneva: England: Longman Ltd.

Millican, J. and J. Smithells, (Ed.), 1992, *Women working for Women's Development: Barriers & Strategies*, Report for a one day Seminar held at the University of Reading, February 1992, Published by Education for Development, in P.R. Reddy and P. Sumangala, *Women in Development, Perspectives from Selected States of India*, Vol. 2, Delhi: B.R. Publishing Corporation.

Raju, Saraswati, 1993, *Women and Work in South Asia: Regional Patterns and Perspectives*, Introduction in Saraswati Raju and Deipica Bagchi, (Eds.), London and New York: Routledge.

Rodda, Annabel, 1994, *Women and Environment*, London: Zed Books.

Sachs, Carolyn E., 1997, *Women Working in the Environment*, Washington: Taylor and Francis.

Shiva, Vandana, 1988, *Staying Alive: Women, Ecology and Survival, Kali for women*, New Delhi.

Venkateshwaran, S., 1995, *Environment, Development and the Gender* Gap, New Delhi: Sage Publications.

18

Environmental Education as a Driver for Sustainable Development Goals

Prabuddh Kr. Mishra

Introduction

Voices around the world are demanding leadership on education, poverty, inequality and climate change. To turn these demands into actions, world leaders gathered on 25 September, 2015, at the United Nations in New York to adopt the 2030 Agenda for Sustainable Development. The 2030 Agenda comprises 17 new Sustainable Development Goals (SDGs) and 169 targets, which will guide policy and funding for the next 15 years to be implemented by "all countries and all stakeholders, acting in collaborative partnership", beginning with a historic pledge to end poverty everywhere permanently and set out quantitative objectives across the social, economic, and environmental dimensions of sustainable development framework for shared action "for people, planet and prosperity". These goals and targets are "global in nature and universally applicable, taking into account different national realities, capacities and levels of development and respecting national policies and priorities." A set of indicators and a monitoring framework will also accompany the goals. The indicators are defined by the Inter-Agency and Expert Group on SDG Indicators (IAEG-SDGs), which will present its recommendations to the UN Statistical Commission in March 2016.

The concept of the SDGs was born at the United Nations Conference on Sustainable Development, Rio+20, in 2012. The objective was to produce a set of universally applicable goals that balances the three dimensions of sustainable development: environmental, social, and economic. The SDGs replace the Millennium Development Goals (MDGs), which in September 2000 rallied the world around a common 15-year agenda to tackle the indignity of poverty. The MDGs established measurable, universally-agreed objectives for eradicating extreme poverty and hunger, preventing deadly but treatable disease, and expanding educational opportunities to all children, among other development imperatives.

With the job unfinished for millions of people—we need to go the last mile on ending hunger, achieving full gender equality, improving health services and getting every child into school. The SDGs must finish the job that the MDGs started, and leave no one behind. The SDGs build on the Millennium Development Goals (MDGs), eight anti-poverty targets that the world committed to achieve by 2015. The MDGs, adopted in 2000, aimed at an array of issues that included slashing poverty, hunger, disease, gender inequality, and access to water and sanitation. Enormous progress has been made on the MDGs, showing the value of a unifying agenda underpinned by goals and targets. Despite this success, the indignity of poverty has not been ended for all.

The new SDGs, and the broader sustainability agenda, go much further than the MDGs, addressing the root causes of poverty and the universal need for development that works for all people. UNDP Administrator Helen Clark noted: "This agreement marks an important milestone in putting our world on an inclusive and sustainable course. If we all work together, we have a chance of meeting citizens' aspirations for peace, prosperity, and wellbeing, and to preserve our planet." The SDGs will now finish the job of the MDGs, and ensure that no one is left behind.

The Sustainable Development Goals (SDGs)

The 17 Sustainable Development Goals form a cohesive and integrated package of global aspirations the world commits to achieving by 2030. Building on the accomplishments of their predecessors the MDGs, the SDGs address the most pressing global challenges of our time, calling upon collaborative partnerships across and between countries to balance the three dimensions of sustainable development—economic growth, environmental sustainability, and social inclusion (The United Nations, 2015).

Fig 18.1: Sustainable Development Goals.

Goal 1: End poverty in all its forms everywhere.

Goal 2: End hunger, achieve food security and improved nutrition and promote sustainable agriculture.

Goal 3: Ensure healthy lives and promote well-being for all at all ages.

Goal 4: Ensure inclusive and equitable quality education and promote lifelong learning opportunities for all.

Goal 5: Achieve gender equality and empower all women and girls.

Goal 6: Ensure availability and sustainable management of water and sanitation for all.

Goal 7: Ensure access to affordable, reliable, sustainable and modern energy for all.

Goal 8: Promote sustained, inclusive and sustainable economic growth, full and productive employment and decent work for all.

Goal 9: Build resilient infrastructure, promote inclusive and sustainable industrialization and foster innovation.

Goal 10: Reduce inequality within and among countries.

Goal 11: Make cities and human settlements inclusive, safe, resilient and sustainable.

Goal 12: Ensure sustainable consumption and production patterns.

Goal 13: Take urgent action to combat climate change and its impacts.

Goal 14: Conserve and sustainably use the oceans, seas and marine resources for sustainable development.

Goal 15: Protect, restore and promote sustainable use of terrestrial ecosystems, sustainably manage forests, combat desertification, and halt and reverse land degradation and halt biodiversity loss.

Goal 16: Promote peaceful and inclusive societies for sustainable development, provide access to justice for all and build effective, accountable and inclusive institutions at all levels.

Goal 17: Strengthen the means of implementation and revitalize the global partnership for sustainable development.

The SDGs Agenda responds to these compound challenges, and is therefore broader and more complex than the MDGs. Most importantly, it adopts sustainable development as the organizing principle for global cooperation, meaning the combination of economic development, social inclusion, and environmental sustainability. Hence, the overarching name "Sustainable Development Goals," as the key message to the world community. Furthermore, the SDGs and related agenda apply to all countries, developed and developing alike. The post-2015 agenda calls for actors to move away from business-as-usual (BAU) approaches towards the sustainable use of resources and peaceful and inclusive societies (Sustainable Development Solutions Network, 2013).The outcome document for the SDG Agenda synthesizes the breadth of these issues by declaring that the SDG framework will stimulate action on five key themes: people, planet, prosperity, peace, and partnerships which are shown in Fig. 18.2. The benefits for goal based planning complement international conventions and other tools of international law by providing a globally shared normative framework that fosters collaboration across countries, mobilizes all stakeholders, and inspires action. Well-crafted goals are able to accomplish a shared narrative of sustainable development and help guide the public understands of complex challenges. Unite the global community and mobilize stakeholders. Community leaders, politicians, government ministries, academics, nongovernmental organizations, religious

Fig 18.2: Sustainable Development: Key Themes

groups, international organizations, donor organizations, and foundations will be motivated to come together for a common purpose around each SDG, support long-term approaches towards sustainable development and Define responsibilities and foster accountability (Sustainable Development Solutions Network, 2013).

Education and SDGs

Education has been identified as an essential component for sustainable development worldwide. The role of education can also positively influence the management of the world's increasingly stressed natural resources through the incorporation of successful techniques of environmental education. Environmental education provides students with the knowledge, skills, and experiences essential to become successful community leaders, as well as making intelligent decisions pertaining to the management of their natural resources.

Education has made many valuable contributions to societies and development globally, and is recognized for the important role it has in improving livelihoods worldwide. Quality education should prepare societies to actively participate in global politics and economics, as well as provide people with the skills necessary to make informed decisions and take responsible actions. Throughout the world, societies have recognized education as a key component of sustainable development. Sustainable development has been promoted since its inception over 30 years ago as an effective means to abate the degradation of human and environmental systems. Sustainable development concentrates on aspects of the economy, society and environment in order to achieve its goals (Hart, 1997). However, it can be an often misused or overused statement in the endorsement of policies worldwide, drawing attention away from the 3 original environmental intentions of the strategy and focusing more attention on the social and/or economic aspects. The economic, social, and environmental aspects of sustainable development and policy formation should be equally represented and balanced (Hart, 1997).

Environmental Education and SDGs

SDGs 4 stand to ensure inclusive and equitable quality education and promote lifelong learning opportunities for all. Achieving inclusive and quality education for all reaffirms the belief that education is one of the most powerful and proven vehicles for sustainable development. This goal ensures that all girls and boys complete free primary and secondary schooling by 2030. It also aims to provide equal access to affordable vocational training, and to eliminate gender and wealth disparities with the aim of achieving universal access to a quality higher education. Ensure all learners acquire knowledge and skills needed to promote sustainable development, including through education for sustainable development and sustainable lifestyles, human rights, gender equality, promotion of a culture of peace and non-violence, global citizenship and appreciation of cultural diversity.

This particular goal cut across all the SDGs horizontally and emerged as one of the most important goal for the achievement of SDGs collectively. As education and human resource development is the key of this goal the different areas related to education viz., education for sustainable development, environmental education, peace education, vocational education, higher education etc. for everyone cutting across all section of society is must for the success of SDGs. In this regard Environmental Education (EE) and Education for Sustainable Development (ESD) is one defined field of specialization which directly deals with environmental conservation and protection without a doubt. The concerned organizations responsible to put into practice the courses and the curriculum in our education systems would very well list down the initiatives undertaken by them towards achieving this. With such overt attention and energy invested to achieve this goal, it is naturally expected that such efforts would bring about environmental literacy and the result would be reflected in our attitude towards the environment and in addressing environmental issues.

Box 18.1

The Role of the UN Sustainable Development Solutions Network (SDSN)

In 2012, UN Secretary-General Ban Ki-moon launched the UN Sustainable Development Solutions Network (SDSN) to mobilize global scientific and technological expertise to promote practical problem solving for sustainable development, including the design and implementation of the Sustainable Development Goals (SDGs). Following their adoption, the SDSN is now committed to supporting the implementation of the SDGs at local, national, and global scales.

To this end, SDSN works with partners in academia, government, business, civil society, and the United Nations to promote practical solutions for sustainable development. We mobilize universities and other knowledge institutions around the world for the implementation of the goals and promote the exchange of lessons and learning.

The SDSN is governed by a remarkable Leadership Council comprised of some 100 global leaders on sustainable development from science, civil society, business, government, and international organizations.

SDSN Priorities

Support for the SDGs

The SDSN provides analysis and technical recommendations to support the implementation of the 2030 agenda, drawing on our global network and the Leadership Council. In particular the work focuses on integrated sustainable development pathways, data, monitoring and review, financing for development, and the climate change agenda.

A global network of problem solvers

More than 20 National and Regional SDSNs have been launched, mobilizing and empowering universities and other knowledge institutions in support of the SDGs. With more than 350 member institutions from over 80 countries, we are building a global network of problem solvers. Our technical expertise is organized across Thematic Networks that foster collaboration and knowledge sharing among expert communities. In addition, SDSN Youth mobilizes young people around the world to prioritize the SDGs and to promote practical youth-led solutions.

Solution initiatives and long-term pathways

Thematic Networks and National and Regional SDSNs are committed to finding novel solutions — often using modern technologies or new business models. This includes helping countries chart long-term pathways for achieving the SDGs. One example, the Deep Decarbonization Pathways Project, supports countries in mapping out how they can transform their energy systems to promote economic growth and reduce emissions, to keep the rise in global temperatures to less than 2°C, as agreed by all countries.

Education for sustainable development

SDSN's flagship online education initiative, SDSNedu, is training the largest-ever cohort of students of sustainable development through free online courses from the world's leading experts. Uniquely, SDSNedu is operated through a consortium of institutions and works with SDSN members around the world to integrate high-quality online education into universities' curricula.

Source: SDSN, 2015

Environmental education is a multidisciplinary field, drawing from the social, physical and biological sciences. According to the Environmental Education and Training Partnership, (EETAP) environmental education encourages citizens to make knowledgeable and informed decisions about their environmental behaviour based on the awareness, knowledge, skills, and attitudes instilled in them (2000). Environmental education relies on both formal and non-formal teaching techniques to accomplish the ultimate goal of encouraging citizens to make informed and positive actions toward the environment. Environmental education makes use of many disciplines, techniques, and resources to accomplish its goals. Since students learn from an array of non-traditional, multiple inte'ligences such as naturalistic, interpersonal, or intrapersonal, environmental education can be a strategy that bridges many learning styles. Environmental education's methodology and goals can be incorporated into SDGs objectives for sustainable development in education. Education that focuses on sustainable development and critical thought has an increased likelihood of success, and environmental education's multidisciplinary nature makes it an ideal strategy for development. However, environmental education in the developing world often has different criteria for success because of different socio-economic factors affecting populations. There is a strong need to link the ideals of environmental quality, human equality and human rights together to increase the effectiveness of environmental education and development.

Environmental education that stresses the preliminary variables of ownership and empowerment are crucial in the promotion of education for sustainable development. The increased participation of youth in environmental investigation and decision-making can lead to an increased sense of empowerment and achievement, thus contributing to sustainable development and the objectives of educational reform. Therefore, if educational programmes want to accomplish the goals of both sustainable development and environmental education, they should stress student participation and action in order to create stronger feelings of ownership and empowerment in the learning process.

For effective implementation and successful endeavour of SDGs, environment education must be taught and our curriculum on environmental courses should focus on local environmental issues which students face daily and empower them with the necessary skill to resolve such issues. Mere discussing greater issues like global warming and climate change will not bring fruitful results. Further, activities which involve exposure of the students to nature must also form a regular feature in the curriculum. Frequent visit of students to nature may instil interest to take-up projects which will give positive results in safeguarding the environment as a whole.

The Way Forward

Many factors are incorporated into environmental education programmes that successfully address both educational reform and sustainable development. The combination of the need for improved education worldwide and rapid environmental degradation has led to increased opportunities for environmental education programmes to enhance both. Programmes that focus on familiar environments and communities promote student success and confidence on a local scale, and provide the foundation for solving larger societal and environmental issues in the future. Basing programmes on sound structural processes supply students with an opportune learning environment to develop the skills necessary for life. Finally, a commitment of time for the long term development of the students, as well on resource conservation, provides students with the opportunity to understand, investigate, and resolve issues they face. However, changing or traditional political environments can directly or indirectly influence the educational process, and need to be accounted for. In order for SDGs to meet its goals, citizens worldwide must be provided with the skills necessary to face future challenges. Using the environment as a unifying educational theme can be a successful strategy in providing citizens with those skills.

Protection of environment is apparently considered to be an important goal under all stages of education as envisaged by environment education for making SDGs a success. Special courses have also been designed to achieve this goal worldwide; however, there is no visible positive impact on the ground. Several reasons can be attributed for the prevailing situation, which includes our lack of concern and commitment for the environment as an individual and lack of skills to tackle environmental problems, due to ineffective environmental courses and policies. To overcome such barriers it is essential to relook and redesign environmental courses that are being imparted in the school and higher education. We cannot wait for the Government to solve all environmental problems. Government takes decisions at the policy level. Often we may even sense a lack of commitment on its part. But ultimately it is we, the citizens, who have to put the policies into practice. And for that matter every individual action counts. Finally, the dictum "*think globally act locally*" will going to deliver the very notion of SDGs through environmental education.

References

Barraza, L., Duque-Aristizabal, A.M. & Rebolledo, G. (2003). EE: From Policy to Practice. *Environmental Education Research*. 9(3): 347-357.

Cheak, M., Volk, T., & Hungerford, H. (2002). Molokai: An Investment in Children, the Community, and the Environment. A CISDE Monograph—The Center for Instruction, Staff Development, and Evaluation: Carbondale, IL.

Environmental Education and Sustainable Development in the New Millennium (17-19). New Delhi, India: Indian Environmental Society.

Hart, R. A. (1997). Children's Participation: The Theory and Practice of Involving Young Citizens in communinity Development and Environmental Care. London, UK: Earthscan Publications Ltd.

http://www.in.undp.org/content/india/en/home/post-2015/sdg-overview.html Process on Localizing the Post-2015. Consultations on the Localization of the Post 2015 Development Agenda—World We Want. Available at https://www.worldwewant2015.org/file/429438/download/467338

Reilly, S. (2008) Environmental Education's Role in Sustainable Development: Three Case Studies from India, South Africa and the United States. http://www.uwsp.edu/forestry/StuJournals/Documents/IRM/Reilly.pdf.

Shimray, C. (2016) Redesigning environmental courses for effective environmental protection. *Current Science*, No. 4, Vol. 110.

Sustainable Development Solutions Network. (2013). *An Action Agenda for Sustainable Development*. Report for the UN Secretary-General. Paris, France and New York, USA: SDSN. Available at http://unsdsn.org/wp-content/uploads/2013/06/140505-An-Action-Agenda-for-Sustainable-Development.pdf

Sustainable Development Solutions Network. (2015). *Data for Development: An Action Plan to Finance the Data Revolution for Sustainable Development*. Paris, France and New York, USA: SDSN. Available at http://unsdsn.org/wp-content/uploads/2015/07/Data-For-Development-An-Action-Plan-July-2015.pdf

The United Nations Development Programme (2015). Key Messages and The United Nations. (2015). *Transforming our world: the 2030 Agenda for Sustainable Development*. Availablable at https://sustainabledevelopment.un.org/post2015/transformingourworld

The United Nations (2015). *Transforming our world: the 2030 Agenda for Sustainable Development*. Available at https://sustainabledevelopment.un.org/post2015/transformingourworld.

The World Bank (2015). *Urban Development: Overview*. Webpage. Available at: http://www.worldbank.org/en/topic/poverty/overview.

United Nations Environment Programme—World Conservation Monitoring Center (2008) R etrieved April 2016 from http://www.unep-wcmc.org/sites/wh/cape_floral.html.

Wilson, H.J. (2002). *Participatory Environmental Education*. In D. Bandhu & R. Ahuja (eds.).

Part III

Spatial Information Technologies in Environmental Management

19

Modelling and Monitoring of Changing Green Space

A Case Study of National Capital Territory of Delhi, India

Seema Sahdev and *Manish Kumar*

Introduction

"Green Infrastructure is a term that is appearing more and more frequently in land conservation and development discussions across the country and around the world. Green infrastructure means different things to different people depending on the context in which it is used. For example, some people refer to trees in urban areas as green infrastructure because of the 'green' benefits they provide, while others use Green Infrastructure to refer to engineered structures (such water treatment facilities or green roofs) that are designed to be environmentally friendly" (Benedict and McMahon, 2002). Nature can be used to provide important services for communities by protecting them against excessive heat, pollution, or helping to improve air, soil and water quality. When nature is harnessed by people and used as an infrastructural system it is called "green infrastructure". Green infrastructure is really a bigger concept and is closely associated with many other things. Green infrastructure also serves to provide an ecological framework for social, economic and environmental health of the surroundings. Even though, Urban Green Infrastructure is a term which has grown in use in recent years and the definitions vary from expert to expert, most stakeholders agreed to the following, "Urban Green Infrastructure is a network of multi-functional open and green space in and around towns and cities, the gardens, trees, rivers, woodland, parkland, nature reserves and urban wild space, and the access to and through them, which support wildlife and biodiversity, provide recreation, access and leisure opportunities and create a sense of place" (MacDonald *et al.*, 2005). The various definitions of Urban Green Infrastructure given by different authors (references) are listed below.

Cities are experiencing increasing signs of environmental stress, notably in the form of poor air quality, excessive noise, and traffic congestion (Ruangrit & Sokhi, 2004). At the same time, irregular and unsustainable extension of cities has caused destruction of urban green areas that has resulted from increasing demand for land (Hassan-Ali Laghai *et al.*, 2012). Urban green infrastructure are an integral part of any city landscape, providing city and its residents with numerous benefits both tangible and in-tangible (Gaodi *et al.*, 2010), ecosystem services like pollutant sequestration and ambient temperature regulation etc. (Nowak *et al.*, 2006) (Jim and Chen, 2008), social services and health (Grahn and Stigsdotter, 2003), and also economic services like tourism, increased property prices etc. (Chaudhry and Tewari, 2010) (Luttik, 2000). But it is ironic that despite realising the numerous benefits availed by green spaces in an urban ecosystem, yet green space is undergoing destruction and degradation in the modern times due to rapid and haphazard urbanization in developing countries, making urban settlements major source of GHG emissions and at the same time making them more vulnerable to global environmental change impacts.

Having realized the importance of urban green space in urban ecosystems, considerable work has been devoted to improve the urban environment and enhancing citizen's quality of life through urban green infrastructure planning. Additionally, issues on urbanization associated land-use change and environmental implications have received increasing research attention. Landscape metrics have been used to quantify land-use change and green space patterns to direct sustainable development and to infer potential ecological processes to guide ecological planning.

Study Area

The Delhi is composed of three geographical regions: Gangetic plains, the ridge, Yamuna flood plains. The Yamuna plains provide agriculture. The Yamuna is only river flowing in Delhi. The average altitude is 293 m above mean sea level which is most dominating feature of this study area. The ridge originates from Aravalli hills in the south and encircles the west, north east and North-West portion in the city. Delhi is separated by Hindon River from eastern side. The national capital territory of Delhi covers an area of 1,484 km^2 (573 sq. mi). The plains are prone to recurrent floods. It has a length of 51.9 km (32 mi) and a width of 48.48 km (30 mi). The city is recorded as development due to proximity of the road, market, and other facilities. The city is recorded great plains at the southern side of the region. Urbanisation and urban sprawl is recorded in this region. The geographical background of the city was recorded as sacred Yamuna river was there from the past. The Delhi is a metropolitan city with very high population.

The National Capital Territory of Delhi is divided into eleven revenue districts. Each district is headed by a District Magistrate and has three subdivisions. A Subdivision Magistrate heads each subdivision. All Deputy Commissioners report to the Divisional Commissioner. These district are meant only for revenue collection

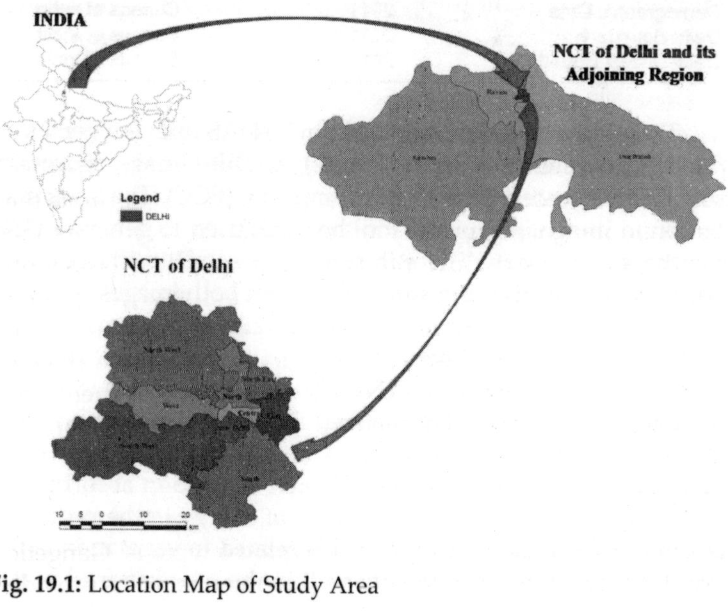

Fig. 19.1: Location Map of Study Area

and Administration. The initial nine districts came into existence from January 1997. Prior to that, there used to be only one district for whole of Delhi with district headquarters at Tis-Hazari. In September 2012, two new districts, viz. South-East and Shahdara were added to the city's map taking the total count to 11.

Data and Methodology

Landsat Satellite Imagery at a resolution of 30 m of 2003 and 2016 were used for land cover classification. The satellite data covering study area were obtained from earth explorer site (http://earthexplorer.usgs.gov/) (Table 19.1).

Table 19.1: Data Used in this Study

Data	*Row/Path*	*Year*	*Spatial Resolution/ Scale(m)*	*Source*
Satellite Images				
Landsat 7	40/146	Feb-2003	30	USGS Earth explorer
Landsat 8	40/146	Feb-2016	30	USGS Earth explorer
Additional Data				
Demographic Data	_	2011	_	Census of India
Delhi Boundary	_	2011	_	Census of India
Delhi District Boundary	_	2011	_	Census of India

These data sets were imported in ERDAS Imagine version 11 (Leica Geosystems, Atlanta, U.S.A.), satellite image processing software to create a false colour composite (FCC). The layer stack option in image interpreter tool box was used to generate FCCs for the study areas. The sub-setting of satellite images were performed for extracting study area from both images by taking geo-referenced out line boundary of Hawalbagh block map as Area of Interest (AOI). For better classification results Normalized Difference Vegetation Index (NDVI) were also created to classify the Landsat images. A Normalized Difference Vegetation Index (NDVI) is an equation that takes into account the amount of infrared reflected by vegetation. Green vegetation absorbs solar radiation, which they use as a source of energy in the process of photosynthesis. The reason NDVI is related to vegetation is that healthy vegetation reflects very well in the near-infrared part of the electromagnetic spectrum. The NDVI is calculated from these individual measurements as follows:

$$NDVI= NIR-RED/NIR+RED$$

where, NIR is a near infrared band such as TM band 4 and Red is a red band such as TM band 3.

The accuracy of classified map was assessed by randomly taking 100 points on the reference image. The accuracy assessment was computed using user, producer, overall and Kappa (Khat/K) statistics. Finally, the resultant classified images were vectored using raster to vector conversion tool with ERDAS IMAGINE software. Quantitative areal data of the overall vegetation change as well as gains and losses between 2003 and 2016 were compiled.

Results and Discussions

Accuracy assessment

In order to access accuracy assessment, 100 ground control points were used to correct the misclassified areas using recode option in ERDAS Imagine software and second, to calculate the mapping accuracy of classified images. The results of the classification accuracy assessment of two images 2003-2016 are presented in Table 19.2.

Table 19.2: Description of Land Cover Mapping Accuracy

Land Use/Cover	*Overall Accuracy (%)*	*Kappa Coefficient*
2003	73.08	0.6218
2016	87.23	0.8247

Source: Based on Landsat 7 and Landsat 8 Satellite Images of 2003 and 2016.

Table 19.3 and Figures 19.2, 19.3 and 19.4 shows district-wise area under vegetation cover. South district which is about 74.43 sq. km. in 2003 and increased up to 108.34 sq. km. in 2016, followed by South-West region with 46.11 in 2003 and raised up to 57.17 sq. km., Central region with 4.63 sq. km. in 2003 and 5.06 sq. km. in 2006, North east district contributes with 13.09 sq. km. in 2003 and 2016 it goes down up to 6.42 sq. km., West region with 16.20 sq. km.

Table 19.3: Distribution of Vegetation Area during 2003 and 2016 in km²

District of NCT of Delhi	*2003*	*2016*	*Vegetation Change in km²*
	Area in km²		
South	74.43	108.34	33.90
South West	46.11	57.17	11.05
West	16.20	9.66	–6.53
New Delhi	22.66	17.55	–5.11
Central	4.63	5.06	0.42
East	10.38	7.27	–3.10
North	13.95	11.07	–2.88
North East	13.09	6.42	–6.67
North West	41.16	36.20	–4.95

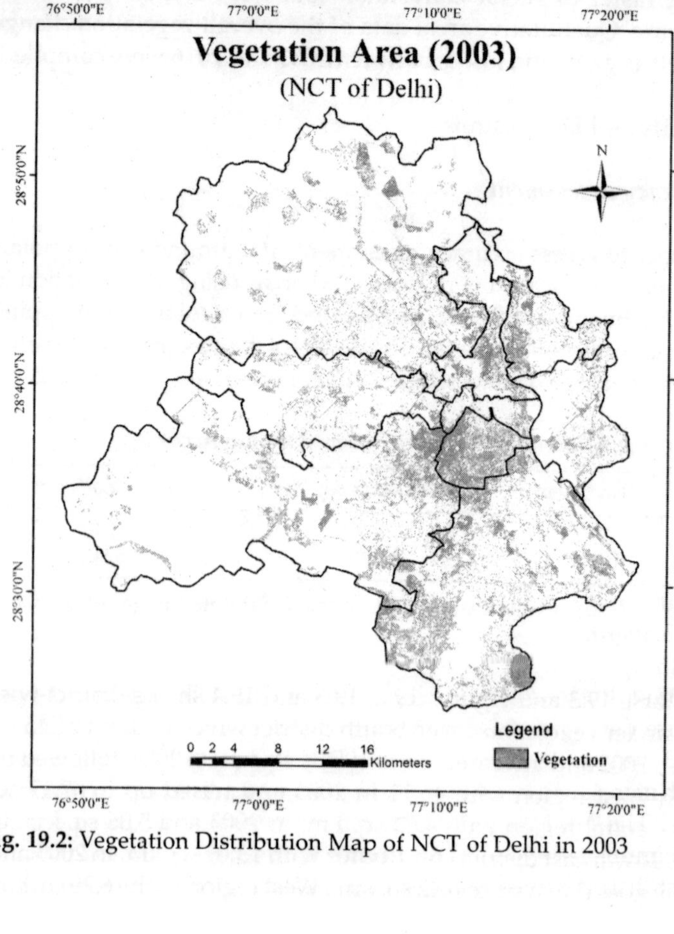

Fig. 19.2: Vegetation Distribution Map of NCT of Delhi in 2003

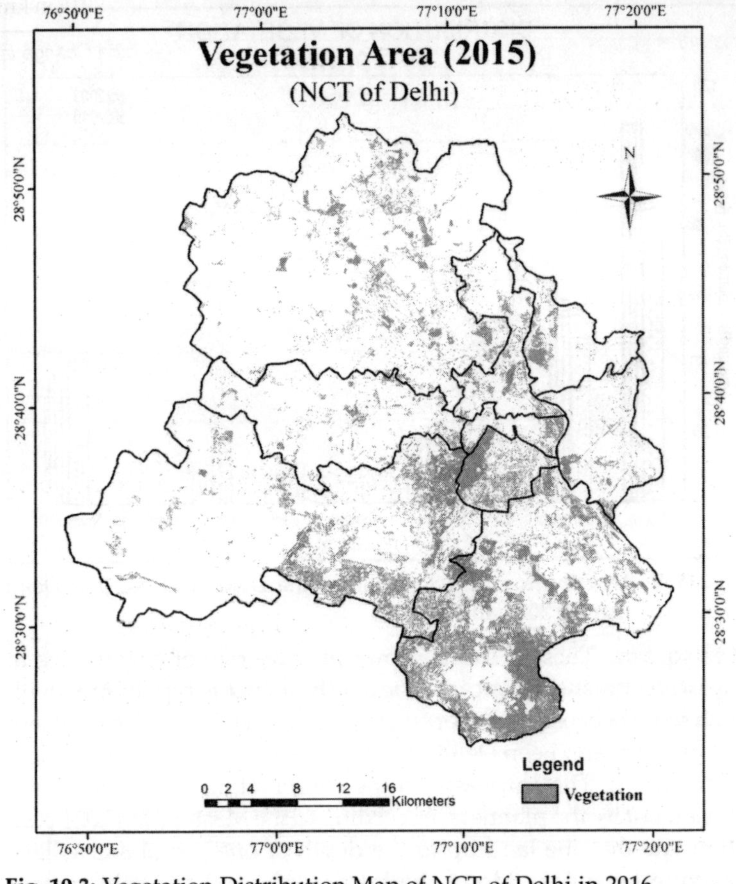

Fig. 19.3: Vegetation Distribution Map of NCT of Delhi in 2016

in 2003 and 9.66 sq. km. in 2016, New Delhi is about 22.66 sq. km. in 2003 and drop down up to 17.55 sq. km. in 2016, North West with 41.16 sq. km. in 2003 and 36.20 sq. km. in 2016, East region is about 10.38 sq. km. in 2003 and 7.27 sq. km. in 2016, North district of Delhi figure outs with area under Vegetation is about 13.95 sq. km. in 2003 and 11.07 sq. km. in 2016. The area under Vegetation cover with increased rate of change district-wise during 2003-2016 periods was: The land cover change under vegetation cover occurred maximum in the south district with 33.90 sq. km. followed by South West district which is about 11.05 sq. km., Central region is about

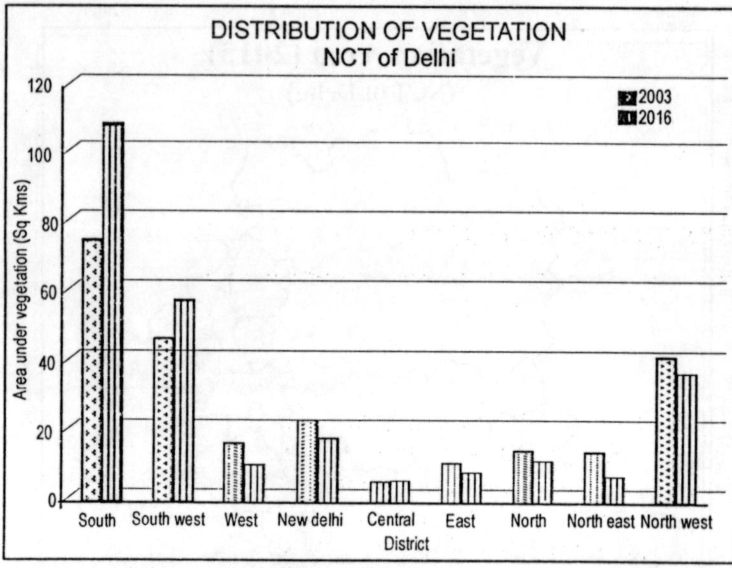

Fig. 19.4: Distribution of Vegetation in the District of NCT of Delhi during 2003 and 2016

0.42 sq. km.. These districts shows positive rate of change due to the urban greenery concept. The south district is highlighted with high score because of the forest enriched in the district. The concept of Go Green and keep Delhi Clean has been accepted by the people of the Delhi. The emphasis on the conservation of the ridge was carried out by the planners. According to the Master plan 2021 plan stimulate that the land-up to the depth of one peripheral village revenue boundary along the border of NCT of Delhi, where available, would be maintained as Green Belt.

The district which shows negative rate of change from 2003 till 2016 among the other districts was: North East is about –6.67 sq. km., West region of Delhi is about –53sq. km., New Delhi scores near about –5.11 sq. km., North West –4.95 sq. km., East district is about –3.10 sq. km. and North not the least gives very less number among all the districts is of –2.88 sq. km. The exact situation is highlighted in Table 19.2 and Figure 19.5 can also gives the visual effect on the analysis during the 2003-2016 period. Urbanization is increasing day-by-day but the negative impact shows on the resources because of the population pressure, over exploitation of the resources and pollution.

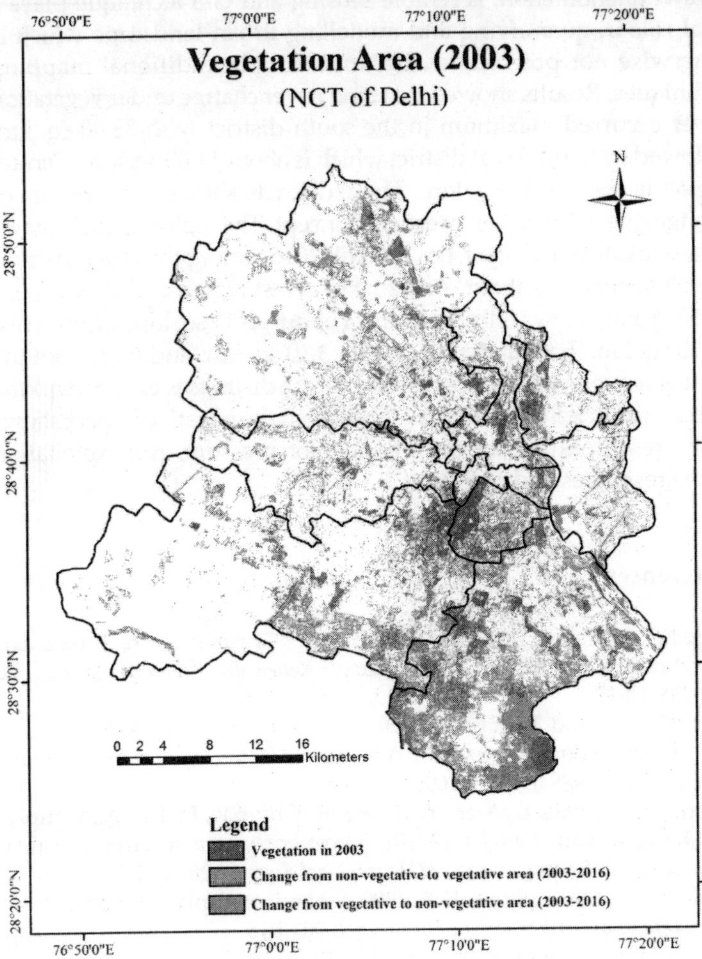

Fig. 19.5: Vegetation Change Map of NCT of Delhi during 2003 to 2016

Conclusion

In this research, an attempt has been made to investigate the usefulness of the remote sensing data and statistical techniques for urban growth dynamics and modelling of spatial and temporal variability. The integration of remote sensing, GIS and database management systems has helped in quantifying, monitoring and modelling the urban sprawl phenomenon. A remote sensing and GIS technique plays a vital role in quantifying and modelling urban landscape which is otherwise not possible to attempt through traditional mapping techniques. Results showed that land cover change under vegetation cover occurred maximum in the south district with 33.90 sq. km. followed by South West district which is about 11.05 sq. km., Central region is about 0.42 sq. km.. These districts shows positive rate of change due to the urban greenery concept. The district which shows negative rate of change from 2003 till 2016 among the other districts was: North East is about –6.67 sq. km., West region of Delhi is about –6.53sq. km., New Delhi scores near about –5.11 sq. km., North West –4.95 sq. km., East district is about –3.10 sq. km. and North not the least gives very less number among all the districts is of –2.88 sq. km.. Urbanization is increasing day-by-day but the negative impact shows on the resources because of the population pressure, over exploitation of the resources and pollution.

References

Benedict, M.A. and E.T. McMahon (2002). "Green infrastructure: smart conservation for the 21st century." *Renewable Resources Journal,* 20 (3): 12-17.

Chaudhry, P. and Tewari, V.P. (2010). Role of public parks/gardens in attracting domestic tourists: An example from City Beautiful of India, *TOURISMOS* (5): 101-109.

Gaodi, X., Wenhua, L., Xiao, Y., Zhang, B., Chunxia, L., Kai, A., Wang, J., Kang X. and Wang, J. (2010). Forest ecosystem services and their values in Beijing. *Chinese Geographical Science,* 20: 51-58.

Grahn, P. and Stigsdotter, U.A. (2003). Landscape planning and stress. *Urban Forestry & Urban Greening* 2: 001-018.

Laghai, H.A. and Bahmanpour, H. (2012). GIS Application in Urban Green space Per Capita Evaluation (Case study: City of Tehran). *Annals of Biological Research* 3(5): 2439-2446.

Luttik, J. (2000) The value of trees, water and open space as reflected by house prices in the Netherlands. *Landscape and Urban Planning,* 48: 161-167.

Nowak, D.J., Crane, D.E. and Stevens, J.C.(2006). Air pollution removal by urban trees and shrubs in the *United States. Urban Forestry & Urban Greening,* 4: 115-123.

Ruangrit, V. and Sokhi, B.S. (2004) Remote Sensing and GIS for Urban Green Space Analysis: A Case Study of Jaipur City, Rajasthan. Institute of Town Planners, *India Journal* 1(2): 55-67.

20

Landslide Hazard Zonation Mapping for Sustainable Development of Hilly Region Using Geospatial Techniques

A Case Study of Uttarkashi District, Uttarakhand, India

Amit Kumar Ray

Introduction

Landslides are one of the most frequently occurring disasters affecting human life and property in Himalaya. The term 'landslide' basically means a slow to rapid downward movement of instable rock and debris masses under the action of gravity which can be categorized into various types on the basis of failure characteristics[1].The term "landslide hazard zonation" applies in general sense to division of the land surface into homogenous areas or user defined domains and the ranking of these areas according to their degrees of actual or potential natural hazards from landslides or other mass movements on slopes[2].According to Geological Survey of India[3] 0.49 million km^2 or 15 per cent of land area of the country is vulnerable to landslide hazard. Out of these 0.098 million km^2 is located in North-eastern Region and rest 80 per cent is spread over Himalayas, Nilgiris, Ranchi Plateau and Eastern and Western Ghats. Predictive modelling of landslide hazard has emerged as a major research field that has been enhanced by the use of new technological advancements such as GI Science[4], remote sensing, GPS data and subsequent incorporation of pair-wise comparison matrix known as AHP applied to spatial data. Hence an increasing number of researchers and institutions are working towards improving of existing modelling procedures relate to landslide hazard mapping at medium and regional scales.

The pair-wise comparison method was introduced by Fechner[5] in 1860 and developed by Thurstone in 1927. Based on pair-wise comparison, Saaty[6] proposes the AHP as a method for multi-criteria decision-making (MCDM) that involves qualitative data. It has been applied during the last twenty-five years in many decision-making situations and has been used on a wide range of applications in many different fields. The method uses a reciprocal decision-matrix obtained by pair-wise comparisons so that the information is given in a linguistic form. It provides a way of breaking down the general method into a hierarchy of sub-problems, which are easier to evaluate. The pair-wise comparison method is more advanced, enabling a relatively reliable examination of real world conditions. Using this method, a matrix is developed in which every criterion attains a value based on its importance in relation to all other criteria and the weight of its relative importance is calculated for each criterion. The application of AHP method, developed by Saaty (1980) for landslide susceptibility mapping has done by Barredo *et al*[7], Mwasi[8], Nie *et al.*[9], and Yagi[10], while the use of weighted linear combination (WLC) technique was reported by Ayalew *et al.*, Nagarajan *et al*[11], used temporal remote sensing and GIS techniques to zonate the landslide hazard in part of western ghat in India. Hassanzadeh[12] has adopted Multiple Regression method and GIS technique for landslides hazard zonation using four factors lithology, slope angle, precipitation and land-use.

The prime objective of the study was to undertake hazard zonation mapping and analysis for rural/urban development and planning in hilly area using GIS, to use spatial AHP Model for making ratio matrix of suitable sites for landslide hazard zonation map, for the disaster management of tehsil and block, for the generation of awareness among decision-makers.

Study Area

The study area, viz., Rajgarhi, Chiniyali and Dunda tehsil are situated in southern part of Uttarkashi district in Uttarakhand, India which extends between 30° 34' 55" N to 30° 56' 33" N

Latitudes and 78°17′11″E to 78°43′28″E Longitudes and encompasses an area of about 3 km^2. The average height of the town is 1,158 metres from mean sea level. These tehsils lies in the lesser Himalayan terrain on the main route to Gangotri and Yamunotri have many Hindu temples, and is also considered as important Hindu pilgrimage centre.

Methodology

Data Collection and Integration

In order to develop a landslide hazard zonation map various thematic layers were generated using 53 J/6 toposheet. Cartosat Satellite data used for creating digital elevation model (DEM) which was further used for preparing drainage and slope map. Information regarding lithological formations of the study area is based on Rai (1993). After a heavy downpour in September 2010 incidence, many landslides occurred. The location of these landslides was captured using GPS. All these information layers were integrated and analysed under ArcGIS Environment.

Selection and Preparation of Criteria Maps

In this study six criteria were selected. The principal criteria that were used for hazard zonation are land-use cover, road proximity, drainage, slope, geology and landslide locations. These criteria were used for preparation of criteria maps and final hazard zonation map.

Scoring/Ranking and Development of Pair-wise Comparison Matrix

For landslide hazard zonation, it is necessary to give some score to each of the criteria as per their suitability for hazard zonation. For this purpose the pair-wise comparison matrix using Saaty's nine-point weighing scale (Table 20.1) was applied. To develop a pair-wise comparison matrix, different criteria are required to create a ratio matrix. These pair-wise comparisons are taken as input and relative weights are produced as an output.

Table 20.1: Nine point weighting scale for pair-wise comparison

Intensity of Importance	*Description*	*Suitability Class*
1.	Equal importance	Lowest Suitability
2.	Equal to moderate importance	Very Low Suitability
3.	Moderate importance	Low Suitability
4.	Moderate to strong importance	Moderately Low Suitability
5.	Strong importance	Moderate Suitability
6.	Strong to very strong importance	Moderate High Suitability
7.	Very strong importance	High Suitability
8.	Very to extremely strong importance	Very High Suitability
9.	Extremely importance	Highest Suitability

Source: Saaty, 1980; ESRI, 1996.

Computation of the Criterion Weights

After the formation of pair-wise comparison matrix, computation of the criterion weights was done. The computation involves the following operations: (a) finding the sum of the values in each column of the pair-wise comparison matrix; (b) division of each element in the matrix by its column total (the resulting matrix is referred to as normalized pair-wise comparison matrix); and (c) computation of average of elements in each row of the normalized matrix, i.e., dividing the sum of normalized scores of each row by the number of criteria. These averages provide an estimate of the relative weights of the criteria being compared.[13]

For preventing bias thought criteria weighting the consistency ratio (CR) was used.

Estimation of the Consistency Ratio

The next step is to calculate a CR to measure how consistent the judgements have been relative to large samples of purely random judgements. The AHP deals with consistency explicitly because in making paired comparisons, just as in thinking, people do not have the intrinsic logical ability to always be consistent[14]. For estimating consistency, it involves the following operations: (a) Determination of the weighted sum vector by multiplying matrix of comparisons on the right by the vector of priorities to get a new column vector. Then, divide first component of new column vector by the first component of priorities vector, the second component of new column vector by the second component of priorities vector, and so on. Finally, sum these values over the rows; and (b) Determination of consistency vector by dividing the weighted sum vector by the criterion weights.

Once the consistency vector is calculated it is required to compute values for two more terms, i.e., lambda (λ) and the consistency index (CI). The value for lambda is simply the average value of the consistency vector. The calculation of CI is based on the observation that λ is always greater than or equal to the number of criteria under consideration (n) for positive, reciprocal matrices and $\lambda = n$, if the pair-wise comparison matrix is consistent matrix. Accordingly, $\lambda - n$ can be considered as a measure of the degree of inconsistency. This measure can be normalized as follows:

$$CI = (\lambda - n) / (n-1)$$

The term CI provides a measure of departure from consistency. To determine the goodness of C.I., AHP compares it by Random Index (RI) and the result is what we call CR, which can be defined as:

$$CR = CI/RI$$

Random Index is the consistency index of a randomly generated pair-wise comparison matrix of order 1 to 10 obtained by approximating random indices using a sample size of 500.[15] Table 20.2 shows the value of RI sorted by the order of matrix.

Table 20.2: Random Index

Order Matrix	*1*	*2*	*3*	*4*	*5*	*6*	*7*	*8*	*9*	*10*
R.I	0.00	0.00	0.58	0.9	1.12	1.24	1.32	1.41	1.45	1.49

The CR is designed in such a way that if $CR < 0.10$, the ratio indicates a reasonable level of consistency in the pair-wise comparisons; if, $CR > 0.10$, then the values of the ratio are indicative of inconsistent judgements. In such cases one should reconsider and revise the original values in the pair-wise comparison matrix.

Rasterization of Criteria Maps

Different criteria maps, viz., slope, landslide locations, geology, drainage, road proximity and LULC were converted into raster data environment for further analysis because in raster data format computation is less complicated than vector data format.

Integration of maps

After rasterization, these classified raster maps were integrated in raster calculator of ArcGIS and multiplying with weightage, final landslide hazard zonation map (Fig. 20.1) was prepared.

Results and Discussions

An effective criterion for landslide hazard zonation is given below in brief with their individual importance: (a) Slope is an important criterion in hilly terrain for landslide hazard zonation. The causes of landslides are usually related to instabilities in slopes which were triggered by heavy or prolonged rainfall. Steep slopes are disadvantageous because mass movement is driven by shear stress which is generated by the mass of the block acting under gravity down the slope. Slope < 15° are considered as gentle slope having high intensity of importance. Slope greater than 15° has been classified as moderate to low suitable areas (Table 20.3). (b) Geology is one of the major causative factors for slope instability. The major rock type observed in Uttarkashi is deformed granite and ramsu formation and others. In general granite is very hard[16] and resistant to erosion but in the case of Uttarkashi area, granite is highly jointed and sheared, therefore, has low suitability and metamorphic interbeded with thin layer of granite's is relatively less susceptible for landslide and erosion has higher intensity of importance (Table 20.3). (c) Landslide Locations experienced locations/areas are the potential sites for landslides in near future, if triggering factors, i.e., heavy or prolonged rainfall occurs again. On 18/19 September, 2010, rainfall, unprecedented in 60 years of record, turned into a massive disaster area. Spatial distribution map of landslide of September 2010 was prepared. Based on these landslide distribution patterns, the Uttarkashi tehsil area is divisible into two categories. These are areas having lowest hazardous and highest hazardous (Table 20.3). With the help of GPS take some GCP's to identify the stable and unstable area. (d) Drainage plays vital role in landslide occurring. In this study we found landslide occurred point near to drainage, so distance from drainage is an important factor. (e) Road Proximity: Road is an important factor in hazard zonation mapping because of the need to transport raw- products and finished materials. Construction of new road is expensive in hilly regions, thus being nearer to an existing road would be advantageous. The distance map shows the distance of each and every pixel in metres from the nearest road. (f) Land-Use Land Cover: According to Onagh *et.al.*[17], land-use is also one of the key factors responsible for the occurrence of landslides, since, barren slopes are more prone to landslides. In contrast, vegetative areas tend to reduce the action of climatic agents such as rain, temperature etc., thereby preventing erosion due to the natural anchorage provided by the tree roots and, thus, are less prone to landslides.

Scoring of Criteria

The scoring used in this study for each of the criteria map and their category at 9 point scale are given in Table 20.3:

Table 20.3: Scoring/Ranking of Criteria

Criteria	*Categories*	*Intensity of Importance*	*LHZ Suitability class*
Slope (Degree)	0<15	8	Very high suitability
	15-30	5	Moderate Suitability
	30-45	3	Low Suitability
	45-60	2	Very Low Suitability
	>60	1	Lowest suitability
Geology	Granite	9	Highest Suitability
	Sheli	8	Very High suitability
	Puga	7	High Suitability
	Metasedimentric	6	Moderate High Suitability
	Ramsuformation	5	Moderate suitability
LULC	Forest	9	Highest Suitability
	Settlement	8	Very high Suitability
	Agriculture	3	Low Suitability
	Barren	2	Very Low Suitability
	River	1	Lowest suitability
	Snow	0	
Drainage	<50	1	Very Low Suitability
	>50	9	Highest Suitability
Road Proximity	<50	3	Low Suitability
	>50	9	Highest Suitability
Landslide	<50	1	Very Low Suitability
	>50	9	Highest Suitability

With the help of the available criteria, a pair-wise comparison matrix has been developed (Table 20.4). After the formation of ratio matrix all criteria were normalised and weights have been computed for each criteria using pair-wise comparison method (Table 20.6).

Calculation of the Consistency Ratio

It is required to check whether our comparisons are consistent. Table 20.6 shows the determination of weighted sum vector and consistency vector.

Calculation of λ = (6.14+6.12+6.13+6.00+6.20+6.50)/6 = 6.18

Note: Lambda (λ) is the average of consistency vector.

Condition 1:

λ should be equal or greater than the number of criteria under consideration. The value calculated above satisfies this condition.

Calculation of CI:

CI = (λ – n)/ (n – 1)

= (6.18-6.00) / (6-1) = 0.036

Calculation of the consistency ratio

Calculation of CR = CI/RI

= 0.036 / 1.24 (Since RI

= 1.24 for n=6) = 0.03

Condition 2:

CR (=0.03) <0.10 indicated a reasonable level of consistency in the

Table 20.4: Pair-wise Comparison Matrix

Criteria	*Pair-wise Comparison matrix*					
	Slope	*Landslide*	*Drainage*	*Geology*	*LULC*	*Road Proximity*
Slope	1	2	4	5	7	8
Landslide	0.5	1	2	4	5	7
Drainage	0.25	0.5	1	2	4	5
Geology	0.2	0.25	0.5	1	2	4
LULC	0.14	0.2	0.25	0.5	1	2
Road Proximity	0.13	0.14	0.2	0.25	0.5	1
Total	**2.22**	**4.09**	**7.95**	**12.75**	**19.5**	**27**

Table 20.5: Normalized Pair-wise Comparison Matrix and Computation of Criterion Weights

Criteria	*Normalized Pair wise Comparison MATRIX*						*Computation of Criterion Weights*
	Slope (a)	*Landslide (b)*	*Drainage (c)*	*Geology (d)*	*LULC (e)*	*Road Proximity (f)*	(a+b+c+d+e+f)/6
Slope	0.45	0.49	0.5	0.39	0.36	0.3	0.42
Landslide	0.23	0.24	0.25	0.31	0.26	0.26	0.26
Drainage	0.11	0.12	0.13	0.16	0.21	0.18	0.15
Geology	0.09	0.06	0.06	0.08	0.1	0.15	0.09
LULC	0.06	0.05	0.03	0.04	0.05	0.07	0.05
Road Proximity	0.06	0.03	0.03	0.02	0.02	0.04	0.03
Total	1	1	1	1	1	1	1

Table 20.6: Computation of Consistency Vector

Criterion	*Weight sum vector*	*Consistency vector*
Slope	[(1)(0.42) + (2)(0.26) + (4)(0.15) + (5)(0.09) + (7)(0.05) + (8)(0.03)]=2.58	2.58/0.42=6.14
Landslide	[(0.5)(0.42) + (1)(0.26) + (2)(0.15) + (4)(0.09) + (5)(0.05) + (7)(0.03)]=1.59	1.59/0.26=6.12
Drainage	[(0.25)(0.42) + (0.5)(0.26) + (1)(0.15) + (2)(0.09) + (4)(0.05) + (5)(0.03)]=0.92	0.92/0.15=6.13
Geology	[(0.2)(0.42) + (0.25)(0.26) + (0.5)(0.15) + (1)(0.09) + (2)(0.05) + (4)(0.03)]=0.54	0.54/0.09=6.00
LULC	[(0.14)(0.42) + (0.2)(0.26) + (0.25)(0.15) + (0.5)(0.09) + (1)(0.05) + (2)(0.03)]=0.31	0.31/0.05=6.20
Road proximity	[(0.13)(0.42) + (0.14)(0.26) + (0.2)(0.15) + (0.25)(0.09) + (0.5)(0.05) + (1)(0.03)]=0.195	0.195/0.03=6.50

pair-wise comparisons. Therefore, the values obtained satisfy the said conditions, which denote that the weights obtained are agreeable.

Landslide Hazard Zonation Map

All three criteria maps were converted into raster format, so that for each pixel, a score can be determined.[18] All the criteria maps

Table 20.7: Distribution of area under different hazard zones in Study Area

Landslide Hazard Zones	*Area*		*Remarks*
	sq. km	*in %*	
Very High	332.87	20.15	Unsafe for development works
High	102.09	6.18	
Moderate	279.68	16.93	Local vulnerable zone of instability
Low	141.74	8.58	Safe for development works
Very Low	795.60	48.16	
Total Area	**1652.63**	**100**	

were integrated and overlaid and final landslide hazard zonation map (Fig. 20.3) was prepared by the following formula:

Landslide Hazard Zonation Map= ε [criteria map * weight]
Landslide Hazard Zonation Index = [(Slope)*0.42] + [(Landslide*0.26] + [(Drainage)*0.15] + [(Geology)*0.09] + [(LU/LC)*0.05] + [(Road proximity)*0.03]

The landslide hazard zonation map (Fig. 20.1) reveals that the study area is divisible into five different hazard zones. These are "very low hazard", "low hazard", "moderate hazard", "high hazard" and "very high hazard" lands. Table 20.6 registers the area under these different categories of hazard zones. About 42 per cent area of the municipal are falls under very high (15%) to high (27%) landslide hazard zones, 19.66 per cent under moderate and about 38.34 per cent falls under low (17.34%) to very low (21%) landslide hazard zones. The study suggests that only 38.34 per cent area of the Almora municipal area is safe for development activities, about 19.66 per cent is vulnerable zone for instability and a large part i.e., 42 per cent is not safe for development works, i.e., mainly engineering works.

Conclusion

Landslide hazard can cause serious damages for people and social economic progress. Therefore, tools for landslide mapping on regional/local scale are needed in order to remedy and prevent these damages. Conventionally, landslide hazard zonation maps

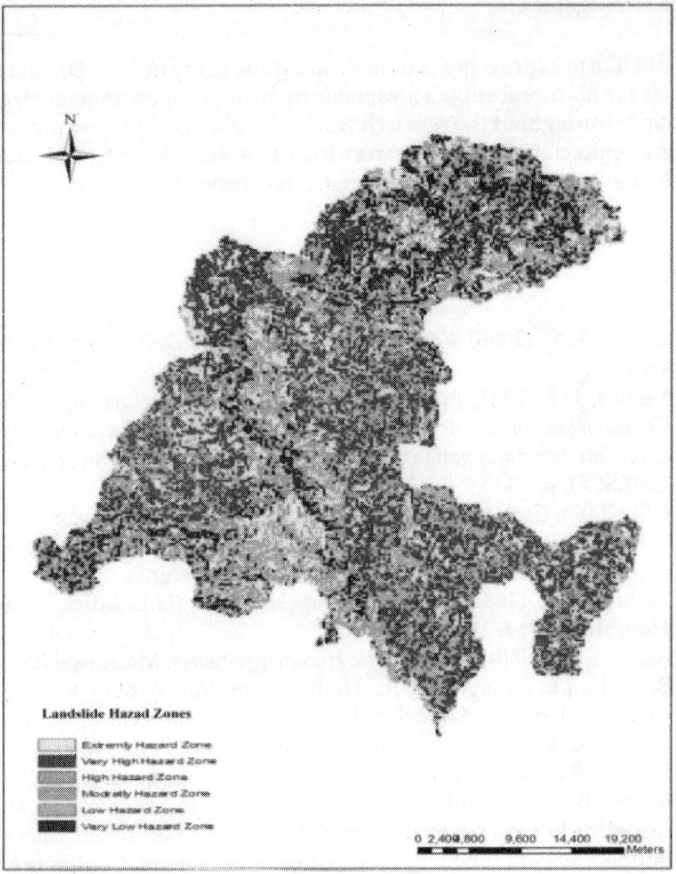

Fig. 20.1: Landslide Hazard Zonation Map of the Uttarkashi Tehsil Area, Uttarakhand, India

are prepare in various ways, which needed a lot of time and effort to obtain the final results, but the GIS based AHP technique is very simple and flexible which can be used for quick analysis of various hazard zones. It provides comprehensive and satisfactory database of availability of suitable land for developmental work. In case of the these tehsil area, the study reveals that a large part of study area (i.e. 20.15%) is unsafe and is not suitable for construction works, 16.93 per cent area is vulnerable for instability and only 48.16 per cent area is safe.

Acknowledgements

I would like to express my extremely gratitude to my mentor Dr. Manish Kumar for his moral support, valuable motivation, encouragement, and guidance throughout the research work. I would also like to express my sincere appreciation to my dearest friends Abha, Mukesh, and Malay for their suggestions and encouragements whenever I needed.

Notes

1. Chang, K.T., (2006). *Raster Data Analysis*, New Delhi: Tata McGraw Hill.
2. Vernes, D.J., 1984, *International Association of Engineering Geology Commission on Landslides and Other Mass Movements on Slopes: Landslide hazard zonation: a Review of Principles and Practice*, Paris: UNESCO, p. 63.
3. GSI (2009). *Geological Survey of India*. www.portal.gsi.gov.in.
4. Wilson, J.P., and A.S. Fortheringham, (2008). *The Handbook of Geographic Information Science*, Blackwell Publishing.
5. Fechner G.T., (1860). *Elements of Psychophysics*, (H.E. Adler, Trans.), Holt, Rinehart & Winston.
6. Saaty, T.L., (1980). *The Analytic Hierarchy Process*, McGraw-Hill.
7. Barredo, J.I., Benavidesz, A., Herhl, J., and Van Westen, C.J., 2000, Coparing heuristic Landslide hazard assessment techniquies using GIS in the Tirajana basin, Gran Canaria Island, Spain, *International Journal of Applied Earth Observation and Geoinformation*, 2 (1), pp. 9-23.
8. Mwasi, B., 2001, Land-use conflicts resolution in a fragile ecosystem using Multi-Criteria Evaluation (MCE) and a GIS based Decision Support System (DSS), In Proceedings International Conference on Spatial Informaton for Sustainable Development, Nairobi, Kenya: FIG-International Federation of Surveyors, p. 11.
9. Nie, H.F., Diao, S.J., Liu, J.X., and Huang, H., 2001, The application of remote sensing technique and AHP-fuzzy method in comprehensive analysis and assessment for regional stability of Chongqing City, China. In Proceeding 22and International Asian Conference on Remote Sensing, Singapore: University of Singapore, pp. 660-665.
10. Yagi, H., 2003 Development of assessment method for landslide hazardness by AHP. *Abstract Volume of the 42and Annual Meeting of the Japan Landslide Society*, pp. 209-212
11. Nagarajan, R., A. Mukherjee, A. Roy and M.V. Khire, 1998, Temporal remote sensing data and GIS application in landslide hazard zonation of part of Western ghat, India, *International Journal of Remote Sensing*, 19(4), pp. 573-585.

12. Hassanzadeh, N. M., (2000). *Landslide Hazard Zonation in Shalmanrood Watershed.* Dissertation, University of Tehran.
13. Malczewski, J., (1999). *Criterion Wighting,* New York, USA: Wiley.
14. Saaty, T.L., (1994). *Fundamentals of Decision Making and Priority Theory with the Analytic Hierarchy Process,* RWS Publications.
15. Saaty, T.L., (2000). *Fundamentals of Decision Making and Priority Theory,* 2nd ed., RWS Publications.
16. S. Singh, (2003). *Rocks,* Prayag Pustak Bhawan, pp. 93-112.
17. Onagh, M., Kumra, V.K., Rai P.K. (2012). Landslide Susceptibility Mapping in a Part of Uttarkashi District (India) by Multiple Linear Regression Method, *International Journal of Geology, Earth and Environmental Sciences,* Vol. 2 (2), pp. 102-120.
18. Jain, K., & Subbaiah, V.Y., 2007, Site suitability analysis for urban development using GIS, *Journal of Applied Sciences,* 7(18), pp.2576-2583.

21

Role of UBUNTU (Open Source Operating System) and QGIS (Open Source GIS Software) in Application of Remote Sensing and GIS in Geographical Studies

Daljit Singh Chhiller

Introduction

Importance of Remote Sensing and Geographical Information System in Geographical Studies

Remote Sensing (RS) is the technology of sensing or acquiring information about other objects or area without being in contact. Electromagnetic radiation either from the sun, earth or from any instrument interacts with objects on the earth, in atmosphere or in space. This interaction results in some unique patterns known as spectral signature. The remote sensing technology records these interactions and helps us in identifying different features on earth. Use of different platforms, different radars and sensors made it possible to have almost real time monitoring of earth and its features. Traditionally, primary data was generated by Geographers, using field observation techniques. As a result, the number of units under observation, geographical area of research, and time period were limited. RS equipped geographers to expand the spatial-temporal coverage of area of research. The repetitive data recorded by RS satellites made it possible to monitor changing geographical patterns like growth of towns, area flooded by rivers, movement of cyclones etc. Use of different sensors and radars at different platforms made it possible to collect information in those spectral bands which were not possible by naked eyes. The vehicles used in RS are able to generate information from dense forests etc., which were earlier inaccessible to geographers. Earlier surveys were conducted for specific purposes only. Now a single satellite image or an aerial photograph is ocean of geographical information.

Geographical Information System (GIS) is the system of acquisition, storing, processing, analyzing and presentation of geo-referenced data. It is basically a computer based application which helps in analyzing large amount of location based data on maps. GIS is capable of storing large amount of data, this data may be updated with the help of remote sensing and census data. The ability to process large amount of data enabled geographers to expand spatial-temporal coverage of the research area. Maps prepared in GIS may be easily updated, edited, and analyzed to prepare maps based on current data. Remote Sensing and GIS are the two Geo-Spatial Technologies, increasingly used in Geographical Research by geographers to keep themselves updated and take the benefits of the technology. There is a wide scope of application of these two techniques in geographical research in field surveying, agriculture geography, urban planning, resource geography, disaster management etc.

The high cost of the software's used to apply these technologies to geographical data did not allow expansion of its use in India except in the projects which are financed by some funding agencies. Moreover, its use for individual research by teachers and students in absence of license access to these technologies was highly restricted. Even if a license is purchased by the educational institution, its maintenance cost further inhibits is use. The present chapter highlights how QGIS open source GIS software helps in overcoming these problems. By adopting UBUNTU a open source operating system and QGIS a open source GIS software any department of Geography can establish a GIS laboratory where not only teachers but students may learn its applications and start using it in a big way. This will enable geography teachers, researchers, and students to understand, analyze and highlight the importance of various indicators of development.

UBUNTU—Open Source Operating System

Introduction: An operating system is a bundle of commands written in computer language to operate the computer. If we leave the history behind and talk about the computers of our time, we are using desktops. We learnt MS-DOS operating system in which commands need to be kept alongside while using the system. Then we learnt the Microsoft Windows, which was user friendly and easy to learn and use. A bundle of utilities were brought in the form of MS-Office to meet the requirement of typing and data utilities. Windows is a proprietary operating system, which need to be purchased along with the desktop. This increases the cost of the desktop. The OS comes with a key and license to use. Once purchased, it needs to be maintained through AMC'S. As a result, use of licensed version is limited to those who can afford to pay or have access in laboratories. Even in institutes it become very difficult to maintain the license conditions. Due to various reasons like virus, deletions of some system file or some mischief by a student the OS keep on crashing. As a layman we have no solution, but to call an expert. It will cost some amount to get the machine start working again. In the process very precious time is lost. Many a time it happens while conducting the practicals. The situations were really embarrassing. Recently, the supports to the older version have been withdrawn. The old desktops are not able to support the newer versions of windows, due to hardware specification requirements. So, the solution for such problems is open source operating systems and one of them is **UBUNTU.**

UBUNTU—open source operating system: UBUNTU is an open source operating system, where we need not to buy a license to use it. It is free to download from their website http://www.ubuntu.com/. The user face is similar to windows and easy to use. We simply need to keep a bootable DVD or pen drive, and we can easily reload it as many time as we need to do it.

Hardware Requirements for UBUNTU: We can easily install UBUNTU in a Pentium 4, and 4.1 GHz system with 256 MB RAM.

Dual OS in a single desktop: If sufficient hard disk space is available, one can install UBUNTU in a desktop along with windows by partitioning the hard disk. This will be very useful while switching from windows to UBUNTU. If there is some problem and urgency, one can switch back to the windows. Once we are familiar to it, we can always stop using the windows.

Why we should use UBUNTU: The following reasons made us to change the operating system and start use of UBUNTU:

1. UBUNTU is license free; we need not to spend money on the purchase of operating system along with the machine.
2. Update is available online and free of cost.
3. Help is available online; one can just search for the problem.
4. At present it is free from all sorts of viruses, so there will be no more virus headaches. One can use the pen drive in as many as desktops. One can check for executable file and delete them as soon as the pen drive is inserted back again. It supports window generated files, as well as creates files which can be easily opened in windows.
5. Using UBUNTU software manager, one can download UBUNTU supported software's.
6. *Libreoffice*: In UBUNTU the MS Office is replaced by Libreoffice. It contains programmes like Libreoffice Writer, Libreoffice Impress, Libreoffice Draw and Libreoffice Calc.
7. *Libreoffice Writer*: It is used to write documents, texts, reports etc. It supports all file extensions of word. After writing the text, we can save it as a document so that it can be opened in MS Office also. Other file extensions are also available like pdf, text, and xml. By default it will save as odt. It will not be possible to open it in MS Office.
8. *Libreoffice Impress*: It is used to prepare presentations. It is similar to power point of MS Office. It is necessary to take care of saving the presentation in ppt extension to use it in MS Office.
9. *Libreoffice Draw*: It is a tool used for drawings.
10. *Libreoffice Calc*: It is a equivalent to excel sheet of MS Office, where one create tables, manipulate data, compute various mathematical and geometrical calculations and draw graphs.
11. *QGIS Software available on UBUNTU*: Another most important reason to use UBUNTU is that GIS software, QGIS is available in UBUNTU operating system. GIS software's are demand of time in Geography, and we can freely use GIS software as per our requirement, at institute and even at home.

QGIS: Quantum Geographical Information System

Open Source Software: GIS software's commonly used, supplied by the company with a soft and a hard key. So, license with a fixed number of users is to be purchased before using these GIS software's. The use of licensed software's is limited to those machines where it is installed along with the hard keys. One cannot use licensed software's in other desktop/ laptop at home or within the institute premises. QGIS, open source software has no such attachments of license. One can download it from their website www.qgis.org, on a bootable CD or pen drive free of cost and install on as many desktops/ laptop, whether in the institute or at home. One needs not to pay any license fee. In this way one can save the cost of software for the laboratory or personal use.

Annual Maintenance Cost (AMC) required: In case we are using licensed GIS Software, we need to spend some money on annual basis to avail maintenance services. This will further increase the burden of cost on the institute or an individual. If we will not pay AMC, the support will be withdrawn. The problem becomes unbearable once the systems are formatted due to some operating system problem. It is next to impossible to reinstall the licensed GIS software's. In case of QGIS, there is no need of AMC, if it is used on UBUNTU operating software. One can again install it without anyone's help.

Open for all to use on any system: QGIS can be used by any one, on any system in the institute or at home. Teachers and students can work on it in the laboratory and at home if they have a system at home. This open source GIS software provides the flexibility of its use at different places, by any number of persons, and on any machine.

Available for Window, UBUNTU and developing for Android: QGIS is available for Windows operating system, UBUNTU and they developing for Android. Once the Android version will be available, use of desktops and laptops will be restricted. One can work on it through smart phones even while travelling.

All Plugins are Available: The cost of other GIS software's depends on the number of applications. Only those applications can be used for which you have paid. Other functions will not work. The QGIS is *a complete bundle with all plug-in* available for educational purposes.

Conclusion

In the fast changing and costly technology, it is necessary for teaching institutes to use cost effective software's. Moreover, the students are increasingly using computers, so to keep the cost of studies lower we need to shift from propriety operating systems and software's to open source software's. *UBUNTU* as an operating system and *Libreoffice and QGIS* as software's offer an option to switch over to save the cost and to increase the accessibility. The use of UBUNTU and QGIS allow access to large number of Geographers and researchers, who were deprived of the technology till now. This will not only lead to application of GIS and Remote Sensing technology in different fields of Geography but also increase the temporal and spatial coverage of research work. The most important aspect is that it will allow students to use data provided by Indian satellites, which they were not able to use till now. Kalindi college is going to start honours course in geography, can save cost of GIS laboratory by adopting UBUNTU and QGIS.

References

1. website http://www.ubuntu.com/.
2. website http://www.qgis.org
3. Dr. Ming-Hsiang Tsou and Jennifer Smith (2011) : Free and Open Source Software for GIS education, A White Paper from Department of Geography, San Diego State University.
4. U. Niethammer, S. Rothmund, U. Schwaderer, J. Zeman, M. Joswig (2011) : Open Source Image-processing Tools for Low-cost UAV-based Landslide Investigations, published in International Archives of the Photogrammetry, *Remote Sensing and Spatial Information Sciences*, vol. xxxviii-1/c22,2011.
5. Stefan Steiniger, Andrew, J.S. Hunter (2013) : The 2012 free and open source GIS software map—A guide to facilitate research, development, and adoption, published in *Computers, Environment and Urban Systems*, Volume 39, may 2013, pages 136–150. available online from 10 november 2012
6. P. K. Yadav, Mohnish Kapoor, Kiranmay Sarma (2012): Land-Use Land Cover Mapping, Change Detection and Conflict Analysis of Nagzira-Navegaon Corridor, Central India Using Geospatial Technology, published in *International Journal of Remote Sensing and GIS*, Volume 1, Issue 2, 90-98.

22

Global Environmental Changes and Indian Ocean Dipole

Netrananda Sahu

Introduction

Global environmental change poses threat to the biophysical systems of the earth. The scientific and research community recognizes the growing need for better understanding of the multifaceted and complex linkages of global environmental changes (including global warming, climate change, and seal level rise) and human habitat, livelihood, and health through climate variability. Climate variability affects virtually all natural systems and human activities. Areas of direct climate impact include agriculture, water quantity and quality, ecosystems, air quality, hydrology and human health (Aceituno 1988; Mechoso and P′erez Iribarren 1992; Marengo 1995; Chiew *et al.*, 1995; Garc′ia and Vargas 1998; Kaplan *et al.*, 1998: Goswami *et al.*, 2006). Understanding and potentially predicting climate changes is therefore needed for affected population, and also to decision-makers within government and industry for resource management and hazard mitigation. Climatc variations may have natural or human-induced causes (Richey *et al.*, 1989; Bang 1995; Vecchi *et al.*, 2006). Improving the understanding of these two causes is achallenging research and societal issue. Also the large-scale and long-term climate variations may be linked to variations in local weather quantities such as temperature, precipitation, cloud cover and storminess, as well as in atmospheric carbon dioxide, ozone, and water vapour (Hastenrath, 1990; Mechoso and

P′erez Iribarren, 1992; Genta *et al.*, 1998; Robertson and Mechoso 1998; Mudelsee *et al.*, 2003). Understanding these links across scales is another major issue.

Anthropogenic activities increasingly affect the structure, process and functioning of ecosystems (Vecchi *et al.*, 2006). It is now clear that every social challenge is in some aspects linked to environment, and that every environmental challenge is in some aspects influences the social ecosystem. Global environmental change is therefore a major contemporary driving force for the socio-economic transformation, and its impacts are expected to influences the entire human society with the global warming stress (Nakamura *et al.*, 2009) in the coming decades. Global change refers to planetary-scale changes in the earth system. The system consists of the land, ocean, atmosphere, poles, life, the planet's natural cycles and deep earth processes, and influence one another. The earth system now also includes human system, so now global change also refers to large-scale changes in society. Until the evolution of IOD, traditional ENSO was treated as the main driving forces of the tropics.

Linkages between Global Environmental Changes and IOD

The Indian Ocean dipole is a coupled ocean–atmosphere phenomenon (Saji *et al.*, 1999) observed in the Indian Ocean in the form of an east-west dipole in the sea surface temperature (SST) anomalies. The Indian Ocean Dipole Mode Index (IODMI) is defined as the difference in SST anomaly between the tropical western Indian Ocean (50–70°E, 10°S–10°N) and the tropical south-eastern Indian Ocean (90–110°E, 10°S-equator). A positive IOD (pIOD) phenomenon is characterized by cooler than normal water in the tropical eastern Indian Ocean and warmer than normal water in the tropical western Indian Ocean (Saji *et al.*, 1999).

A negative IOD (nIOD) is characterized by warmer than normal water in the tropical eastern Indian Ocean and cooler than normal water in the tropical western Indian Ocean. The IOD usually begins to develop in boreal summer, peaks in fall, and decays rapidly in winter, which is seasonally modulated by the Asian monsoon wind and the Indian Ocean rim countries (Saji *et al.*, 1999; Xiang *et al.*, 2011). Ashok *et al.*, (2001) suggested that the Indian Ocean dipole mode plays an important role as a modulator of the Indian monsoon rainfall and influences the Indian summer monsoon-ENSO relationship.The recently discovered IOD mode (Saji *et al.*, 1999; Webster *et al.*, 1999; Fischer *et al.*, 2005) has considerable influence on the climates of many regions around the globe (Saji *et al.*, 1999; Ashok *et al.*, 2001; Guan and Yamagata, 2003; Saji and Yamagata, 2003).The instrumental record of climate variability in the tropics is essentially limited to the last few decades during which the global environmental changes has been noticed, however, the stable isotopic composition of living corals provides an effective means for extending the instrumental observations (Urban *et al.*, 2000, Pfeiffer and Dullo 2006; Abram *et al.*, 2007).

Techniques and Modelling for Understanding of IOD and Global Environmental Changes

The changes in the SSTs during the IOD phenomenon are found to be linked with the similar changes in the surface winds and rainfall. During the peak phase of the pIOD Equatorial winds change direction from westerlies to easterlies that creates heavy rainfall over the western Indian Ocean, i.e. East Africa and very less rainfall over the eastern Indian Ocean, i.e. Indonesia (Rao *et al.*, 2002). This is quite similar that of Bjerknes type of air-sea interaction in the tropical Pacific (Bjerknes 1969). Saji and Yamagata (2003) claimed that IOD has climatic impacts on several regions remote from the Indian Ocean. They found that there is a strong correlation of IOD events over Europe, northeast Asia, North and South America and South Africa (Saji and Yamagata 2003). Black *et al.*, (2003) and Clark *et al.* (2003) have demonstrated that that IOD modulates rainfall over few African countries during boreal fall.Like the case of ENSO, the Coupled General Circulation Models (CGCMs) are very useful in predicting IOD. Wajsowicz (2005) has succeeded to predict IOD at three months' lead time with the help of NASA Seasonal-to-Interannual Prediction Project (NSIPP). Luo *et al.* (2007) have provided a higher skill of predictability of IOD using SINTEX-F for a four months lead time.

The growth of the IOD depends on a positive feedback mechanism between anomalous equatorial easterly winds (Rao *et al.*, 2002), upwelling equatorial, thermocline changes in response to the equatorial winds and coastal Kelvin waves (Feng and Meyers, 2003) reducing the thermocline depth and sea surface temperature off the coast of Sumatra, and the atmospheric dynamical response to the subsequently reduced convection, heat content and sea level anomalies (Rao *et al.*, 2002), outgoing long-wave radiation anomalies (Behera *et al.*, 1999). The ocean Rossby waves are essential in linking the anomalous wind and SST off Sumatra and subsurface temperature variations in southwest Indian Ocean (Feng and Meyers, 2003; Xie *et al.*, 2003; Gualdi *et al.*, 2003; Yamagata *et al.*, 2004).

Interactions of ENSO and IOD

The ENSO and IOD along with Asian Monsoon and other local patterns have influenced the climate pattern of Indian Ocean rim countries. IOD, ENSO and ENSO Modoki have wide range of environmental and socio-economic impacts on the global to regional climate. The basin-wide warming during the ENSO (Charles *et al.*, 1997; 2003) events and similar atmospheric circulations in the Indian Ocean is easier to understand and predict. The mechanism of interactions between ENSO and IOD cannot be explained easily. The interaction between IOD and ENSO can be explained through the zonal Walker circulation (Yamagata *et al.*, 2003). They claimed that Walker cell exists in the Indian Ocean only in the case of pure IOD events only. With the unprecedented occurrence of the IOD events from 2006-2008 also raises many questions about the IOD/ENSO relationship with weekening ENSO events years. Behera *et al.* (2006) have extensively studied the interactions between IOD and ENSO with the help of SINTEX-F coupled model. Meyers *et al.* (2007) in their impirical research stated that there are cases of independent existance of IODs. Sahu *et al.* (2013) from the impirical investigation found the independent existance of few cases of IODs impacts on extremely-low streamflow events in the Citarum river in Indonesia in their recent studies, however, most of the IOD events particularly pIOD events occurred along with the El Nino events, which needs to be further invesigated.

Impacts of IOD

From last few decades it has been seen that climate variability modes played important role for the large scale environmental and societal effects across the globe. With the unprecedented occurrence of thre IOD events from 2006-2008 also raises many questions about the IOD/ENSO relationship with weekening ENSO events years. The tropical Indo-Pacific region is the main driving force behind these modes. The east and south east Asia are influenced by Pacific dynamics along with Indian Ocean dynamics. Hence, this region is totally influenced by the climate change induced ocean–atmosphere variability modes.

Recent studies have found that IOD events have strong influence of the climate of East Asia (Saji and Yamagata, 2003), East Africa and Indonesia (Saji *et al.*, 1999; Behera and Yamagata, 2003; Black *et al.*, 2003; Conway *et al.*, 2007), Indian summer monsoon (Shukla and Paolino, 1983; Ashok *et al.*, 2001, 2007), Australia (Cai *et al.*, 2009), Brazil and the Mediterranean region (Saji and Yamagata, 2003; Yamagata *et al.*, 2004), the southeast Australian "Black Saturday" bushfire in the state of Victoria in February 2009 also caused by the positive IOD (Cai *et al.*, 2009). Associated with the pIOD, the normal convection situated over the eastern Indian Ocean warm pool shifts to the west and brings heavy rainfall over the east Africa, India, Bangladesh and Vietnam and severe droughts/forest fires over Indonesia, Australia and dry as well as hot summer in Europe, Japan, Korea and East China (Saji *et al.*, 1999). A negative IOD sea surface temperature pattern often results in an increase of rainfall over parts of Australia and Indonesia whereas droughts in East of Africa and Indian Subcontinent. Historically, ENSO has a strong relationship with Indian Monsoon (Bjerknes, 1969; Wright, 1979, Deser and Wallace, 1987; Charles *et al.*, 1997; Neelin *et al.*, 1998; Torrence and Webster, 1999; Charles *et al.*, 2003; Gadgil *et al.*, 2004; Swapna and Krishna 2008). However, in the last couple of decades the frequent IOD occurrence has weakened the ENSO and Monsoon relationship (Kumar *et al.*, 1999; Saji *et al.*, 1999; Webster *et al.*, 1999; Behera *et al.*, 1999, Behera and Yamagata, 2003).

Implications of IOD in Asian Countries

A number of studies have documented that the changes in the IOD exert great impacts on climate variability in South Asia, East Asia, and other regions (Ashok *et al.*, 2003, 2004; Saji and Yamagata 2003). Many IOD events in the recent past occurred independently of the El Nino/La Nina. Even independent effects of IOD and ENSO have been established in the Asian region though both events occurred in the same year at few occasions. The zonal oxygen isotopic gradient in the Indian Ocean coral records was significantly correlated with central Pacific sea surface temperature on different timescales (Abram *et al.*, 2007). Thus, it is likely that this 'coral dipole' was a product of strong ENSO-like teleconnections over the Indian Ocean, as opposed to being the result of unique Indian Ocean or monsoonal dynamics.

Concluding Remarks

From last few decades it has been seen that climate variability modes played important role for the large scale environmental and societal effects across the globe.The tropical Indo-Pacific region is the main driving force behind these modes. The east and south-east Asia are influenced by Pacific dynamics along with Indian Ocean dynamics. Hence, this region is totally influenced by the climate change induced ocean–atmosphere variability modes. The impact assessment analysis based on the previous studies shows that the extreme natural events are increasing from last few decades, though causes are still not scientifically proved, however, it is a fact that from 1990s onwards IOD dominants with frequent occurrence compared to ENSO in the climate modes history. However, its impact ranges from regional to global scale. The link of these economic and human losses have direct implications to the IOD/ENSO climate modes which needs further scientific investigations.

List of Abbreviation Used

IOD	Indian Ocean Dipole
IODMI	Indian Ocean Dipole Mode Index
ENSO	El Niño–Southern Oscillation
SST	Sea Surface Temperature
NSIPP	NASA Seasonal-to-Interannual Prediction Project.

References

Abram, N.J., Gagan M.K., McCulloch M.T., Chappell J., Hantoro W.S.

(2003) Coral reef death during the 1997 Indian Ocean Dipole linked to Indonesian wildfires, *Science*, 301: 952–955.

Abram, N., Gagen M., Liu Z., Hantoro W., McCulloch M., Suwargadi B. (2007) Seasonal characteristics of the Indian Ocean Dipole during the Holocene epoch, *Nature*, 445: 299–302.

Aceituno, P. (1988) On the fluctioning of the Southern oscillation in the South America sector, *Monthly Weather Review*, 116: 505–524.

Ashok, K., Guan Z., Yamagata T. (2001) Impact of the Indian Ocean Dipole on the relationship between the Indian Monsoon rainfall and ENSO, *Geophys. Res. Lett.*, 26: 4499-4502.

Ashok, K., Saji, N.H. (2007) On impacts of ENSO and Indian Ocean Dipole events on the sub-regional Indian summer monsoon rainfall, *Natural Hazards*, Volume 42, Number 2, pp. 273-285.

Ashok, K., Yamagata, T. (2009) Climate change: The El Niño with a difference. *Nature*, 461: 481-484.

Ashok, K., Guan, Z., Yamagata, T. (2003) Influence of the Indian Ocean Dipole on the Australian winter rainfall. *Geophys. Res. Lett.* 30, 1821 (2003).

Ashok, K., Guan, Z., Saji, NH., Yamagata, T. (2004) Individual and combined influences of ENSO and the Indian Ocean Dipole on the Indian summer monsoon. *J. Clim. 17*, 3141–3155.

Ashok, K., Behera, S.K., Rao, S.A., Weng H., Yamagata, T. (2007) El Niño Modoki and its possible teleconnection, *JGR-Ocean*, **112**, C11007, doi:10.1029/2006JC003798.

Black, E., Slingo J., Sperber K.R. (2003) An observational study of the relationship between excessively strong short rains in coastal East Africa and Indian Ocean SST. *Mon Weather Rev.*, 131:74–94.

Behera, S.K., Krishnan, S., Yamagata, T. (1999) Unusual ocean-atmosphere conditions in the tropical Indian Ocean during 1994, *Geophys. Res. Lett.*, 26, 3001-3004, 10.1029/1999GL010434.

Behera, S.K., Yamagata, T. (2003) Influence of the Indian Ocean dipole on the Southern Oscillation, *J. Met. Soc. Japan*, 81, 1, 169-177, doi: 10.2151/jmsj.81.169.

Bjerknes, J. (1969) Atmospheric teleconnections from the equatorial Pacific, *Mon. Wea. Rev.*, 97, 163-172.

Cai, W., Cowan, T., Raupach M (2009) Positive Indian Ocean Dipole events precondition southeast Australian bushfires, *Geophys. Res. Lett.*, 36, L19710, doi:10.1029/2009GL039902.

Charles, C.D., Hunter, D.E., Fairbanks, R.G. (1997) Interaction between the ENSO and the Asian monsoon in a coral record of tropical climate. *Science* 277, 925–928.

Charles, C.D., Cobb, K.M., Moore, M.D., Fairbanks, R.G., (2003) Monsoon–tropical ocean interaction in a network of coral records spanning the 20th century. *Mar. Geol.* 201, 207–222.

Chiew, F., Whetton, P., McMahon, T. (1995) Detection of climate changes in recorded runoff volumes in South-east Australian rivers, *International Journal of Climatology,* **13**: 643–653.

Clark, C.O., Webster P.J., Cole JE (2003) Interdecadal variability of the relationship between the Indian Ocean Zonal Mode and East African coastal rainfall anomalies. *J. Clim., 16:* 548-554.

Conway, D., Hanson C.E., Doherty R., Persechino, A. GCM simulations of the Indian Ocean dipole influence on East African rainfall: Present and future. *Geophys. Res. Lett.,* 34, L03705 (2007).

Deser, C., Wallace J.M. (1987) El Nino events and their relation to the Southern Oscillation:1925-1986, *J. Geophys. Res.,* 92, 14, 189-14, 196.

Feng, M., Meyers G. (2003) Interannual variability in the tropical Indian Ocean: a two-year time scale of IOD. *Deep-Sea Res.,* II 50:2263–2284.

Fischer, A.S., Terray P., Guilyardi E., Gualdi S., Delecluse P. (2005) Two independent triggers for the Indian Ocean Dipole/Zonal Mode in a coupled GCM. *J. Clim.,* 18, 3428–3449.

Gadgil, S., Vinayachandran, P.H., Francis, P.A., Gadgil, S. (2004) Extremes of the Indian summer monsoon rainfall, ENSO and equatorial Indian Ocean oscillation. *Geophys. Res. Lett.,* 31, L12213.

Garc'ia N.O., Vargas W.M. (1998) The temporal climatic variability in the Rio de la Plata basin displayed by the river discharges, *Climatic Change,* **38**: 359–379.

Genta, J.L., P'erez Iribarren G., Mechoso, C.R. (1998) A recent increasing trend in the streamflow of rivers in Southeastern South America, *Journal of Climate,* **11**: 2858–2862.

Goswami, B.N., Venugopal, V., Sengupta, D., Madhusoodanan, M.S., Xavier, P.K. (2006) Increasing trend of extreme rain events over India in a warming environment. *Science,* 314, 1442–1445.

Gualdi, S., Guilyardi, E., Navarra, *et al.* (2003) The interannual variability in the tropical Indian Ocean as simulated by a CGCM, *Climate Dynamics,* 20, pp. 567-582.

Guan, Z., Yamagata, T. (2003) The unusual summer of 1994 in East Asia: IOD teleconnections. *Geophys Res Lett.,* 30, DOI:10.29/2002 GL 016831.

Hastenrath, S. (1990) Diagnostic and prediction of anomalous river discharges in northern South America, *Journal of Climate* 3:1080–1096.

Kaplan, A., *et al.* (1998) Analysis of global sea surface temperature 1856–1991. *J. Geophys. Res.,* 103, 18567–18589.

Kumar, K.K., Rajagopalan, B., Cane, M.A. (1999) On the weakening relationship between the Indian Monsoon and ENSO, Science, 284, 2156-2159, doi: 10.1126/*Science*.284.5423.2156.

Luo, J.J., Masson, S., Behera, S.K., *et al.* (2007) Experimental forecasts of Indian Ocean dipole using a coupled OAGCM, *J.Climate,* 20, 10, pp. 2178-2190.

Luo, J.J., Behera, S.K., Masumoto, Y., Sakuma, H., Yamagata, T. (2008) Successful prediction of the consecutive IOD in 2006 and 2007. *Geophys. Res.* Lett., 35, L14S02.

Marengo, J.A. (1995) Variations and changes in South America streamflow, *Climatic Change,* **31**: 99–117.

Mechoso, C.R., P'erez Iribarren, G. (1992) Streamflow in Southeastern America and the Southern oscillation, *Journal of Climate,* 5:1535–1539.

Meyers, G., McIntosh, P., Pigot, L., Pook, M. (2007) The years of Niño, La Niña and interactions with the tropical Indian Ocean. *J. Clim.,* 20, 2872–2880.

Mudelsee, M., Börngen, M., Tetzlaff, G. and Grunewald, U. (2003) No upward trends in the occurrence of extreme floods in central Europe. *Nature,* 425, 166–169.

Nakamura, N., Kayanne, H., Lijima, H., McClanahan, T.R., Behera, S.K., Yamagata, T. (2009) Mode shift in the Indian Ocean climate under global warming stress, *Geophys. Res. Lett.,* 36, L23708, doi: 10.1029/2009GL040590.

Neelin, J.D., Battisti, D.S., Hirst, A.C., Jin, F.F., Wakata, Y., Yamagata, T., Zebiak, S. (1998) ENSO theory, *J. Geophys. Res.,* 103, 14, 261-14, 290.

Pfeiffer, M., Dullo, W.C. (2006) Monsoon-induced cooling of the western equatorial Indian Ocean as recorded in coral oxygen isotope records from the Seychelles covering the period of 1840–1994? *Quat. Sci. Rev.* 25, 993–1009.

Rao, A.S., Behera, S.K., Masumoto, Y., Yamagata, T. (2002) Inter-annual variability in the subsurface tropical Indian Ocean. *Deep-Sea Res II* 49:1549–1572.

Richey, J.E., Nobre, C., Deser, C. (1989) Amazon river discharges and climate variability: 1903–1985, *Science,* **246**: 101–103.

Robertson, A.W., Mechoso, C.R. (1998) Interannual and decadal cycles in river flows of Southeastern South America. *Journal of Climate,* **11**: 2570–2581.

Sahu N., Behera, S.K., Yamashiki, Y., Takara, K. and Yamagata, T. (2012) Large Impacts of Indo-Pacific Climate Modes on the Extreme Streamflows of Citarum River in Indonesia, *Journal of Global Environmental Engineering,* Vol.17, pp. 1-8.

Sahu, N., Behera, S.K., Yamashiki, Y., Takara, K., Yamagata, T. (20133) IOD and ENSO impacts on the extreme stream-flows of Citarum river in Indonesia, *Climate Dynamics,* doi:10.1007/s00382-011-1158-2, 39(7-8), 1673-1680.

Sahu, N., Behera, S.K., Ratnam, J.V., Silva, R.V., Parhi, P., Duan, W., Takara, K., Singh, R.B., Yamagata, T. (2014) El Niño Modoki connection to extremely-low streamflow of the Paranaiba River in Brazil, 2014: 42, 1509-1516, DOI 10.1007/s00382-013-2006-3.

Saji, N.H., Goswami, B.N., Vinayachandran, P.N., Yamagata, T. (1999). A dipole mode in the tropical Indian Ocean, *Nature,* 401, 360-363.

Saji, N.H., Yamagata, T. (2003) Possible impacts of Indian Ocean dipole mode events on global climate, *Climate Research,* 25, 151-169.

Saji, N.H., Yamagata, T. (2003) Structure of SST and surface wind variability during Indian Ocean Dipole Mode events: COADS observations. *J. Clim.* 2735–2751.

Shukla, J., Paolino, D. (1983) The southern oscillation and long-range forecasting of summer monsoon rainfall over India, *Mon.Wea. Rev.*, 111, 1830-1837.

Swapna, P., Krishnan, R. (2008) Equatorial undercurrents associated with Indian Ocean Dipole events during contrasting summer monsoons. *Geophys. Res. Lett.* 35, L14S04.

Torrence, C., Webster, P. (1999) Inter-decadal changes in the ENSO-Monsoon systems, *J. Clim.*, 12, 2679-2690, doi:10.1175/1520-0442 (1999)012.

Urban, F.E., Cole, J.E., Overpeck, J.T. (2000) Influence of mean climate change on climate variability from a 155-year tropical Pacific coral record. *Nature*, 407, 989–993 (2000).

Vecchi, G.A. *et al.* (2006) Weakening of tropical Pacific atmospheric circulation due to anthropogenic forcing. *Nature*, 441, 73–76 (2006).

Wang, B. (1995) Inter-decadal changes in El Niño onset in the last four decades, *J. Climate*, 8, 267-285.

Wajsowicz, R.C. (2005) Potential predictability of tropical Indian Ocean SST anomalies, *Geophys. Res. Lett.*, 32, L24702, doi: 10.1029/ 2005GL024169.

Webster, P.J., Moore, A.M., Loschinigg, J.P., Leben, R.R. (1999) The great Indian Ocean warming of 1997-98: Evidence of coupled oceanic-atospheric instabilities, *Nature*, 401, 356-360.

Weng, H., Ashok, K., Behera, S.K., Rao, S.A., Yamagata, T. (2007) Impacts of Recent El Niño Modoki on Droughts/Floods in the Pacific Rim during Boreal Summer. *Climate Dyn*, 29: 113-129. doi:10.1007/s00382-007-0234-0.

Wright, P. (1979) Persistence of rainfall anomalies in the central Pacific, *Nature*, 277, 371-374.

Xie, S.P., Annamalai, H., Schott, F.A., McCreary, J.P. (2003) Structure and mechanisms of South Indian Ocean climate variability. *J. Clim.*, 15:864–878.

Yamagata, T., Behera, S.K., Luo, J.J., Masson, S., Jury, M.R., Rao, S.A. (2004) Coupled Ocean-Atmosphere Variability in the Tropical Indian Ocean. "Earth Climate : The Ocean-Atmosphere Interaction" Wang, C., Xie, S.P., Carton, J.A. (ed.) *Geophysical Monograph*, 147, *American Geophysical Union*, pp. 189-212.

23

A Model of Sustainable Agriculture and Environmental Protection for an Agriculturally Rich District of Punjab

Neha Arora

Introduction

In Punjab, various legal and technological responses are directly or indirectly affecting the environment. The policies like free power supplies to farmers and subsidies on canal irrigation water have provided incentives for farmers to over use water in their production practices, thereby exacerbating the problems of groundwater depletion, burning of crop residue and declining soil fertility in different parts of the State especially pertaining to Patiala district. The different legal and policy responses and other technological responses surely has an impact on the use of various natural resources especially water and land in agricultural activities. Hence, in the chapter some of such responses are studied in greater details in order to assess the sustainability of agriculture in one of the rich agricultural district of Punjab, Patiala district. Patiala district, located in the south-eastern part of the State of Punjab truly suffers from the changes in environment due to its recurring agricultural practices especially sinking of ground water and reducing soil fertility. Negligible area under forest is also one of the major reasons for deteriorating soil and water condition in the district. Uncontrolled irrigation, monoculture of rice-wheat rotation, excessive usage of chemical fertilizers and insecticides and pesticides together with increasing area under high-yielding varieties of seeds are questioning the future sustainability of agriculture in the region. Therefore, it is essential to incorporate and develop, at this stage, a model for sustainable agriculture and environment protection for the future of agricultural development of the district or for any part of the country.

Understanding Sustainable Agriculture

Definition and Concept

The idea of sustainable agriculture has been around a long time. Since the very first crop was sown and animal was penned, farmers have tried to ensure that their land produces a similar or increasing yield of products year after back-breaking year; recent attempts to popularize the concept build on this tradition. Sustainable agriculture is the activity of growing food and fibre in a productive and economically efficient manner, using practices that maintain or enhance the quality of the local and surrounding environment-soil, water, air and living things.

One definition is as follows:

Sustainable agriculture is the use of farming systems and practices which maintain or enhance:

- The economic viability of agricultural production;
- The natural resource base; and

Other ecosystems which are influenced by agricultural activities. This definition can be supplemented by some fundamental principles of sustainable agriculture:

- That farm productivity is enhanced over the long term;
- That adverse impacts on the natural resource base and associated ecosystems are ameliorated, minimised or avoided;
- That residues resulting from the use of chemicals in agriculture are minimised;
- That net social benefit (in both monetary and non-monetary terms) from agriculture is maximised; and
- That farming systems are sufficiently flexible to manage risks associated with the vagaries of climate and markets.

Advantages of Sustainable Agriculture

Sustainable agriculture inherits ecological sustainability, economic sustainability and social sustainability that reflects the advantages of sustainable agriculture.

- *Ecological sustainability*: It encourages ecological sustainability by improving fertility of the soil, helps in water retention capacity, raising bio-diversity, controlling land and water pollution and preventing climate changes leading to global warming.
- *Economic sustainability*: Agriculture cannot be sustainable unless it is economically viable over the long term. It tends to avoid any risk of farmers to be exploited by mediators. The organic products are lucrative in nature and will earn higher profits to the farmers and will also help to generate employment.
- *Social sustainability*: Sustainable agricultural practices are based on local social customs, traditions, norms etc. and local people are more likely to accept them. It aims at enhancing indigenous knowledge of farmers by using their traditional know how and local innovation. It improves the food security by improving the quality and nutritional value of the food, and by producing a bigger range of produce throughout the year.

The model could be analyzed through the flow chart presented in Fig. 23.1. Sustainable agriculture is the need of the hour. It can be achieved only through the protection of our environment and in this effort a model is developed with the help of a flow chart.

Land, water and air needs to be protected from the ill effects of its over-exploitation for the fulfillment of the needs of human beings. Land/Agricultural land can be protected only through organic farming. Organic farming understands the principles of nature, which are self-sustaining developing systems. It respects the environment's own systems for controlling pests and diseases in raising crops and livestock, and avoids the use of synthetic pesticides, herbicides, chemical fertilizers, growth hormones, antibiotics or gene manipulation. Through its emphasis on high production, conventional agriculture has contributed to degrading

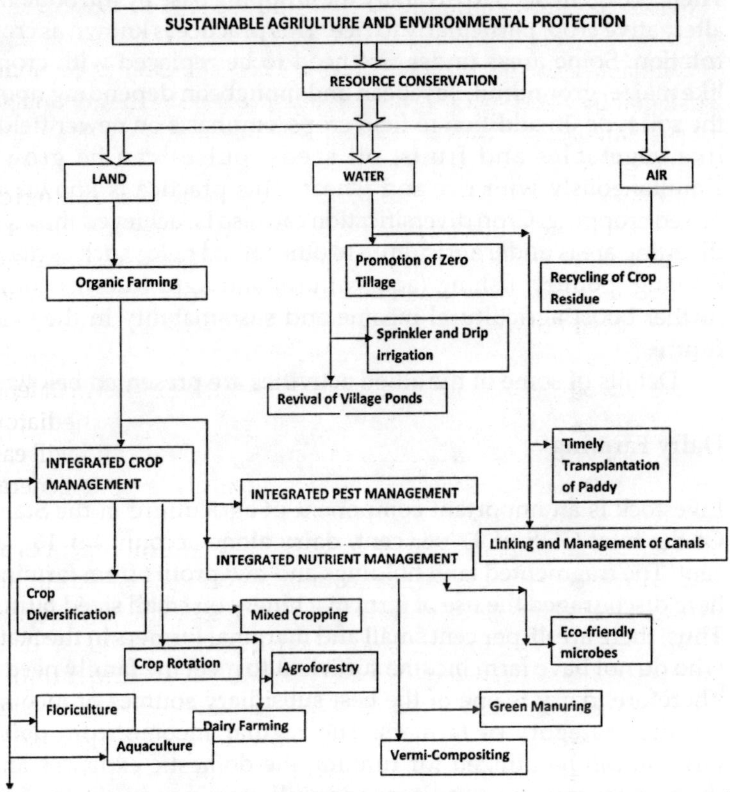

Fig. 23.1: A Model of Sustainable Agriculture and Environmental Protection

soil and water and reducing biodiversity, which is the key element in assuring food security. It includes integrated crop management, integrated nutrient management and integrated pest management.

Integrated crop management can be achieved through crop diversification, crop rotation and mixed cropping. Crop or agricultural diversification refers to the shift from one particular cropping system to a varied and multiple cropping system to stabilize farm income (particularly on small holdings) and protect our natural resources. The cropping pattern of Punjab is entirely dominated by only two crops rice and wheat. If such trend continues, our land and water resources will be further degraded and depleted and will not be able to sustain the production level.

There is urgent need to diversify the cropping base by introducing alternative crop, particularly to rice. This practice is known as crop rotation. Some areas under rice need to be replaced with crops like maize, groundnut, soyabean and mungbean depending upon the soil type. In addition to field crops, emphasis on newer fields like vegetables and fruits, oil seeds, pulses can be grown simultaneously with rice and wheat. This practice is known as mixed cropping. Crop diversification can also be achieved through diverting areas under agriculture to other allied fields such as dairy farming, poultry, fishing (aquaculture) and agro-forestry could further boost agricultural income and sustainability in the near future.

Details of some of the allied activities are presented below:

Dairy Farming

Livestock is an important component of agriculture in the State. Of the total GDP of 41 per cent, dairy alone account for 16 per cent. The fragmented land holdings and low profits from farming here discouraged the use of farm machinery on small sized farms. Thus, there are 45 per cent small and marginal farmers in the State who do not have farm income sufficient to meet the family needs. Therefore, dairy is one of the best subsidiary sources of income for such category of farmers. The regular income from dairy farming can be utilized for running the domestic expenses and thus consumption credit needs will decline. By involving themselves in dairy profession, the farmers can get regular gainful employment throughout the year. The fodder and feed produced on the farm are always cheaper. Additionally, farm yard manure obtained from animal waste can be put to use to improve the health of soil which is deteriorating day-by-day. It can be put to use for power and light by installing gobar gas plant in the villages.

Agro-Forestry System

This includes the following:

- Tree Species have ameliorative capacity for land restoration. The plantation adds sufficient residues to soil reduce run off and soil loss besides providing economic returns to the farmers.

- Multipurpose tree species can be introduced into agro-forestry systems to regenerate soil health without any appreciable investments.
- Ameliorative capacity of trees can be utilized by mixed cropping of trees with crops: the common system is called agro-forestry.

Over the years, farmers have been integrating tree, crop and animal components for sustenance. With the passage of time the agricultural component received priority over woody elements for sustaining self-sufficiency in foodgrains. The population pressure resulted in small holdings and consequently lesser number of trees of the farms providing food, fodder, fibre, fuel, fertilizer, fruit, etc. Agro-forestry is defined by some as a dynamic, ecologically-based natural farm management system that, along with agriculture and the integration of trees on farms, has many environmental benefits. Put simply, agro-forestry is using trees on farms. Trees can provide many products such as timber, fodder, fuelwood, medicines, and oils. It also helps to conserve soil, enhance soil fertility, and provide shelter belts for crops and fruit trees. As per climate conditions of Punjab the trees like Poplar, Eucalyptus (*safeda*), Dek (*dhrek*), Subabul, Kikar etc. can be successfully grown with the main crops Poplar is considered to be the best agro-forestry species for intercropping, having high rate of growth, short rotation, good economic returns and has less effect on intercrops. Farmers can plant this species on their cropland and within 6-7 years harvest and market it to the industry. During the *Kharif* season soybean, maize and grain legume can be grown while during the *Rabi* season wheat, potato, peas, etc., can grow successfully. The Punjab Agricultural University has released seven clones of poplar for growing in Punjab. These are PL-l, PL-2, PL-4, PL-5 (for the central plain region), PL-6, PL-7 (for semi-arid region) and PL-3 (both for central plain and semi-arid region[7]. Along with financial benefits to farmers, agro-forestry can play a vital role in balancing our ecology. Pollution can be mitigated by planting good biomass producing tree like *Arjun, Jamun, Karanj* , *Neem, Guava, Siris, Aonla* , *Babool, Sheesham*, Ironwood, Bamboo, and *Khamer* etc. in Punjab.

- These systems make available to people the required

quantity of timber, fruit, firewood, fodder etc. for which they traditionally depend on forests. Thus, the system helps in reducing the pressure on reserve forests and helps in their conservation and development. They optimize the physical conditions (permeability, water holding capacity and acidity or alkalinity) of soil to a level which is supportive for the growth and production of the standing crops. The tree species grown along with the crops in waterlogged areas helps maintain water-table up to a certain extent.

- *In situ* stabilization of high sand dunes by planting species like *Sarkanda* (*Saccharum munja*), *Ber* (*Zizyphus nummularia*), *Pahari Kikar* (*Prosopis juliflora*), *Jand* (*Prosopis cineraria*), *Subabul* (*Leucaena leucocephala*), *Kikar* (*Acacia nilotica*) along the periphery of fields to check the movement of sand by wind action.
- Reclamation of salt affected cum waterlogged area and bring them under plantation with species such as *Safeda* (*Eucalyptus* spp.), *Pahari Kikar* (*Prosopis juliflora*), *Kikar* (*Acacia nilotica*) and *Neem* (*Azadirachta indica*), which act as biopumps.
- In alluvial plain areas with brackish ground waters, Eucalyptus and Dek can also be grown, however, if there is assured availability of canal water, agriculture can be the best practice.

Agro-forestry has come-up as an important and economical component in land-use technologies which must be incorporated in the land management system of productive and unproductive land by the farmers of Punjab.

Integrated Nutrient Management

Integrated Nutrient Management is the key to organic farming. It uses management practices such as crop rotation, green manuring, recycling of residues, water management and so on, to ensure that available nutrients are used on the farm to grow crops and raise livestock. The most influential nutrient management techniques to enrich the fertility of the soil are:

Vermi-compost

Vermi composting denotes the use of earthworms for efficient bio-degradation of organic solid waste into organic manures. It is an environment friendly technology. Application of vermi compost improves soil health by supplying nutrients such as NPK, micro-nutrients and plant growth harmones. Besides efficient waste management, it provides excellent employment opportunities to small farmers through sale of worms and compost. Besides enriching the soil it also helps in reducing weeds from growing along the crop. Punjab farmers are opting for vermin composting technology in order to bring their crops under organic farming and saving the environment.

Promotion of Biofertilizers

Biofertilizers, like vermicomposting, are also eco friendly, low cost and maintain soil health. The commonly used biofertlizers are Rhizobium, Azotobacter and blue green algae. The first two occur naturally in soil and the latter generally grows on the surface of stagnant waters. Their efficient strains are being isolated, commercially grown, dried and made available in the market.

Resorting to Green Manuring

Green manures offer good alternative to costly chemical fertilizers. But, there is hardly any adoption of green manuring for paddy in Punjab. The scope for its adoption has further declined among farmers in spite of strong recommendations from the Punjab Agricultural University. Moreover, efforts are not being made at present to popularize this practice to boost production of crops while conserving soil fertility. Crops meant for green manuring have been identified by PAU and are given in the package of practices of crops. Such recommendations of PAU must be implemented to restore deteriorating soil health and to minimize the use of costly chemical fertilizers. Chemical fertilizers only provide one or two major nutrients, while the soils are becoming deficient in micro-nutrients. Our efforts should be on gradual reduction of chemical use while sustaining productivity. An important way is the use of bulky organic manures, which can improve the organic content of soil, thereby enhancing its physical, chemical and biological properties. Organic manures improve the nutrient balance. Bulky organic manures can be supplied through farmyard manure, farm compost, 'own compost, night soil, sludge, green manure, etc. Out of these sources only farmyard manure and green manure are widely used. Farmyard manure is prepared from dung, yet about 60 to 70 per cent of dung is used as fuel in rural areas. Also, the dung is not managed properly and the quality of manure is not good. This practice adds organic matter to the soil, improves the physical properties of soil in terms of aeration, porosity, water-holding capacity, and facilitates penetration of rainwater. Green-manure crops hold plant nutrients that would otherwise be lost by leaching. Leguminous green manure crops add nitrogen to the soil. This practice increases the availability of nutrients like phosphorus, calcium, potassium, magnesium and iron. In the rice-wheat cropping system the use of chemical fertilizers can be reduced by one-third if green-manuring is done before the rice crop. In Punjab and Haryana, wheat is harvested in April and rice is transplanted in June. The fields thus remain vacant for about two months, which can be utilised for green-manuring. Scientists have developed a package of practices for this. The green manure crop *dhaincha* (*Sesbaina aculeata*) should be sown in the second half of April using 10 kg of seed per acre. The dose of phosphate fertilizers meant for the rice crop should be applied in *dhaincha* at the time of sowing. This green-manure crop should be ploughed into the field at 6-7 weeks of age. The transplanting of rice seedlings can be done easily after a week.

Integrated Pest Management

The pest problem in Punjab agriculture has undergone a tremendous change due to adoption of green revolution technology. The widespread cultivation of short statured high yielding varieties of seeds, increase use of fertilizers and pesticides has accentuated pest problems. To mitigate the ill-effects of excessive and indiscriminate use of pesticides, particularly insecticides and herbicides, stress should be laid to popularize the judicious use of highly toxic chemicals. The excessive use of pesticides have not only polluted our environment, but posed several uncontrollable problems like the development of pesticide resistance in insects, weeds and pathogens, resurgence in pests and appearance of new pests in our crop ecosystem. The plant protection expenditure needs to be curtailed to minimize the cost of production. The judicious use of pesticides based on economic threshold values coupled with other non-chemical methods needs to be popularized to mitigate the ill-effects of pesticides and to harvest profitable yield of crops.

Conclusion

There is no doubt that Punjab government as well as premier institutions like Punjab Agricultural many other are leaving no stone unturned for sustaining agriculture in the state and preventing the environment as well. Numerous soil and water conservation measures can be used to achieve the above goals but the effort lies in the hand of public hence public participation at the grassroots level that is the village level is essential. But nevertheless at a macro-level agricultural development with focus on agricultural production has lead to ignoring of ecological balance and social scene in the state. To deal with the current situation, an agricultural strategy to concentrate on important areas for research to alleviate or eliminate these adverse effects for attaining sustainable development are identified as below:

- Development of sound land-use system based on soil capabilities.
- Water budgeting in relation to planting period, soil type and water availability.
- Development of management practices for use of marginal and poor quality irrigation water on long term basis.
- Long term impact of wheat – rice system on physical, chemical and biological properties of the soil.
- Monitoring excessive use of agro-chemicals in relation to ecology and economy.
- Integrated pest management systems for minimizing pesticide problems.
- Preservation of biodiversity, including an appropriate legislation.
- Encouraging crop diversification.

It seems that the prolonged dominant monoculture of wheat-rice rotation has now resulted in deceleration of agricultural growth as well as productivity per ha. Fatigue in technology may be another reason for this phenomenon as no major break through in the improvement of rice and wheat varieties has occurred since the green revolution. Development of high value products, namely fruits, vegetables, horticulture and floriculture offer good opportunities but adequate agro-processing facilities, marketing structure and other infrastructure are required to be build-up to render them successful. In brief, at present a strong political will, proper guidance by agricultural institutions and equally remunerative alternatives should be made available to substitute area under wheat and rice in the state. Organic farming, crop diversification and proper irrigation techniques like canal water management are the essential requirements for the depleting ground water and declining quality of soil in order to achieve sustainability of agriculture for present and future generations in the district.

References

Chand, R., 1999, *Agricultural Diversification in India: Potentials and Prospects in Developed Region*, New Delhi: Mittal Publications.

Chawla, J.K., Khepar, S.D., Siag, M. and Kumar, D., 2001, Quality status and optimum utilization of village pond water—A case study, *Indian Journal of Environment Health*, Vol. 43, No.3, pp. 114-122.

Dhaliwal, G.S., Arora, R. and Dhawan, A.K., (Eds.), 1999, *Emerging Trends in Sustainable Agriculture*, Commonwealth Publishers, New Delhi, pp. 104-131.

Dhaliwal, G.S., et al., (Eds.), 1998, *Ecological Agriculture and Sustainable Development*, Chandigarh: Indian Ecological Society and Centre for Research in Rural and Industrial Development.

FAO, 1994, *Development and Education Exchange Papers (DEEP): Sustainable Agriculture and Rural Development*: Part 1: Latin America and Asia, Rome, p. 5.

Hira, G.S., Chibba, I.M. and Singh, V., 2006, *Save Water: Save Punjab, Department of Soils*, Ludhiana: PAU.

Johl, S.S. and Ray, S.K., 2002, *Future of Agriculture in Punjab*, Chandigarh: Centre for Research in Rural and Industrial Development.

Punjab State Landuse Board, 2003, *News Letter*, November, Vol. 1, Punjab State Council for Science and Technology, Chandigarh, State of Environment, Punjab, 2007.

Punjab Agricultural University, Ludhiana, 2006, Department of Soil Science, Package and Practices for Crops of Punjab—*Kharif* and *Rabi*.

Singh, P., and Singh, I., 1996, Groundwater Depletion in Haryana and Punjab: A Threat to Sustainability in Agriculture, *Agricultural Situation in India*, Vol. 53 (7), pp. 485-490.

Singh, R.B., 1999, Land-use change, diversification of agriculture and agro-forestry in north-west India. In: Haque, T., (Eds.), *Land Use Planning in India*, New Delhi: National Centre for Agricultural Economics and Policy Research.

Singh, R.B., 2000, Environmental consequences of agricultural Development: a case study from the Green Revolution State of Haryana, India, *Agriculture Ecosystems and Environment, Elsevier Science*, pp. 97-103.

Sengupta, R., and Sinha, K., (Eds.), 2003, *Challenges of Sustainable Development: The Indian Dynamics*, New Delhi: Manak Publications.

Vanloon, W. Garry, Patil, S.G. and Hugar, L.B, 2005, *Agricultural Sustainability Strategies for Assessment*, New Delhi: Sage Publications, pp. 19 to 55.

24

Socio-economic Impact Assessment of Corridor Development Along the Delhi-Agra Axis (1991-2011)

Awadh Narayan Choubey and *Taruna Bansal*

Introduction

The contemporary process of urbanization has mainly been influenced by the 'Industrial Revolution'. The industrial towns that emerged were dynamic in nature characterised with consistent and continued growth unlike the settlement of the past. They witnessed major changes as a new set of production and process started operating at the global and regional levels; which started impinging on the cities. These phenomena, together with the development of modern means of transport and communication gave rise to a new urban system.

In this new system, the city became part of complex system consisting of interrelated urban regions rather than being an independent settlement. Such systems were now so inter-dependent that any major change in the population, economy, employment or service provisions in any one city had repercussions on other urban places (Pacione, 2001). This became more dominant with the spread of the functional influence of the cities beyond the limits of the build-up area. The advancement is directly associated with the development of the transportation links between these urban settlements. Sometimes an almost continuous ribbon of 'concrete structures' with humanity and occupation are found stretched nearly for hundreds of kilometers between two cities. Such *corridor cities* have emerged as one of the prevalent bi-centric urban systems at the regional level. For Roy (2000), the concept of 'urban corridors' is a model based on synthetic philosophy. These cities have a functional and a locational relationship, which provides them with holistic and competitive advantage over mono-centric cities.

Various studies have shown that some of these are still in the incipient stage of formation while others are quite advanced in form and connectivity. Whatever be the stage, these are an intricate web of growing 'modern urban cities' whose functional and locational relationship provide them comparative advantage over other mono-centric cities. Hence, corridor cities are an intricate web of cities that are the spaces of urban influence which are generated on the basis of spatial arrangement and functions of rural-urban duality. In simple words, urban corridors are primarily those contiguous areas which are spaced usually around large cities and towns articulating urban and rural liaison at various levels.

In the above framework the present chapter analysis one such corridor between Delhi and Agra and how the process of urbanization has influenced and changed the land cover as well as land-use along the axis from 1991 to 2011. At the outset some understanding is required of the term 'corridor', before its development potential can be determined, this constitutes the first section of the chapter. In the second section, the authors have tried to construct a conceptual model for the socio-economic impact assessment of corridor development along the Delhi-Agra axis from 1991 to 2011. The major land cover changes that have occurred along the corridor in last 20 years have been examined in the third section. The fourth section presents the conclusions drawn from the study.

SECTION 1
THEORETICAL BACKGROUND OF THE STUDY

Today, half the world's population lives in urban areas and by the middle of this century all regions will be predominantly urban. According to current projections of UN-Habitat, virtually the whole of the world's population growth over the next 30 years will be concentrated in urban areas. Although many countries have a hostile attitude to the process of urbanization because of its negative consequences, it appears that this process is inevitable throughout the world. But generally, the process is considered positive, as it brings a number of vital changes. These changes are in the employment sector (from agricultural activities to mass production and service industries); in societal values and modes of governance; in the structure and functionality of human settlements; in the spatial scale, density and activities of cities; in the social, cultural and ethnic composition of urban dwellers and also in the extension of democratic rights, particularly with relation to empowerment of women. As a result, cities are merging together to create urban settlements on a massive scale taking the form of either mega-regions or urban corridors or city-regions. They are emerging as the new engines of both global and regional economies reflecting the emerging links between urban expansion and new patterns of economic activity. (***State of the World's Cities Report, "Bridging the Urban Divide" UN Habitat Report, 2010/11)***

*The concept of corridor development is relatively old especially in developed regions but*still holds a great respect as an effective regional development strategy in the developing countries. In the industrially developed countries a new type of metropolitan expansion took place in the form of conurbation as a result of technological advancement and economic restructuring in the late nineteenth and early twentieth centuries.With the advent of the densely populated concentric industrial city about a century ago, city growth in a linear shape was presented as an alternative (Priemus and Zonneveld, 2003). This is nothing but an analogous in concept to the modern urban corridors though the latter are at much larger scale spatially. Priemus and Zonneveld refer to a corridor as consisting of bundles of infrastructure that link two or more areas (2003).

The term 'urban corridors' as a concept, first appeared when Geddes (1915) used it to refer to 'town aggregates' or 'city regions'. These are urban areas embracing several contiguous built up areas with ribbons of factories along the main roads out of the city spreading into neighbouring areas. In addition, transport system has been extended so that the metropolis is well connected with its hinterland. This gives rise to what Soria, Y. Mata (1882) calls a "ribbon city" – a conscious form of urban development. He felt that such linear settlements along transport routes would solve both urban and agrarian economic problems.

Berry (1967) identified a number of differing types of urban forms under the headings of 'ribbons'. The first type is the well-established shopping street, which usually runs from the nucleated centre to the lower order centers. The second form is the highway oriented ribbons. This is characterized by the assembly of motels, petrol pumps and restaurants. The third type is the urban arterial location, which consist of stores that require excessive space like furniture stores, building materials and lumber yards. Thus, ribbon development is an initial stage of corridor development wherein a narrow and linear growth takes place along the traffic artery with open land behind or on either side of the road.

Corridor cities are therefore, those bi-centric urban centers where close links have existed between two places of complementary function rather than simply on the basis of physical proximity. These cities may have the same hierarchy of functions but are functionally independent. And when considered together they make functionally integrated (though spatially separated) entities; in other words a 'truncated central place hierarchy' (Kidwai, 1968).

In simple words, corridors directly support the principles of urban integration, intensification and containment of regional urbanization. A corridor is not an elongated node rather it is a continuous link between two metropolitan nodes that provide a focus for public transport services and a arrangement along which high density mixed land-use can be promoted (Warnich and Verster, 2005).

SECTION 2

Study Area

The Delhi-Agra corridor extends from Delhi to Agra covering a distance of 208 Kms through the four districts of Haryana and Uttar Pradesh. In Haryana, parts of the Faridabad and Palwal districts form part of this axis. While in Uttar Pradesh some areas of Mathura and Agra districts fall under this axis. In total, this corridor comprises of 8 tehsils, 81 villages and 13 urban centres.

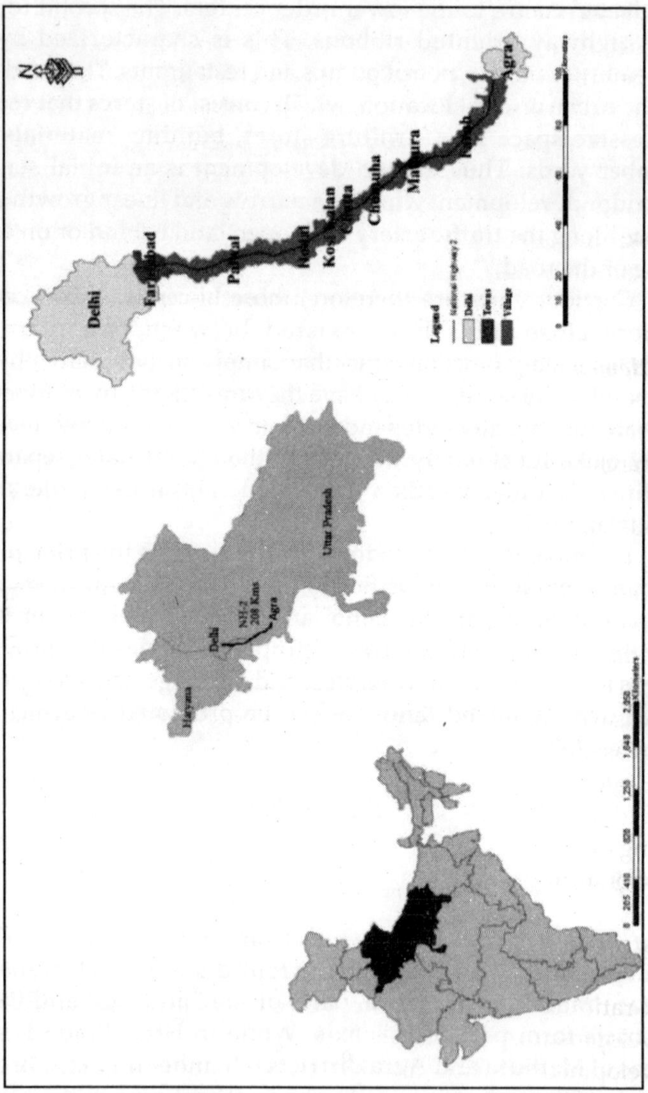

Map 24.1: Location of Delhi-Agra Corridor

Socio-economic Impact Assessment of Corridor Development along the Delhi-Agra Axis (1991-2011)

In this section of the chapter the authors have tried to analyze the impact of corridor development on the socio-economic conditions of the villages along the corridor. For this purpose at the initial stage the hierarchy of urban settlements has been examined. This will provide us a clear understanding that if such a development is possible along this axis. Further, the socio-economic indicators (sex-ratio, female literacy rate, workforce participation rate, female workforce participation rate, workers in agricultural and non-agricultural activities) have been investigated to comprehend this process and its impact along the corridor.

Settlement Hierarchy along the Corridor

On the basis of classification provided by the Census of India, the hierarchy of urban settlements along the corridor has been studied. The data in Table 24.1 clearly shows a lop-sided picture of urbanization in the region. But still leaves some hope as the concentration of population is class I cities is somewhat stagnant with minor alterations. Secondly the number of large towns is also somewhat constant (3 in 1991; 4 in 2001 and 2011) – Agra, Mathura, Faridabad; Palwal became Class I in 2001. The picture that emerges is that nearly 20 per cent of population resides in small and medium towns (Classes II, III, IV and V); the number of these towns have increased from 29 in 1991 to 35 in 2001 to 52 in 2011. This clearly indicates that minor growth centres can be developed along the corridor which can initiate the process of corridor development along the axis. This impact is distinctively visible in the social and economic indicators of the villages along the corridor.

Distribution of Sex-Ratio

Sex-ratio has always been regarded as a positive indicator of development. An improved sex ratio indicates a better level of development which is usually associated with urbanization. The data in Table 24.2 clearly indicates an improvement in sex-ratio. In 1991, nearly 58 per cent of villages had a sex-ratio in the range of 751 to 850; the per cent of villages in this range ha subsequently

Table 24.1: Hierarchy of Urban Settlements along the Corridor (1991-2011)

Classes	1991	2001	2011
Class I	77.73 (3)	79.54 (4)	78.14 (4)
Class II	2.64 (1)	3.13 (2)	5.08 (4)
Class III	8.05 (4)	6.53 (8)	7.74 (14)
Class IV	7.24 (12)	5.23 (10)	6.56 (22)
Class V	3.68 (12)	4.93 (15)	2.06 (12)
Class VI	0.65 (4)	0.64 (3)	0.42 (5)
Total	**100.00 (37)**	**100.00 (42)**	**100.00 (61)**

Note: The numbers in parenthesis denote the number of towns in each class.

Source: Data generated from Census of India (2011).

Table 24.2: Distribution of Sex-Ratio (1991-2011)

Range	Number of villages	Percent	Number of villages	Percent	Number of villages	Percent
<750	9	4.37	2	1.00	3	1.55
751-850	120	58.25	96	47.76	34	17.53
851-950	73	35.44	87	43.28	148	76.29
>950	4	1.94	18	8.96	9	4.64
Total	**206**	**100.00**	**203**	**100.00**	**194**	**100.00**

Source: Data generated from Census of India (2011).

decreased to 17.53 per cent. On the other hand the per cent of villages in the range 851-950 has increased from 35.44 in 1991 to 43.28 in 2001 and 76.29 in 2011. This shows that the process of corridor development has a positive impact on these villages as male selective migration is decreasing.

Distribution of Female Literacy Rate

Women education is also an important indicator of development. Studies worldwide have shown that there is a special relation between female education and development. In fact, if female schooling raises human capital, productivity and economic growth as much as that of male education than the gender gap in education is undesirable (Schultz, 1993). The above statement undoubtedly implies that progress in female literacy has a positive correlation with development. The data in Table 24.3 can be related to this and it can be opined that the corridor is experiencing affirmative influences of the process of urbanization.

Table 24.3: Distribution of Female Literacy Rate (1991-2011)

Range	1991		2001		2011	
	Number of villages	*Percent*	*Number of villages*	*Percent*	*Number of villages*	*Percent*
< 20 %	138	66.99	8	3.98	0	0.00
21 – 40 %	49	23.79	178	88.56	30	15.46
41 – 60 %	14	6.80	9	4.48	158	81.44
61 – 80 %	5	2.43	6	2.99	1	0.52
> 81 %	0	0.00	0	0.00	4	2.06
Total	**206**	**100.00**	**201**	**100.00**	**193**	**100.00**

Source: Data generated from Census of India (2011).

In 1991, nearly 67 per cent of villages have female literacy rates below 20 per cent, but the proportion has significantly decreased. In 2001 about 88 per cent villages had female literacy rates between 21 to 40 per cent and this figure too decreased as in 2011 most of the villages (approximately 81 per cent) had female literacy rates between 41 to 60 per cent.

Distribution of Workers

In today's globalised economy the proportion of workers engaged in formal market is an important sign related to a region's economic growth. Here in this chapter we have taken the workforce participation rate (WPR) of villages to comprehend that workers are working *in situ* or are migrating to nearby urban areas for jibs. Corridor development as a concept says that equal opportunities should develop along the axis as a result of regional urbanization. The data in Table 24.4 again confers that this particular axis is experiencing and witnessing development along with urbanization as workforce participation rates have shown improvement. This indicates that jobs are being generated and people are able to enter the labour market,

The most striking figures are that villages with less than 20 per cent WPR have drastically reduced while villages with WPR

Table 24.4: Distribution of Workers (1991-2011)

Range	*1991*		*2001*		*2011*	
	Number of villages	*Percent*	*Number of villages*	*Percent*	*Number of villages*	*Percent*
< 20 %	15	7.28	9	4.48	3	1.55
21 – 40 %	179	86.89	155	77.11	126	64.95
41 – 60 %	7	3.40	31	15.42	52	26.80
61 – 80 %	4	1.94	6	2.99	12	6.19
> 81 %	0	0.00	0	0.00	0	0.00
Total	**206**	**100.00**	**201**	**100.00**	**194**	**100.00**

Source: Data generated from Census of India (2011).

between 61 to 80 per cent have significantly increased from 3.4 per cent in 1991 to 15.42 in 2001 and 26.8 in 2011.

Distribution of Female Workforce Participation Rate

One of the strongest determinants of labour market outcomes in both developed and developing countries is educational attainment. Education is a key factor behind the U-shaped hypothesis of female employment: once women's education levels catch up and job opportunities emerge, women start to participate in greater numbers (Verick, 2014). This is important to understand because Female workforce participation (FWP) is an important driver (and outcome) of growth and development. Here too we have chosen this indicator within this perspective and we were able to analyse that as education or literacy among females show improvement; their participation in the labour marke also shows upward trends.

The data in table 24.5 shows that in 1991 nearly the entire corridor had poor performance with regard to this indicator as about 92 per cent of villages had FWP rate below 20 per cent. The figures have changed for better as now this proportion has significantly decreased (53.09% in 2011). This change can be attributed to number of factors, but the crucial factor is access to quality education (beyond secondary) as it directly leads improved employment outcomes for women. But this is a one side story as in most of the developing countries like India; high female labour force participation rates typically reflect poverty. Moreover, women earn less than men and are more likely to be engaged in

Table 24.5: Distribution of Female Workforce Participation Rate (1991-2011)

Range	*1991*		*2001*		*2011*	
	Number of villages	*Percent*	*Number of villages*	*Percent*	*Number of villages*	*Percent*
< 20 %	189	91.75	109	54.23	103	53.09
21 – 40 %	09	4.37	43	21.39	41	21.13
41 – 60 %	07	3.40	45	22.39	45	23.20
61 – 80 %	01	0.49	04	1.99	04	2.06
> 81 %	00	0.00	00	0.00	00	0.00
Total	**206**	**100.00**	**201**	**100.00**	**193**	**100.00**

Source: Data generated from Census of India (2011).

unprotected jobs, such as domestic work. Education raises the expectations of women, but it needs to be matched by job creation. Underreporting is common, so data on women's participation rates do not accurately reflect women's work. This issue becomes more transparent when we analyse the participation of women in agricultural and non-agricultural activities.

7. Distribution of Workers in Agricultural Activities

The basic definition of urbanization states that urbanization is a process where population shifts from agricultural economic activities to non-agricultural economic activities. Therefore, it can be perceived that if this particular axis is witnessing development of urban corridor which can also be termed as regional urbanization, where metropolitan cities are declining. According to Soja (2011), three major forces have been driving this process of regional urbanization; which is leading to the formation of city regions. These forces are—the globalization of capital, labour, and culture; economic restructuring and the formation of a new economy; and the facilitative effects of the revolution in information and communications technologies (Soja, 2011). This process can be replicated here as Indian economy underwent major restructuring after 1991 when the economy was opened up and the phenomenon of liberalization was adopted. This led to major structural adjustments throughout the country.

Therefore, this can be said for the study region too, as here too we see shifts in the economic structure both for men and women (Tables 24.6 and 24.7). In 1991, prior to globalisation, men in nearly 37 per cent of villages and women in nearly 53 per cent of villages were engaged in agricultural activities. The figures show a declining trend in 2001 as well as in 2011. This distinctively shows that the process of urbanization in the region has gone hand in hand with the structural adjustments that the country has witnessed in the last 26 years. Now, the proportion of workers in non-agricultural activities has significantly improved.

The above analysis of the various social and economic indicators for the villages along the corridor clearly show the changes that the region has undergone in the last twenty-twenty five years. In accordance with the process of corridor development the region has witnessed positive changes as there has been remarkable improvement in sex ratio, female literacy rate and female workforce participation rate. Moreover, the study also illustrates the shift from the agricultural to non-agricultural activities for both men and women. This process of development in harmony with urbanization becomes more apparent when one studies the changes in land cover along the axis; which has been discussed in the next section.

SECTION 3
LAND COVER CHANGES ALONG THE DELHI-AGRA AXIS (1996-2016)

In the modern age of technology, the entire earth surface is undergoing changes with regard to its land cover and its usage. This is the result of high man-land ratio which instigates the human community to alter the land cover for their use especially in the form of built up area. This process is triggered when a particular region undergoes rapid urbanization especially in developing countries like India. In this particular study we have tried to analyze the changes in land cover that this corridor has witnessed in last twenty years with the help of GIS techniques. Here we have analyzed the land cover that existed along the axis in 1996 (Map 24.2) and in 2016 (Map 24.3); the changes that have occurred have also been analyzed.

Table 24.6: Distribution of Workers in Agricultural Activities (1991-2011)

Range	*1991*				*2001*				*2011*			
	Number of villages		*Percent*		*Number of villages*		*Percent*		*Number of villages*		*Percent*	
	M	*F*	*M*	*F*	*M*	*F*	*M*	*F*	*M*	*F*	*M*	*F*
< 20 %	2	20	0.97	9.71	19	28	9.45	13.93	19	28	9.79	14.43
21 – 40 %	13	12	6.31	5.83	32	27	15.92	13.43	32	27	16.49	13.92
41 – 60 %	38	37	18.45	17.96	60	43	29.85	21.39	60	43	30.93	22.16
61 – 80 %	77	27	37.38	13.11	52	42	25.87	20.90	52	43	26.80	22.16
> 81 %	76	110	36.89	53.40	38	61	18.91	30.35	31	53	15.98	27.32
Total	**206**	**206**	**100.00**	**100.00**	**201**	**201**	**100.00**	**100.00**	**194**	**194**	**100.00**	**100.00**

Table 24.7: Distribution of Workers in Non-Agricultural Activities (1991-2011)

Range	*1991*				*2001*				*2011*			
	Number of villages		*Percent*		*Number of villages*		*Percent*		*Number of villages*		*Percent*	
	M	*F*	*M*	*F*	*M*	*F*	*M*	*F*	*M*	*F*	*M*	*F*
< 20 %	59	89	28.64	43.20	23	59	11.44	29.35	19	41	9.79	21.13
21 – 40 %	87	74	42.23	35.92	62	31	30.85	15.42	35	42	18.04	21.65
41 – 60 %	40	28	19.42	13.59	66	61	32.84	30.35	65	43	33.51	22.16
61 – 80 %	11	12	5.34	5.83	31	28	15.42	13.93	52	28	26.80	14.43
> 81 %	9	3	4.37	1.46	19	22	9.45	10.95	23	40	11.86	20.62
Total	**206**	**206**	**100.00**	**100.00**	**201**	**201**	**100.00**	**100.00**	**194**	**194**	**100.00**	**100.00**

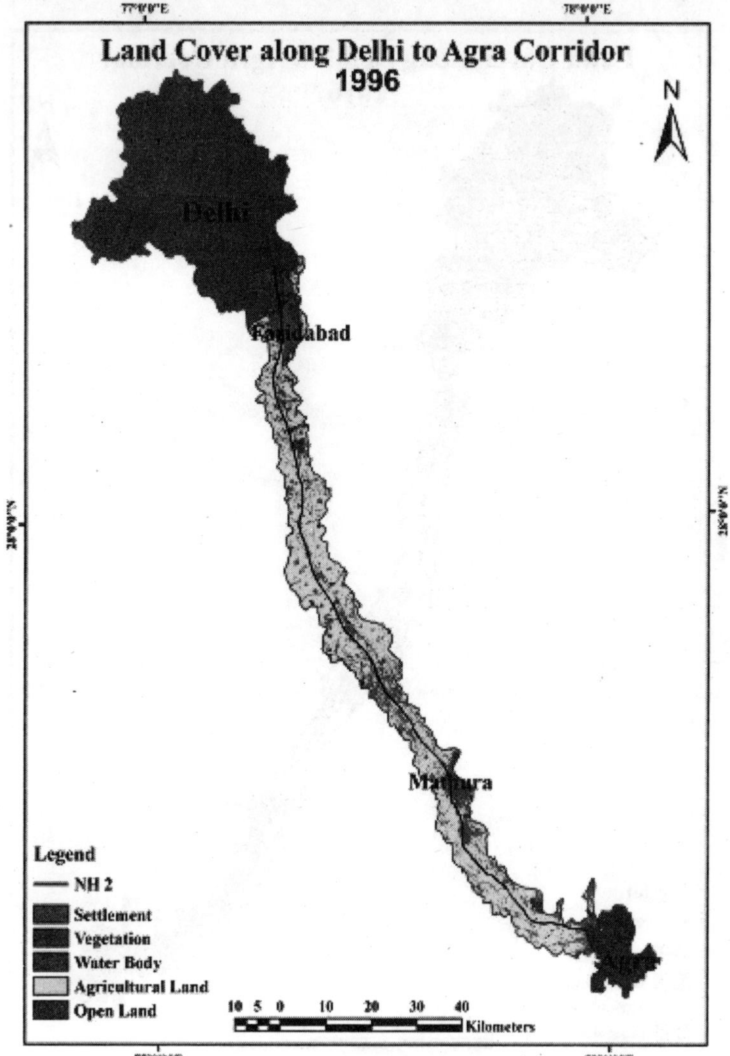

Map 24.2: Land Cover along Delhi to Agra Corridor 1996

The changes are apparent and the most significant is the increase in the proportion of settlements from 26 per cent in 1996 to nearly 46 per cent in 2016. Another remarkable change is that the entire open land has been converted mainly into settlement.

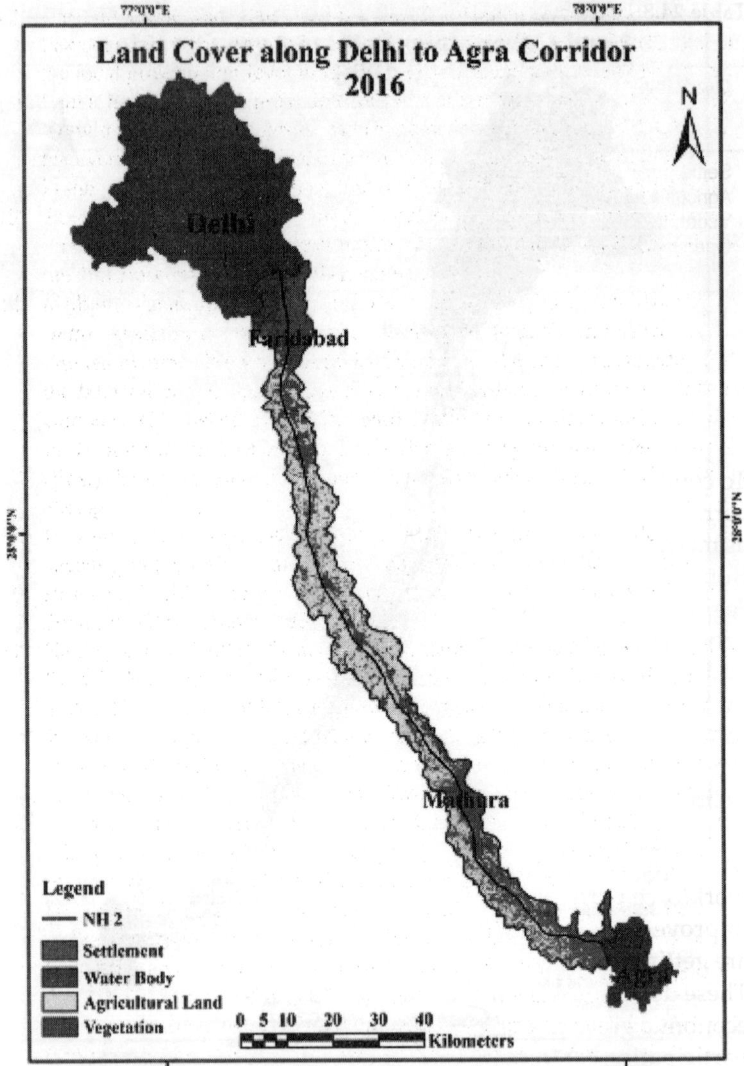

Map 24.3: Land Cover along Delhi to Agra Corridor 2016

The trend is very similar to the urbanization process where agricultural land, vegetation and water bodies are converted into concrete to meet the demands of the increasing population (Table 24.8).

Table 24.8: Proportion of Different Land Cover Classes along the Delhi-Agra Axis (1996-2016)

Land Cover Classes	1991		2001	
	In Hectares	*In Per cent*	*In Hectares*	*In Per cent*
Settlement	408743	26.07	2934525	46.80
Agriculture Land	965859	61.61	3056366	48.74
Vegetation	107387	6.85	240590	3.84
Open land	71442	4.56	0	0.00
Water body	14158	0.90	38806	0.62
Total	**1567589**	**100.00**	**6270287**	**100.00**

SECTION 4
CONCLUSIONS

To conclude, the Delhi-Agra Axis is going through the process of corridor development. Both Delhi and Agra are fulfilling their roles as metropolis; which are diffusing spread effects along the NH-2. But to give all the credit to these two metropolis in the era of regional urbanization is not right. The axis has witnessed this rapid process because of the presence of second tier cities like Faridabad and Mathura. These cities have been in harmony with their metropolis and have been able to disseminate the positive influences of the process of urbanization. This holds true because the changes witnessed by villages along this axis confer to the basic definitions of urbanization as a process. Firstly, as stated earlier, there has been significant improvement in the social indicators of development like sex-ratio, female literacy late and female-workforce participation rate. These indicators depict that there is improvement in the basic standard of living for women as they are getting educated and even participating in the labour market. These developments are crucial drivers for balanced regional and economic growth. But this is not a complete picture as increasing participation of women in the labour market is often associated with poverty and over exploitation. Since this is not our concern here, we leave these questions unanswered.

Another important change that the corridor has witnessed in accordance with the process of urbanization is the shift from agricultural or primary activities to non-agricultural and secondary or tertiary activities. The analysed data as well as the land cover changes clearly portray these changes. In short it can be said that there have been encouraging and progressive modifications along the Delhi-Agra Axis which represent the development of urban corridor along the National Highway-2.

Bibliography

Books

Berry, B.J.L. (1967). *Geography of the Urban Centres and Retail Distribution: The Urban Case,* New York: Engelwood Cliffs, 42-58.

Butola, B.S. (1995). Urbanization and Under-development in the North-Eastern India, in J. B. Ganguly (ed.) *Urbanisation and Development in North-East India: Trends and Policy Implications,* Delhi: Deep & Deep Publications, 39-47.

Carter, H. (1972). *The Study of Urban Geography,* London: Edward Arnold Publishers Ltd.

Dutt, A. K. (1994). *The Asian City: Processes of Development, Characteristics, and planning,* The Netherlands: Kluwer Academic Publishers, Dordrecht.

Dreze, J. and Gazdar, H. (1996). Uttar Pradesh: The Burden of Inertia in A. Sen and *et al.* (eds.) *Indian Development,* Bombay: Popular Publisher.

Harvey, D. (1988) Urban Places in the Global Village: reflections on the Urban Condition in late Twentieth Century Capitalism in L. Mazza (ed.) *In World Cities and the Future of the Metropolis,* New York: Milano, 21-33.

Jain, A. K. (1990). *The Making of a Metropolis: Planning and Growth of Delhi,* New Delhi: National Book Organisation.

Kundu, A. (1996). *Measurement of Urban Processes,* New Delhi: Oxford University Press.

Pacione, M. (2001). *Urban Geography: A Global Perspective,* London: Routledge.

Prakasa Rao, V.L.S. (1973). The Process of Urbanization, Fulbright *Newsletter,* March, 10-14.

Prasad, L. (1985). *The Growth of a Small Town: A Sociological Study of Ballia (U.P.),* New Delhi: Concept Publishing Company.

Soja, E.W. (2000). *Post-metropolis: Critical Studies of Cities and Regions,* London: Blackwell Publishers.

——(2011). Regional Urbanization and the end of Metropolis Era in G. Bridge and S. Watson (eds.) *The New Blackwell Companion to the City,* London: Wiley-Blackwell, pp. 679-689.

Articles

Berry, B. J. L. (1976) The Counter Urbanisation Process: Urban America since 1970, *Urban Affairs Annual Review*, 11, 17-30.

Gilbert, A. (1993) Third World Cities: The Changing National Settlement System, *Urban Studies*, 30 (4/5), 721-40.

Hill, E. W. and Wolman, H. L. (1997) City-suburban Income Disparities and Metropolitan area Employment: Can Tightening Labour Market Reduce the Gaps, *Urban Affairs Review*, 32 (4), 558-82.

Priemus, H. and Zonneveld, W. (2003) What are corridors and what are the issues? Introduction to special issue: the governance of corridors, *Journal of Transport Geography*, No. 11, pp. 167 -77.

Roy, B. K. (2000) About a Synthetic Model: In Indian Urbanization (The Urban Corridors) *Annals of the National Association of Geographers*, India, 96-101.

Schwanen, T., Dieleman, F. M. and Dijst, M. (2001) Travel Behaviour in Dutch Mono-centric and Poli-centric Urban Systems, *Journal of Transport Geography*, 9, 173-186.

Schultz, T. P. (1993) Reruns to Women Education in E. King and M. Hill (eds.) *Women's Education in Developing Countries*, Washington D.C.: John Hopkins for the World Bank.

Tammaru, T. (2001) Sub-urban Growth and Suburbanization under Central Planning: The Case Study of Estonia, *Urban Studies*, 38(8), 1341-57.

Other Documents

Bansal, T. (2002) Emerging Development Corridors in India: A Comparative study of Kanpur-Lucknow and Ghaziabad-Meerut Axes (1971-91), M.Phil. Dissertation submitted to Centre for the Study of Regional Development, JNU, New Delhi.

State of the World's Cities Report, "Bridging the Urban Divide" UN Habitat Report, 2010/11.

Kidwai, A. H. (1968) Study of the Functional Linkages between Lucknow and Kanpur, MRP Thesis submitted to IIT, Kharagpur.

Roy, B. (1993) India-Urban Corridors, Monograph No. 12, National Atlas and Thematic Mapping Organization, Kolkata.

Warnich, S. and Verster, B. (2005) The Answer is Corridor Development, but what is the Question. In: (SATC2005) Proceedings of the 24th Southern African Transport Conference, 11-13 July, 2005, Pretoria: Conference Planners, pp. 343-351.

Index